D1617568

Managing Conflict in the New Europe

# Managing Conflict in the New Europe

## The Role of International Institutions

Fergus Carr
*Principal Lecturer in International Politics*
*University of Portsmouth*

and

Theresa Callan
*Lecturer in International Politics*
*University of Portsmouth*

© Fergus Carr and Theresa Callan 2002

First published 2002 by
PALGRAVE MACMILLAN
Houndmills, Basingstoke, Hampshire RG21 6XS and
175 Fifth Avenue, New York, N.Y. 10010
Companies and representatives throughout the world.

PALGRAVE MACMILLAN is the global academic imprint of the Palgrave Macmillan division of St Martin's Press, LLC and of Palgrave Macmillan Ltd. Macmillan® is a registered trademark in the United States, United Kingdom and other countries. Palgrave is a registered trademark in the European Union and other countries.

ISBN 0–333–75013–6

This book is printed on paper suitable for recycling and made from fully managed and sustained forest sources.

A catalogue record for this book is available from the British Library.

Library of Congress Cataloging-in-Publication Data
Carr, Fergus
    Managing conflict in the new Europe: the role of international institutions/ Fergus Carr and Theresa Callan.
        p. cm.
Includes bibliographical references and index.
ISBN 0–333–75013–6 (cloth)
    1. Europe–Foreign relations–1989- 2. International agencies. 3. Security, International. I. Callan, Theresa, 1967- II. Title

JZ1570 .C37 2002
341.5'23'094–dc21

2001058504

10  9  8  7  6  5  4  3  2  1
11  10  09  08  07  06  05  04  03  02

Printed and bound in Great Britain by
Antony Rowe Ltd, Chippenham and Eastbourne

*To the memory of*
*Sean Carr and Francis Callan*

# Contents

# Acknowledgements

We would like to thank the Centre for European Studies Research at the University of Portsmouth under whose auspices research for this book was undertaken. We would also acknowledge the assistance given at the relevant international institutions in the provision of information and clarification. Particular thanks go to Carolyn for all her help with the manuscript and its preparation. We would also say thank you to Madeleine and Poe for their assistance in the production of the text.

# Preface

This book examines the challenges facing security providers in the present European order. The fundamental question pursued is the degree to which the institutional security architecture can rise to the challenges of instability and insecurity currently besetting Europe. It addresses the appropriateness of practice in light of the reconfiguration of power since 1989, examining the changing nature of security, cooperation and conflict in the new Europe. It analyses the roles of the European Union (EU), the Western European Union (WEU), the North Atlantic Treaty Organization (NATO) and the Organization for Security and Cooperation in Europe (OSCE). The approach is to establish the place of international institutions within prevailing analyses of international politics and then assess the evidence pertaining to the European security architecture in practice.

Particular attention is paid to the varieties of conflict, actual and potential, in Europe. The nature of conflict in the contemporary era is contrasted with that prevalent in the Cold War. The transition from Cold War bipolarity and 'threats' to a new order and 'risks' contextualizes the analysis. The changing conflict paradigm is examined and the increasing salience of substate conflicts assessed. Methods of conflict management and resolution – both theoretical and empirical – are reviewed. The structural and perceptual dimensions of intra-state conflict, such as those in Kosovo and Northern Ireland, are examined.

The development of the new European security architecture forms a key theme of the book. The interrelationship and security contributions of the EU, the WEU, NATO and the OSCE are analysed. The degree to which each institution has sought to define its competency in security management and the methodology of security provision is assessed. The central concern is to ascertain the prevailing understandings of conflict and conflict resolution held by the institutions. We examine the degree to which an institutional interdependence of security provision has developed, providing for 'interlocking' political, military and economic functions. The book also considers the emergent 'division of labour' between NATO and the WEU/EU, the significance of the European Defence and Security Identity, and the policies of both the EU and NATO toward the wider Europe with particular attention being given to Russia.

We examine institutional responses to inter-state conflict in Europe. The book addresses a number of themes concerning the nature of security provision. It examines the capacity of institutions to manage the conflicts of their own members. The significance of integration in the European Community/European Union for the resolution of inter-state economic and political conflicts in Western Europe is assessed. NATO's capacity to manage the conflicts of its members is examined including Greek and Turkish relations. The role of the United States with respect to mediation and negotiation within the Alliance is analysed. A second theme is consideration of the 'outreach' of institutions to promote security and stability. The effectiveness of liberal 'norm-setting' promoted by the OSCE and the European Union is assessed. The significance of accession to membership of the European Union and NATO is also analysed. NATO's relationship with its former adversaries is traced through the North Atlantic Cooperation Council (NACC), Partnership for Peace and on to enlargement policy. NATO–Russian relations are of prime importance to this analysis. The potential of the 'Founding Act on Mutual Relations' between NATO and Russia to serve as the basis for a 'security regime' between East and West is examined. The record of arms control also informs this discussion.

The analysis of institutional responses to conflicts within states focuses upon the former Yugoslavia. The intra-state and inter-state complexity of conflict in Bosnia and Croatia is thoroughly examined and the effectiveness of the EU, WEU, NATO and UN responses is assessed. The problems of intervention in ethnic conflicts, the difficulties of implementing strategies of deterrence and the challenges of institutional coordination under media scrutiny are analysed. The compatibility of humanitarian intervention with strategies of peace enforcement is also considered. This case study reviews the post-Dayton peace process and the potential of peacemaking in Bosnia. The crises in Kosovo and Macedonia conclude our analysis with an assessment of the role of international institutions as security providers.

# List of Abbreviations

| | |
|---|---|
| ABM | Anti-Ballistic Missile |
| ALA | Albanian Liberation Army |
| CEEC | Central and East European Countries |
| CEPSD | Common European Policy on Security and Defence |
| CFE | Conventional Forces in Europe |
| CFSP | Common Foreign and Security Policy |
| CIO | Chairman in Office |
| CJTF | Combined Joint Task Force |
| CMEA | Council for Mutual Economic Assistance |
| CPC | Conflict Prevention Centre |
| CPSU | Communist Party of the Soviet Union |
| CSCE | Conference on Security and Cooperation in Europe |
| CSO | Committee of Senior Officials |
| DDR | German Democratic Republic |
| DPC | Defence Planning Committee |
| DSACEUR | Deputy Supreme Allied Commander Europe |
| EAPC | Euro-Atlantic Partnership Council |
| EFTA | European Free Trade Association |
| EMU | Economic and Monetary Union |
| EPC | European Political Cooperation |
| EPU | European Political Union |
| ERP | European Recovery Programme |
| ESDI | European Security and Defence Identity |
| EU | European Union |
| FAWEU | Forces Answerable to the Western European Union |
| FRY | Federal Republic of Yugoslavia |
| GNP | Gross National Product |
| HCNM | High Commissioner for National Minorities |
| HDZ | Croatian Democratic Union |
| IAEA | International Atomic Energy Agency |
| ICTY | International Criminal Tribunal for the Former Yugoslavia |
| IFOR | Implementation Force |
| IMS | Integrated Military Structure |
| INF | Intermediate-Range Nuclear Forces |

| JCS | Joint Chiefs of Staff |
|---|---|
| JNA | Yugoslav National Army |
| KFOR | Kosovo Force |
| KLA | Kosovo Liberation Army |
| KPC | Kosovo Protection Corps |
| KVM | Kosovo Verification Mission |
| LDK | Popular Movement for Kosovo |
| MAD | Mutually Assured Destruction |
| MAP | Membership Action Plan |
| MRC | Major Regional Conflict |
| MTCR | Missile Technology Control Regime |
| NAC | North Atlantic Council |
| NACC | North Atlantic Cooperation Council |
| NATO | North Atlantic Treaty Organization |
| NLA | National Liberation Army |
| NPG | Nuclear Planning Group |
| NSG | Nuclear Suppliers Group |
| ODIHR | Office for Democratic Institutions and Human Rights |
| OFE | Office for Free Elections |
| OHR | Office of the High Representative |
| OSCC | Open Skies Consultative Commission |
| OSCE | Organization for Security and Cooperation in Europe |
| PfP | Partnership for Peace |
| PIC | Peace Implementation Conference |
| PJC | Permanent Joint Council |
| PPEWU | Policy Planning and Early Warning Unit |
| QMV | Qualified Majority Voting |
| SACEUR | Supreme Allied Commander Europe |
| SALT | Strategic Arms Limitation Talks |
| SDA | Party for Democratic Action |
| SDI | Strategic Defense Initiative |
| SDS | Serbian Democratic Party |
| SEA | Single European Act |
| SFOR | Stabilization Force |
| SHAPE | Supreme Headquarters Allied Powers Europe |
| START | Strategic Arms Reduction Treaty |
| UN | United Nations |
| UNEF | United Nations Emergency Force |
| UNHCR | United Nations High Commissioner for Refugees |
| UNIP | United Nations International Police |

| | |
|---|---|
| UNMIK | United Nations Interim Administration Mission in Kosovo |
| UNPROFOR | United Nations Protection Force |
| UNSCR | United Nations Security Council Resolution |
| WEU | Western European Union |

# 1
# Managing Conflict in the New Europe

The objective of this book is to examine the role of international institutions as security providers in the European order. The fundamental question to be pursued is the degree to which the new institutional security architecture can respond to the challenges of instability and insecurity currently besetting the European order. The focus will be upon political and military conflict and the role of NATO, the OSCE, the EU, the WEU, and the UN. The contextual backdrop will be the changing nature of security and conflict in Europe in the post-Cold War world.

We want to examine the varieties of conflict, actual and potential, in the new Europe. The salience of intra-state conflict in contemporary Europe will be assessed and contrasted with inter-state conflict. Ethnicity and substate forces will be explored to advance understandings of intra-state conflict and its potential for resolution and management. The process of institutional adaptation to these new forms of insecurity will be assessed. The challenge for international institutions founded to meet the security needs of states is to respond to both new levels and new forms of conflict. The Cold War presented what, in retrospect, was a relatively straightforward, if all-pervasive, threat to the international system. World politics was dominated by superpower bipolarity, and military and nuclear threats. This 'threat system' overlay other conflicts and set the agenda for international institutions. In Europe alliances operated within the Cold War rationale and reinforced bloc politics and confrontation. In the global system the UN's security role was equally conditioned and inhibited by the Cold War. In the wake of the Cold War, security can be seen to be not only the preserve of states but a concern as well for societies, minorities and individuals (see Dalby, 1997; Krause and Williams, 1997; Buzan et al.,

1

1998). Indeed, it can be strongly argued that state–society relationships now form an important dimension to security politics within which the rights of individuals and minorities become prominent issues. The recent history of the former Yugoslavia has highlighted the politics of separatism, secession and 'ethnic cleansing' and set a new agenda for Europe's security architecture. At the same time as the level of security need broadened, so too did its forms. Security ceased to be dominated solely by military forms, as societal, economic and environmental attributes grew in importance. In contrast to the Cold War era, international institutions now had to embrace multi-level conflicts and a multi-issue agenda.

The current European order is characterized, as we shall see, by both inter-state and intra-state conflicts. In addition, just as in the Cold War, Russia's relations with the West is a key feature. NATO enlargement, arms control, nuclear deterrence and the 'management' of European security have been important elements of Europe's international relations since 1991. Other regional conflicts have transcended the demise of the Cold War, such as Greek–Turkish relations and conflict over Cyprus. Integration has formed another theme with the 'pull' of the European Union. The EU process of both 'deepening' commitments for its existing member states while 'broadening' its potential membership has raised questions for states, their domestic politics and the appropriate extent of institutional governance. Economic management can also be seen in this context with the EU and G8 providing fora for the resolution of conflict and the enhancement of stability. While Balkan fragmentation starkly highlights the crisis confronting weak states when their legitimacy is challenged, the politics of identity is not confined to the former socialist states. Northern Ireland, for example, has deeply embedded domestic conflicts which have, to date, defied resolution. Threats to identity and social groups are perceived in a number of settings and manifest themselves in domestic politics in a number of ways, violence being just one. The politics of immigration, asylum and citizenship now assume a new significance in the European regional order.

This book will argue that the space for international institutions to make a difference, to enhance security, is facilitated by the end of the Cold War. It will seek to substantiate this assertion by examining the nature of conflict and the factors inhibiting international institutions in the Cold War and contrasting this with conditions in contemporary Europe. Chapter 2 on conflict in the Cold War and post-Cold War worlds opens this argument by examining: the nature of the new secu-

rity environment; the changing concepts of security, conflict and stability; and the transition from 'threat' to 'risks'. It further argues that
the nature of contemporary security makes international institutional
responses more relevant. Issues of economic and political stability,
human rights and law can be seen to transcend the competence of
individual states. The need, moreover, for interventions which are
deemed legitimate underwrites the importance of international institutions as means for norm-setting and consensus building.

The opportunity for international institutions to enhance security in
the new Europe is not, however, without difficulty. The breadth of
security challenges and their complexity require a response from more
than one institution. The concept of a security architecture of overlap-
ping institutions has been established but is yet to be fully cohesive in
practice.

The competence of the European security architecture in managing
inter-state and intra-state conflict and its consequences is also yet to be
fully established. The focus of this book is political and military
conflict and we examine the way in which institutions have adopted
strategies to deal with such forms of conflict. The third chapter of the
book on conflict and its management analyses the changing conflict
paradigm and the increasing importance of substate conflict. The
nature of ethno-political conflict is explored and the potential spectrum of responses for its resolution is noted. This basis facilitates an
evaluation of the evolution of the European security architecture, its
capacity and potential. Our approach is both historical and analytical.
The role of international institutions is best understood with reference
to both their internal dynamics and the external international system
in which they operate.

## International institutions, states and cooperation

The role of international institutions in the maintenance of international order and promotion of security has long been the subject of
debate in the study of international politics. The capacity of individual
institutions to address the security concerns of their members has
formed one line of enquiry. Studies, for example, have examined the
competence of the United Nations to implement its Charter (see
Nicholas, 1975; Luard, 1982; Roberts and Kingsbury, 1993; Baehr and
Gordenker, 1999). A related form of analysis has been to assess the
effectiveness of alliances such as NATO to develop strategies which
meet their members' needs (see, for example, Hunter, 1969; Treverton,

1985; Gompert and Larrabee, 1997). Such investigations examine the structure, decision-making, resources and cohesion of institutions. The analyses have concluded upon the effectiveness of institutions in light of their members' compliance with organizational norms and/or the credibility of institutional strategies toward non-members. Underlying these approaches has been a second line of enquiry which has been concerned to ascertain the place of international institutions within the overall nature of international order. In some respects this enquiry has been central to the development of international relations as a discipline because it involves questions about the nature of actors, conflict and the international system. As we shall see the analytical assumptions adopted in these debates critically affect authors' views of the relevance of institutions to international politics in general and security provision in particular.

In the realist approach to international politics the role of international institutions is circumscribed by the dominance of states and their interests. In his classic *The Twenty Years Crisis: 1919–39*, E. H. Carr challenged the liberal case that 'reason could demonstrate the absurdity of international anarchy ...' (Carr, 1989, p. 26) and that the force of public opinion was the voice of reason (ibid., p. 34). Carr rejected as 'inadequate and misleading the attempt to base international morality on an alleged harmony of interests which identifies the interest of the whole community of nations with the interest of each individual member of it' (ibid., p. 66). He saw the failure of the League of Nations as an inability to provide an absolute and disinterested standard for the conduct of international affairs.

> What matters is that those supposedly absolute and universal principles were not principles at all, but the unconscious reflections of national policy based on a particular interpretation of national interest at a particular time.
>
> (Ibid., p. 87).

The classic realist case is that international institutions are permeated by national interests. Such interests are seen to act as a major constraint upon the role of organizations such as the League of Nations or the United Nations. Morgenthau, for example, interpreted Soviet behaviour in the Cold War as differing only in 'manner and form, but not in substance, from the attitude all great powers have traditionally taken with regard to international agreements' (Morgenthau, 1971, p. 350). That is, the 'iron law of international politics, that legal obligations must yield to the national interest' (ibid., p. 351). So Morgenthau argued that

> while it is true that the Russians have violated those agreements the keeping of which they do not deem to be in their interest, it is also true that they have kept those agreements which they thought it to be in their interest to keep ...
>
> (Ibid., p. 350)

At the United Nations, however, the conflict between the West and Russia, 'instead of being seen in terms of relative power, is conceived in the absolute terms of peace, law and order *vs* aggression, crime and anarchy' (ibid.). For realists international institutions should be seen as part of the struggle for power rather than some sort of arbiter of it or entity independent from it.

> It is roughly the case that, while in domestic politics the struggle for power is governed and circumscribed by the framework of law and institutions, in international politics law and institutions are governed and circumscribed by the struggle for power.
>
> (Wight, 1979, p. 102)

Conflict in the realist world view is the norm and its underlying cause is the structural anarchy of the state system and the absence of international government. This is critical to neorealism and described by Waltz as a 'self-help system ... in which those who do not help themselves, or who do so less effectively than others, will fail to prosper, will lay themselves open to dangers, will suffer' (Waltz, 1986, p. 117). The consequent security dilemma is seen as a constant feature of the system and has been stressed by both classical and neorealists.

> In such a situation, mutual mistrust is fundamental and one power can never have an assurance that another power is not malevolent. Consequently with the best will in the world no power can surrender any part of its security and liberty to another power. This is the situation of Hobbesian fear ...
>
> (Wight, 1979, p. 102)

For neorealists it is the structure of the system that 'shapes and shoves (its) units' (Waltz, 1995, p. 78). In Waltz's neorealist conception the anarchic system is more than a condition as it constitutes a distinct structure. This was seen to impart two effects: 'states are made functionally similar by the constraints of structure, with the principal differences among them defined according to capabilities' and 'structure mediates the outcomes that states produce' (ibid., p. 80).

State-level explanations of conflict were not embraced by Waltz who rejected 'reductionist' accounts. This approach proved contentious with other theorists (see Keohane et al., 1986) and Waltz later conceded that, 'structures do not determine behaviours and outcomes, not only because unit-level and structural causes interact, but also because the shaping and shoving of structures may be successfully resisted' (Waltz, 1986, p. 343). While the concession has received mixed reaction (see McSweeney, 1999, p. 216) it does point to a more complex relationship between agency and structure. Nonetheless conflict remains integral to the international system for both classical and neorealists and the issue of relative capabilities is central to the analysis. In this context the prospects for order and cooperation among states appear limited.

The realist analysis of relative capabilities makes order a product of power balances and concentrates on the dominant role of great powers in the international system. The idea of a balance of power was seen by Wight to arise 'naturally in considering any relationship between competing human units ...'(Wight, 1979, p. 168) and for Waltz it requires 'no assumptions of rationality or of constancy of will on the part of all of the others' (Waltz, 1986, p. 117). Competition between states is understood to be constant and if 'the drive of some of the units appears to promise success, it is blocked by other units whose similar motives cause them in turn to counter and thrust' (Waltz, 1959, p. 209). So for Morgenthau 'the balance of power and policies aiming at its preservation are not only inevitable but are an essential stabilizing factor in a society of sovereign nations....'(Morgenthau, 1967, p. 161). The concept of equilibrium or balance 'signifies stability within a system composed of a number of autonomous forces' (ibid., p. 162). Bull stresses that the 'chief function of the balance of power, however, is not to preserve peace, but to preserve the system of states itself' (Bull, 1979, p. 107). This may involve the use of force, and war then becomes a legitimate instrument to preserve the balance.

> Wars initiated to restore the balance of power, wars threatened to maintain it, military interventions in the internal affairs of another state to combat the encroaching power of a third state, whether or not that state has violated legal rules, bring the imperatives of the

balance of power into conflict with the imperatives of international law. The requirements of order are treated as prior to those of law ...

(Ibid., p. 109)

The balance of power does not presume a collectivity of interest. It is not a system 'in the sense that the states involved necessarily have the common end in mind of preserving the independence of the rival participants ...' (Hartmann, 1969, p. 311). If there arises a collectivity of interest it is sectional, temporary in character and represented by alliances as 'exclusive institutions'.

To say that a state enters an alliance (follows the pattern of the balance of power) is simply another way of saying that it institutionalizes its belief that its power problem is similar to that of its alliance partner. If several join together, it implies that they all agree on the compatibility or identity of their own vital interests with each other, agree on the essential nature of the common threat, and wish to counter the power of the rival nation or group.

(Ibid., p. 309)

The function of alliances is to block or counter rival groupings. For Hartmann this means that 'neither group is particularly interested in "balancing" the other as such'; instead balance is 'an accidental by-product of the existence of two alliance groupings, each formed to counter the power and ambitions of the other' (ibid., p. 371). A 'balance' therefore may or may not result from the competition of alliances or powers. The literature on the subject, in fact, debates the conditions which would lead to successful deterrence or trigger war (see, for example, Claude, 1962). The role of great powers in this equation is clearly critical. They form the core of alliances, can exercise hegemony in regions and dictate the international agenda. The 'inequality of states in terms of power has the effect, in other words, of simplifying the pattern of international relations, of ensuring that the say of some states will prevail while that of others will go under, that certain conflicts will form the essential theme of international politics while others will be submerged' (Bull, 1979, p. 206). Bull further points to the existence of a general balance of power and local regional balances (ibid., p. 103). In the Cold War a dominant balance was moreover clearly discernible with subordinate regional balances. Morgenthau described the decline of Europe's great power system and the domination of the superpowers in the Cold War in the following terms:

> Today the balance of power of Europe is no longer the centre of
> world politics around which local balances would group themselves,
> either in intimate connection or in lesser or greater autonomy.
> Today the European balance of power has become a mere function
> of the world-wide balance of which the United States and the Soviet
> Union are the main weights, placed on opposite scales.
>
> (Morgenthau, 1967, p. 194)

In a related series of debates analysts have looked at the role of dominant or hegemonic forces in the provision of stability. The hegemonic
stability thesis holds that 'hegemonic structures of power, dominated
by a single country, are most conducive to the development of
strong international regions whose roles are relatively precise and well
obeyed ...' (Keohane, quoted in Guzzini, 1998, p. 143). The approach
moreover suggests public good can result from the actions of the hegemony although theorists have differed in its definition from the liberal
international economy, to international order and international
regimes (see Guzzini, 1998, pp. 144–6). Young refers to the idea of
'imposed orders' that 'are fostered deliberately by dominant forces or
consortia of dominant actors' who 'succeed in getting others to
conform to the requirements of these orders through some combinations of coercion, cooperation, and the manipulation of incentives'
(Young, 1993, p. 100). In this approach, United States leadership of the
international economy in the post-1945 era was institutionalized in
the Bretton Woods system and associated regimes. Hegemonic leadership resulted in a more stable international economy.

The realist approach, therefore, prescribes against state cooperation
save in alliances against a common foe or under the leadership of a
hegemonic power, and looks to conflict as the norm. Not all analysts,
however, are so negative in their appraisal of the potential for state
cooperation. Keohane and Nye challenged the realist depiction of state
relations with the concept of complex interdependence (Keohane and
Nye, 1989). Three elements were seen to characterize complex interdependence: the existence of multiple channels connecting societies;
multiple issues without a clear hierarchy affecting the inter-state
agendas; and lastly, the minor or non-use of military force within the
region where complex interdependence prevails (ibid., pp. 24–9). These
characteristics 'softened' and 'permeated' the realist state, eroded the
distinction between foreign and domestic policies and set new challenges for governments, particularly in the management of economic
interdependence. International institutions and regimes assumed a

new significance in this context. In a 'world of multiple issues imperfectly linked, in which coalitions are formed transnationally and transgovernmentally, the potential role of international institutions in political bargaining is greatly increased' (ibid., 1989, p. 35). While Keohane and Nye did not argue that complex interdependence reflected the whole spectrum of international politics, they did suggest that it represented aspects of the contemporary international system neglected in realist analysis.

> We do not argue, however, that complex interdependence faithfully reflects world political reality. Quite the contrary: both it and the realist portrait are ideal types. Most situations will fall somewhere between these two extremes.
>
> (Ibid., p. 24)

The conditions of American hegemonic decline led to a new research focus on state cooperation and regimes. The stress of analysis was not on institutions as the embodiment of values or standards but on interests. The potential for state cooperation and its institutionalization has been argued to be a product of interest and preference. International politics has been described as 'typically characterized by independent self-interested decision-making, and states often have no reason to eschew such individualistic behavior' (Stein, 1993, p. 117). It is when reason exists that Stein and others believe 'individualistic self-interested calculation leads [states] to prefer joint decision-making because independent self-interested behavior can result in undesirable or suboptimal outcomes' (ibid., p. 120). The classic case can be presented in terms of a 'Prisoner's Dilemma', 'in which individuals have a dominant strategy of defecting from common action but in which the result of this mutual defection is deficient for all' (ibid., p. 122). In this case, collective good will not be produced or will 'be under produced, despite the fact that its value to the group is greater than its cost' (Keohane, 1984, p. 69). Regimes and institutions can realize such common interest and avoid common aversions. The essential argument is that regimes are interest-based and can solve the dilemmas of independent decision-making. Stein saw that the same 'terms of autonomously calculated self-interest that lie at the root of the anarchic international system also lay the foundation for international regimes as a form of international order' (Stein, 1993, p. 132). Keohane underlines the point with the observation that 'cooperation takes place only in situations in which actors perceive that their policies are actually or potentially in conflict, not where there is harmony' (Keohane, 1984, p. 54). Cooperation can therefore be seen as 'when actors adjust their behaviour to the actual and anticipated preferences of others, through a process of policy coordination' (ibid., p. 51). Regimes facilitate this process and are more than the sum of individual agreements. The classic definition is:

> Regimes can be defined as sets of implicit or explicit principles, norms, rules and decision-making procedures around which actors' expectations converge in a given area of international relations.
> (Krasner, 1993, p. 2)

For Stein, the critical condition for a regime to exist is that 'interaction between the parties is not unconstrained or is not based on independent decision making' (Stein, 1993, p. 117). Keohane emphasizes the 'contract' nature of regimes 'when these involve actors with long-term objectives who seek to structure their relationships in stable and mutually beneficial ways' (Keohane, 1993, p. 146). The value of such arrangements is seen to 'vary directly with the desirability of agreements to states and with the ability of international regimes actually to facilitate the making of such agreements' (ibid., p. 152). Keohane underlines the centrality of hegemonic power in the creation of regimes (Keohane, 1993, p. 142, and Keohane, 1984, pp. 33–46) but does not believe 'that hegemony is either a necessary or a sufficient condition for the emergence of cooperative relationships' (Keohane, 1984, p. 31). In light of the arguments posed by Stein and Keohane concerning the self-interest of states, both post- and non-hegemonic cooperation is seen as possible and facilitated by regimes.

International institutions may conform to regime characteristics but also may not. Stein argues that the United Nations is not a regime because 'membership generates no convergent expectations that constrain and shape subsequent actions' (Stein, 1993, p. 134). The notion of convergence and consequently compliance is central to the development of regime theory. It is the decentralized nature of regimes that is highlighted by Keohane who argues that if 'we view international regimes, and their international organizations, as attempts to construct hierarchies, or quasi-governments, they will appear weak to the point of ineffectiveness' (Keohane, 1984, p. 237).

Regimes are seen less 'as centralized enforcers of rules than as facilitators of agreement among governments' (ibid., p. 238). Rules remain important in this approach as standards or guidelines (ibid., p. 239) rather than as hierarchies above states. For Keohane, 'strong regimes are those with clear rules and effective incentives to comply with them (ibid.).

State compliance with regime principles, norms and rules is then fundamental to the credibility of regime analysis. Stein stresses that a preference for joint decision-making results from the dilemmas of common interests and common aversions (Stein, 1993, p. 120). Regimes are seen to be the means to realize common interests and avoid common aversions by collaboration and coordination. In Keohane's analysis incentives result from the value of regimes. Firstly, in terms of individual regimes, 'it may be rational to obey their rules if the alternative is their breakdown, since even an imperfect regime may be superior to any politically feasible replacement' (Keohane, 1984, p. 100). Secondly, in terms of regimes as part of a larger network of regimes and issues, 'by linking issues to one another, regimes create situations that are more like iterated, open-ended Prisoner's Dilemma, in which cooperation may be rational, than like single-play Prisoner's Dilemma, in which it is not' (ibid., p. 103). In the global economy, interdependence and a multiplicity of issues has led to the creation of numerous regimes so 'disturbing one regime does not merely affect behaviour in the issue-area regulated by it, but it is likely to affect other regimes in the network as well' (ibid., p. 104). Governments have then to view compliance in a number of related issue areas. Keohane also argues that compliance is linked to the constraints faced by decision-makers who are 'in practice subject to limitations on their own cognitive abilities, quite apart from the uncertainties inherent in their environments' (ibid., p. 111). Actors in this view are not 'perfectly rational' but subject to 'bounded rationality'; 'they cannot compile exhaustive lists of alternative courses of action, ascertaining the value of each alternative and accurately judging the probability of each possible outcome' (ibid., p. 112). So Keohane argues that the choice governments face is 'not whether to adhere to regimes at the expense of maximizing utility through continuous calculations, but rather on what rules of thumb to rely' (ibid., p. 115). Regime rules constrain others, 'signpost' courses of likely behaviour and provide information. Regimes 'provide information and reduce the cost of transactions that are consistent with their injunctions, thus facilitating inter-state agreements and their decentralized enforcement' (ibid., p. 246).

The primary focus of regime theory was developed in relation to global political economy and not classic security studies. Jervis has agreed that, 'if the connections between outcomes and national power are indirect and mediated, there is more room for choice, creativity, and institutions to restrain and regulate behaviour, and to produce a regime' (Jervis, 1993, p. 174). Such connections are seen to be 'less direct' in non-security areas like communications or trade. The security dilemma has been seen to inhibit regimes in the security domain.

> The primacy of security, its competitive nature, the unforgiving nature of the arena, and the uncertainty of how much security the state needs and has, all compound the prisoner's dilemma and make it sharper then the problems that arise in most other areas.
>
> (Jervis, 1993, p. 175)

Jervis saw a security regime as possible only when the great powers wanted a regulated environment (ibid., p. 176), were supportive of the status quo, saw war as too costly and also believed that others share the value they place on mutual security and cooperation (ibid., p. 177). These conditions were hard to realize in the Cold War even when the constraints of mutually assured destruction pointed to strategic arms limitation as a necessary regime for the superpowers. The benefits of such a regime included: information about each other's capabilities, planning and ultimately strategic rationales. The difficulty arose in sustaining the regime when other policy sectors were in competition, not least in the Third World. Jervis has acknowledged that regimes can bring benefit to security situations by enhancing information but stresses 'much depends on the nature of the situation: the changes required when a status quo power faces an expansionist power are very different from the changes that could increase cooperation among status quo powers that face one another' (Jervis, 1999, p. 52). The problems that surround the clash of interest between revisionist and status quo powers clearly cannot be resolved by enhancing information flows and reducing transaction costs. In these cases, realists would point to the role of coercive diplomacy, deterrence and, ultimately, force in the maintenance of order. Such scenarios do not represent a Prisoner's Dilemma but a zero sum game.

Other commentators have argued that cooperation in the security domain has been limited by the notion of 'relative' as opposed to 'absolute' gains. They argue that 'anarchy impedes cooperation not only because it generates cheating problems but also because it causes states to worry that partners might achieve relatively greater gains from collaboration and, thus strengthened, become more domineering friends in the present or possibly more formidable foes in the future' (Grieco, 1993, p. 729). This issue of relative gains, it is claimed, hinders security cooperation in particular because the balance of power is seen to motivate the desire for relative gains (Mearsheimer, 1994, in Brown et al., 1998, p. 334). Grieco has concluded that

> a state will decline to join, will leave, or will sharply limit its commitment to a cooperative arrangement if it believes that partners are achieving, or are likely to achieve, relatively greater gains. It will eschew cooperation even though participation in the arrangement was providing it, or would have provided it, with large absolute gains.
> (Grieco, 1988, p. 161)

Concerns about cheating, about reneging on an agreement, too are seen to hinder cooperation as such behaviour may also lead to relative gains (see Mearsheimer, 1994, in Brown et al., 1998, p. 338).

In this vein of understanding, the role of international institutions and regimes in promoting stability and security is severely doubted. For Mearsheimer, 'institutions have minimal influence on state behaviour, and thus hold little promise for promoting stability in the post Cold War world' (ibid., p. 332). Keohane and Martin, in direct contrast, argue that 'just as institutions can mitigate fears of cheating and so allow cooperation to emerge, so they can alleviate fear of unequal gains from cooperation' (Keohane and Martin, 1995, in Brown et al., 1998, p. 390). Neoliberal thinking does not deny the importance of relative gains but asks 'under what conditions such distributional conflicts are severe' (ibid.). One answer is that the strategic setting can be seen as critical to the issue of relative gains. The era of Cold War bipolarity with its zero sum rationality made for particular concern with relative gains. In different strategic environments and 'where there are more than two states or where states care about a mixture of absolute and relative gains, the institutionalist case for the possibility of decentralized cooperation remains strong (Snidal, 1991, p. 701).

Indeed, the debate on relative gains has become rich in qualifications and in addition to the strategic setting, influential variables identified include: the number of parties to an issue (Snidal, 1991); the nature of the parties – adversaries or like-minded states; the nature of the issue; the question of cumulative gains (Matthews III, 1996); and whether military advantage favours offence or defence (Glaser and Kaufmann, 1998). In this wider context, institutions can be seen to be important to processes of bargaining between states. The significance of their role, however, needs to be carefully measured.

In some variants of contemporary realism, similar conclusions have been reached. Glaser's 'contingent realism' finds that choices between cooperation and competition are highly conditioned with no general preference for competition (Glaser, 1994, in Brown et al., 1998, p. 134). Jervis has also identified the potential for state cooperation under 'defensive realist' understanding (Jervis, 1999, pp. 48–55). Institutions in this approach have the potential to facilitate cooperation depending upon the severity of the security dilemma and the intentions of the actors. The institutionalization of international policies is therefore seen as 'fragile' unless institutions 'produce or are accompanied by deeper changes in what actors want and how they conceive of their interests' (ibid., p. 61). In short, the degree to which institutions become embedded in the affairs of states is clearly critical to their influence upon behaviour.

## Conclusions

The above review of some of the debates concerning state cooperation and the place of international institutions generates a number of questions for the analysis of contemporary European security architecture.

Our focus is on military and political conflict which first invites an examination of the relative distribution of power among the leading states in the European order and their policy orientation. The transformation of the bipolar system to a new order in which Europe is no longer divided and subject to the politics of confrontation has directly affected the role, actual and potential, of international institutions. The Soviet Union played a critical role in shaping the old European order, and account needs to be taken of this record and its demise in analysis of current policies emanating from the states of Eastern and Central Europe. Russia's role as the strategic successor to Soviet leadership also requires historical contextualization to inform understandings of Moscow's contemporary strategies. The pattern of continuity and change in Washington's policies as the surviving 'superpower' informs our understandings of NATO, arms control and the regionalization of security. The reunification of Germany and its impact upon the European order is also significant in the development of Europe's institutional network. In short, the changing nature of the European order and the role of the great powers is seen as fundamental to the potential influence of international regimes and institutions.

We shall seek to demonstrate that, in the wake of the Cold War, many states have experienced a dramatic change often summarized as being from 'threats' to 'risks' in the security sector. A new European strategic environment has emerged in which many states are pursuing convergent policies, demonstrating 'a like-minded' orientation and seeking regulation of security issues. In this changed security environment with its changed and arguably reduced security dilemma new roles for institutions have developed. Both NATO and the European Union have begun processes of 'outreach' and enlargement while the Organization for Security and Cooperation in Europe (OSCE) may finally fulfil its rationale as a pan-European security provider. NATO will be seen to be less of an 'exclusive' alliance while the European Union may be more than a regime and a form of governance (see Carr and Massey, 1999). A central component of our enquiry is to trace this institutional development, adaption and augmentation and to analyse the role of the leading powers in the process.

In post-Cold War Europe, it is not just the strategic setting that has changed but the concept of security itself. The demarcation lines between what in the Cold War was deemed to be security and the 'softer' world of political economy have blurred as states now view their stability in a broader sense. Additionally processes of democratization, human rights and law have rendered security a much more complex concept. As Manfred Wörner argued:

> We must come to terms with a more diffuse concept of security in which economic integration and assistance and the internal democratization of states become as important as traditional military defence in maintaining security and preventing the degeneration of instabilities into tensions liable to cause conflicts.
>
> (Wörner, 1991, p. 8)

As the 'space' for institutions has grown in post-Cold War Europe, so too has their potential role in facilitating cooperation in a broad range of issue areas. In our analysis of the development of the new European security architecture, we shall seek to ascertain the significance of relative gains to states when the security dilemma has been so radically redefined. We shall further seek to establish the importance of institutions as centres for bargaining.

International institutions will be examined in two ways: firstly, consideration will be made of their internal dynamics – their impact upon members; and, secondly, their external role will be assessed in their impact upon non-members. Distinction will be drawn between 'exclusive' and 'inclusive' organizations. The approach allows for an evaluation of the extent to which cooperative strategies are sustained by core powers and/or by mutual interests and the impact of those policies on members and non-members alike. The degree to which institutions can be agents of international socialization will be assessed. For some, such institutionalization is likely to be limited, as the 'effects that international institutions may have on national decisions are but one step removed from the capabilities and intentions of the major state or states that gave them birth and sustain them' (Waltz, 2000, p. 126). Our approach is to consider the form of institution, the issue area and the degree to which the institution's norms and approaches have become embedded in the state's policy process.

By pursuing the above areas of enquiry, this book seeks to contribute to the analysis of state cooperation. The weakness of the traditional approach is that at its base is the assumption that conflict among states is the sole challenge for international institutions. We, however, argue that conflicts within states form another key challenge. Intra-state conflict now deserves greater recognition in the analysis of institutions as security providers.

A significant feature of the new European security agenda has concerned the relationship of states and societies. The violent wars of secession and separatism in the former Yugoslavia have forcibly brought nationalist politics and the problems of statehood to the forefront of security challenges. The relationship of societal and political security has come to form a particular problematic:

> Societal security is closely related to, but nonetheless distinct from political security which is about the organizational ability of states, systems of government, and the ideologies that give governments and states their legitimacy.
>
> (Buzan, Wæver and Wilde, 1998, p. 119)

Societal security has instead been seen as concerning 'identity, the self conception of communities and individuals identifying themselves as members of a community' (ibid., p. 119). Threats to identity therefore may be posed by states and/or other communities. A key problem is that identity is socially constructed, it is 'not a fact of society; it is a process of negotiation among people and interest groups' (McSweeney, 1996, p. 85). This dynamic process makes clashes between competing identities inherently political. The relationship between state and societal security also has to incorporate individual security. Individual human rights may be imperilled by states or by communities pursuing their societal security at the expense of others. In its worst form as 'ethnic cleansing', the pursuit of exclusive security for defined ethnic groups fundamentally denies the rights of others.

It can be argued that the classic realist security dilemma is a highly appropriate concept to explain ethnic conflict within states.

In areas such as the former Soviet Union and Yugoslavia, 'sovereigns' have disappeared. They leave in their wake a host of groups – ethnic, religious, cultural – of greater or less cohesion. These groups must pay attention to the first thing that states have historically addressed – the problem of security – even though many of these groups still lack many of the attributes of statehood.

(Posen, 1993, p. 28)

Security is firstly defined by identity and its cohesion. In a weak or collapsing state the cohesion of one group can be seen as a threat to another. So 'unless proven otherwise, one group is likely to assume that another group's sense of identity, and the cohesion that is produced, is a danger' (ibid., p. 31). As we shall argue, the role of elites, the media and the production of fear are also important elements in the spiral of group conflict. In essence, however, the security dilemma is easily applied to the basic uncertainty of group relations.

As we shall see in the case of the former Republic of Yugoslavia, international institutions entered an environment akin to the classic realist anarchical system. The European Community/European Union, the United Nations, NATO and the OSCE all sought to implement strategies in a context often far removed from the new European order. Such approaches – including mediation and negotiation, truces and ceasefires, peacekeeping and humanitarian aid – led to questions on their suitability for conflicts involving 'national survival'. As the international community sought to enforce its decisions in Bosnia and Kosovo, questions grew about the nature of deterrence in ethno-political conflicts and its credibility when applied to inter-communal violence.

The relationship of peacekeeping to peace-enforcement became a new problematic, as did the relationship of 'mandate' organizations, the United Nations or OSCE, to those charged with enforcement, NATO. International institutions whose role had hitherto been primarily judged in terms of state conflict were now being judged in terms of intra-state conflict. The examination has been thorough and raised questions about: firstly coherence, the ability of states in an institution to agree, mount and sustain a strategy; secondly, capability, the resources needed to support strategies for intervention in ethno-political conflict; and thirdly, collectively, the ability of the European security architecture to act together effectively with the United Nations to respond to such cases. The issue of time is, moreover, important as such conflicts typically are not of limited duration but demand long-term commitments.

Many aspects of the challenge of intra-state conflict for international institutions are not new. The United Nations, for example, encountered in its Congo operations in the 1960s many of the features which would pertain in the Croatian and Bosnian conflicts in the 1990s. Both Cyprus and the Lebanon also provide evidence of inter-communal violence and the constraints upon international solutions to domestic strife. What was and is new, is the challenge for institutions whose focus is European security: NATO, the European Union and the OSCE. Our analysis is of these institutions and their response to European crises.

The order of the book seeks to pursue the enquiry launched here, namely the role of international institutions as security providers in the new Europe. It commences in Chapter 2 with a comprehensive analysis of the security environment in the Cold War and post-Cold War worlds. Chapter 3 assesses the increased salience of intra-state conflict within the contemporary international system and reviews contending theories of conflict management and resolution. Chapter 4 examines the development of the new European security architecture – its key institutions, their organization and adaptions to the new security challenges. Chapter 5 analyses these institutions' responses to inter-state conflict in the new Europe and is followed by Chapter 6 which concentrates upon the challenges of intra-state conflict. The conclusion in Chapter 7 seeks to evaluate the overall competence of the European security architecture in light of inter-state and intra-state conflict. It seeks to address the issues of conflict and cooperation introduced in this chapter and the presented evidence of institutional performance. Finally, we shall seek to ask for whom have institutions enhanced security – states, societies or individuals?

# 2
# Conflict in the Cold War and Post-Cold War Worlds

## Introduction

The end of the Cold War heralded a revolution in European security. A Europe divided into rival alliances, separated by an 'Iron Curtain' and overshadowed by nuclear confrontation, gave way to a new order. The transition was remarkably swift and far reaching in its consequences. Security understandings were transformed from the notion of 'threats' to 'risks'. The conceptualization of security moved from a military focus to include societal, economic and institutional perspectives. The concern of this book is to examine the challenge faced by security providers in this new, yet transitional, environment. It seeks to analyse the degree to which the European institutional architecture can respond to contemporary challenges of political and military instability.

   The purpose of this chapter is to provide a conceptual and historical basis for the investigation of international institutional security management. In particular the chapter will focus upon the changing concepts of security, conflict and stability in the new Europe. The nature of conflict in the contemporary era will be contrasted with that of the Cold War.

## Conflict and the international order in the Cold War

This section explores the key features of conflict in the Cold War. The analysis traces the evolution of superpower conflict and its projection into the international system. A primary concern is to examine the manner in which this central conflict came to 'overlay' others linking the local with the regional and the global. The pattern can be traced to the end of the Second World War when the respective security concerns of the Soviet Union and the United States led to diplomatic inertia, disputes, confrontation and crises which critically affected the wider international order and international institutions.

## Soviet security interests

Soviet security embraced a spectrum of interests ranging from the revolutionary imperatives bequeathed by Lenin to the survival of the Soviet state. The fusion of communist ideas and realpolitik meant in practice both ideological and pragmatic responses to international politics. Stalin's doctrine of 'Socialism in One Country' cemented the integration of Soviet state interests and ideology (see Deutscher, 1967, pp. 281–93). Stalin argued that the Soviet Union had to be sufficiently strong in economic and military terms to survive the encirclement of a hostile capitalist world. He made it the duty of every communist to defend the Soviet state as it constituted the basis of revolution. In the interwar years 'isolation as a communist nation and a limited capacity to extend its power and influence ... dictated a practical policy of prudence, but without abandonment of ideological militancy' (Crockatt, 1996, p. 32). In the post-1945 era the maintenance of the Soviet bloc, confrontation with the Western Alliance and the dynamics of the arms race preoccupied the Soviet leadership. In this context Soviet security interests moved from a European to a global level.

### Soviet security in Europe: Germany and the sphere of influence

Germany was of central strategic importance to the Soviet Union. The threat posed by Hitler's Germany led to a pragmatic solution in 1939, the Soviet–German Non-Aggression Pact. The Pact enhanced Soviet security by deflecting German aggression and its secret protocol granted Moscow a sphere of influence including Finland, Estonia, Latvia, Bessarabia and a part of Poland. Following the German invasion of the Soviet Union in 1941, Moscow looked for a strategic alliance with the Western powers. Stalin's objectives were to secure the defeat, dismemberment and occupation of Germany. At the Moscow Foreign Ministers Conference and Tehran Summit in 1943 the Soviet line on Germany was pressed and Stalin sought Alliance recognition of Soviet interests in Eastern and Central Europe. As the Red Army moved westward Stalin began to accomplish his objectives. In February 1945 when the Allies met in Yalta Soviet troops were advancing on Berlin. At the Yalta Conference Stalin looked for significant reparations from Germany, the destruction of German power and recognition of Soviet security interests in the future of Poland. The United States and Britain deferred a decision on Germany until the Potsdam summit in July 1945 and sought to widen the Polish provisional government to include non-communist democratic representatives. The Potsdam summit agreed to the principles of an occupation regime for Germany, that reparations should be taken by each occupying power from its own zone with the Soviet Union receiving an additional 25 per cent of reparations from the Western zones. The de facto consequence of this decision was to divide responsibility for the transition period and, as 'with the settlements in other areas, temporary and transitional expedients became the basis for permanent arrangements' (Crockatt, 1996, p. 54). Stalin did not, however, abandon the idea of a unified Germany and through diplomacy at the international level and the Socialist Unity Party on the ground in the Eastern zone tried to exert maximum influence over as much of the country as possible. Soviet policy was to seek a reunified demilitarized Germany in which Communist influence could prevail rather than accept a divided country in which the 'greater and more powerful state would be assured of Western protection and would develop a booming capitalist economy (Windsor, 1969, p. 58). When the Western powers introduced currency reform into their respective zones of Germany in 1948 it politically divided the country. This directly challenged Moscow whose response was to blockade Berlin. It was only after the birth of the West German state in 1949 that East Germany was constituted as a state.

As the Second World War concluded Stalin began the construction of an 'external' or 'informal' empire from the Balkans to Eastern and Central Europe. Brzezinski has surmised that the Soviet Union had five major objectives with regard to the region (Brzezinski, 1967, p. 4). The first was to deny the area to Germany which was 'in the past a source of major threat to Russian security' (ibid., p. 4). The second was to ensure that Eastern Europe was not controlled by political forces hostile to Moscow. Stalin sought the establishment of 'friendly' regimes in Eastern Europe and, as the Western powers were to discover, reserved the right to determine enemies of the USSR. The third Soviet objective was to use the area for Soviet economic recovery. The fourth objective was to deny the region to the capitalist world since 'no doubt the Soviet leaders, even at the height of the Grand Alliance, must have considered the possibility that some day after the conclusion of the War the capitalist world would again be arrayed against the USSR' (ibid., p. 5). The final objective, Brzezinski believed, was linked to the former in that 'if ideological assumptions played a role in the crystallization of Soviet defensive interests in East Europe, then it's likely that the other part of the ideological orientation, namely its offensive component, was also present' (ibid., p. 5). The addition of territory to the base of socialism would in itself be seen as a progressive step.

The Sovietization of Eastern Europe did not match the degree of centralization pursued in the 'internal empire', the Soviet Union, but was institutionalized nonetheless. In September 1947 the Cominform was founded to coordinate the activities of East European Communist Parties. At its inaugural meeting, Zhdanov the Chief Soviet spokesman stressed that the United States had divided the world into two camps which necessitated closer relations among Communist parties 'on the basis of a common anti-imperialist and democratic platform' (Zhdanov, 1947, quoted in Stokes, 1991, p. 42). Zhdanov identified a new alignment of political forces.

> The more the war recedes into the past, the more distinct become two major trends in postwar international policy, corresponding to the division of the political forces operating on the international arena into two major camps: the imperialist and anti-democratic camp, on the one hand, and the anti-imperialist and democratic camp, on the other. The principal driving force of the imperialist camp is the United States of America … The cardinal purpose of the imperialist camp is to strengthen imperialism, to hatch a new imperialist war, to combat socialism and democracy and to support reactionary and anti-democratic pro-fascist regimes and movements everywhere.
>
> (Zhdanov, ibid., p. 40)

The Cominform marked the end of 'pluralist Sovietization' and the beginnings of what is 'most satisfactorily identified as Stalinism – a period of total conformity in the relations among Communist states (Brzezinski, 1967, p. 62). In 1948 a series of bilateral treaties linked the Soviet Union and East European States and provided for defence arrangements. In February 1948 the coalition Czech government was ousted and a Communist takeover was completed (Kennedy-Pipe, 1995, p. 122). When Tito refused to accept Stalin's leadership Yugoslavia was expelled from the Cominform in June 1948 for taking a nationalist road (see Stokes, 1991, pp. 58–65). The split with Tito sharpened Soviet resolve to ensure conformity in Eastern Europe which in turn meant a 'far greater degree of Soviet involvement would be necessary, with one of its costs being a further decline in the domestic sources of support for the Communist parties (Brzezinski, 1967, p. 64).

Soviet fear of a Titoist contagion led to purges throughout Eastern Europe, show trials and terror. Stalinist policy linked security to ideology, territory and military factors. The interrelationship of these factors led to a structure of relationships in which the Soviet Union sought to determine political development, and Soviet interests were paramount in this system.

After Stalin's death in 1953, the 'thaw' in East–West relations and Moscow's new leadership encouraged the growth of political diversity in the Soviet bloc. Malenkov's 'New Course' (see Brzezinski, 1967, p. 159) and Khrushchev's condemnation of Stalin at the Communist Party of the Soviet Union's (CPSU) Twentieth Party Congress came to be interpreted in Eastern Europe as permitting political variance. The consequences were a second Soviet split with Tito, tensions over Gomulka's leadership in Poland and military intervention in Hungary. Khrushchev had sought change in Soviet bloc relations but remained committed to a 'socialist commonwealth' in which there are 'different paths' but 'among the different paths, there is one general path' (Khrushchev, Prague, July 1957, quoted in Brzezinski, 1967, p. 269). The Warsaw Pact founded in 1955, in response to West German inclusion in NATO, and a revitalized Council for Mutual Economic Assistance (CMEA) were the institutional bases of the Socialist Commonwealth. Unrest and discontent in Hungary became a major crisis for Moscow when Imre Nagy, the Party leader, in October 1956 accepted the principle of a multi-party system and withdrew from the Warsaw Pact. Soviet military intervention commenced on 4 November which violently suppressed the anti-communist movement and forcibly maintained Hungary's membership of the Soviet bloc. After the events of 1956, Soviet policy was to place more emphasis on conflict prevention but 'efforts to foster military, political and economic integration of the "Commonwealth" were, however, only marginally successful during Khrushchev's tenure' (Shafir, 1987, p. 172). Khrushchev's successors also faced challenges in maintaining the cohesion of the Soviet bloc. Yugoslavia remained a socialist 'outsider', the Sino-Soviet split generated tensions and Romania balanced its relations with Moscow with openings to the West. Soviet difficulties in dealing with Ceausescu were, however, eclipsed by the crisis in Czechoslovakia in 1968. Alexander Dubcek became the Czech leader in January and was supported by the progressive faction of the Communist Party. As reformism grew in strength the Czech leadership began to liberalize the regime and seek economic linkages with West Germany. The problems for the Soviet leadership were first 'that the reform faction was independent of Moscow, and the second was that the reform movement initiated democratic charges which threatened to erode Party control' (Kennedy-Pipe, 1998, p. 137). After a series of political initiatives failed to redress the situation, Brezhnev ordered a military intervention in August 1968. In the wake of the invasion the Soviet Union determined a private settlement with the Czech Party and declared its public position on relations with Eastern Europe as a whole, the so-called 'Brezhnev Doctrine'. In November 1968 Brezhnev addressed the Polish United Workers Party on the themes of sovereignty and intervention.

> Socialist states stand for strict respect for the sovereignty of all countries. We resolutely oppose interference in the affairs of any state and the violation of their sovereignty. At the same time, affirmation and defence of the sovereignty of states that have taken the path of socialist construction are of special significance to us communists. The forces of imperialism and reaction are seeking to deprive the people first in one, then another socialist country of the sovereign right they have earned to ensure prosperity for their country and well-being and happiness for the broad working masses by building a security free from all oppression and exploitation. And when encroachments on this right receive a joint rebuff from the socialist camp, the bourgeois propagandists raise the cry of 'defence of sovereignty' and 'non-interference'. It is clear that this is the sheerest deceit and demagoguery on their part.

On the question of intervention, Brezhnev argued:

> ... that there are common natural laws of socialist construction, deviation from which could lead to deviation from socialism as such. And when external and internal forces hostile to socialism try to turn the development of a given socialist country in the direction of restoration of the capitalist system, when a threat arises to the cause of socialism in that country – a threat to the security of the socialist commonwealth as a whole – this is no longer merely a problem for that country's people, but a common problem, the concern of all socialist countries.
>
> (Brezhnev, 1968, quoted in Stokes, 1991, p. 133)

The principles of the 'Brezhnev Doctrine' – limited sovereignty and the overriding interests of the 'socialist commonwealth' – structured Soviet relations with Eastern Europe until the Gorbachev era. The pursuit of détente with the United States and West Germany was predicated upon the maintenance of the bloc, not its erosion. The recognition of the legitimacy of the German Democratic Republic (DDR) was critical to this policy as it signified a wider legitimacy for the Soviet sphere of influence. The 1972 treaty entailing mutual recognition by the two Germanies was therefore a high point of détente both for Moscow and for the division of Europe.

## United States security in Europe

As Germany's defeat became certain the wartime Alliance between Russia and the United States began to disintegrate. The security interests of the two powers led to different and often conflicting policies. As Crockatt has observed 'the United States and the Soviet Union had little in common prior to the war – indeed much had divided them – and from a long term perspective the Alliance was an aberration in their relations' (Crockatt, 1996, p. 46). For the United States Joint Chiefs of Staff (JCS) world peace depended upon the continued cooperation of Russia and the West but this was suspect at best. The JCS believed that a commitment of armed forces should be made to the United Nations (UN) but it 'will be only a small part of the military forces which will be required in any event for national security against the in no way remote possibility of a breakdown in the relation of major powers' (*Foreign Relations of the United States*, 1946, 1, pp. 1160–5, quoted in Etzold and Gaddis, 1978, p. 41). The JCS's sceptical view of postwar relations was in contrast to the State Department's approach which looked to the United Nations as the basis for the future order (see *Foreign Relations of the United States*, 1946, 1, pp. 1125–8, quoted in Etzold and Gaddis, 1978, p. 45). In a sense both viewpoints reflected President Roosevelt's wartime policy of seeking a postwar order based upon great power cooperation but dressed in Wilsonian universalism (see Aron, 1975, p. 4). Yergin has argued that to secure public support Roosevelt disguised his policies in 'Wilsonian garb' (Yergin, 1980, pp. 44–5). At Yalta Roosevelt sought acceptance of liberal principles of self-determination and free elections. The Declaration on Liberated Europe envisaged the formation of 'interim governmental authorities broadly representative of all democratic elements in the population and pledged to the earliest possible establishment through free elections of governments responsive to the will of the people' (Yalta Conference, 1945, quoted in Morgan, 1974, p. 58). With regard to Poland, which became the symbol of East–West relations, it was agreed to reorganize the Communist Lublin administration to include democratic leaders from within Poland and abroad. Despite the language, the share of power given to non-Communists was undetermined and no guarantees were provided for the exiles in London. After Yalta, Stalin's power on the ground in Eastern Europe determined outcomes rather than liberal conference commitments. When Roosevelt informed Stalin that 'there has been a discouraging lack of progress made in carrying out, which the world expects of the political decisions which we reached at the conference, particularly those relating to the Polish question', Stalin's response was to blame America's envoys and to announce that Polish discussions had reached a 'dead end' (Harriman and Abel, 1976, pp. 430–1).

Roosevelt's parallel objectives of securing the maximum possible self-determination for Eastern Europe while not impairing the unity of the Russian alliance became increasingly strained. While Roosevelt remained optimistic that compromises could be found, the problems of reconciling Soviet behaviour with liberal expectations mounted. Roosevelt's death in April 1945 left his Vice President, Truman, with the task of finding policies to secure America's security interests in Europe.

President Truman's initial policy toward Moscow varied between confrontation and conciliation. The clash between Truman and the Soviet Foreign Minister Molotov over the Yalta accords (see Yergin, 1980, p. 83) represented one extreme and the Hopkins Mission to Stalin the other. The Potsdam summit in July 1945 provides further evidence of Washington's willingness to compromise and postpone divisive issues (see Yergin, 1980, pp. 114–17). For Alperovitz this was really a 'delayed showdown' until nuclear intimidation could be brought to bear (Alperovitz, 1985, pp. 110–38). Truman had inherited Roosevelt's decisions to build the atomic bomb, to exclude the Soviet Union from the project and to reject proposals for an international agreement to control nuclear power. When, in April 1945, Secretary of War Stimson briefed Truman on the political implications of the atomic bomb, the use of the weapon against Japan was not questioned but the need for a select committee to consider postwar control was stressed (Bernstein and Matusow, 1966, p. 3). In Sherwin's view, 'what emerges from a careful reading of Stimson's diary, his memorandum of April 25th to Truman, a summary by Groves of the meeting and Truman's own recollections is a case for overall caution in American diplomatic relations with the Soviet Union – it was an argument against any showdown' (Sherwin, 1975, p. 163). Truman did, however, set the date of the Potsdam summit to coincide with the first atomic test (Yergin, 1980, p.

101). Stimson too clearly saw the bomb as a 'master card' in its diplomatic potential for the resolution of territorial disputes with Moscow (Sherwin, 1975, p. 190). The use of the bomb against Japan was then both to secure a prompt American victory and to provide a salutary lesson to Moscow. American policy-makers assumed that such an awesome demonstration of power would induce Soviet concessions in the negotiation of postwar settlements in Europe and Asia. The failure of this 'atomic diplomacy' soon, however, became evident in the Council of Foreign Ministers meeting when American rather than Soviet concessions on European issues became more likely (Yergin, 1980, p. 129). Stalin's policy toward Eastern Europe was not, as we have seen, deterred but rather consolidated in the period of American atomic monopoly. The problem for the Truman administration was to find an effective policy response when diplomatic bargaining, even when backed by atomic power, appeared ineffectual. It was in this context that Kennan's 'Long Telegram' assumed particular significance.

Kennan's 'Long Telegram' argued that the primary motivation of the Kremlin was Russian insecurity reinforced by Marxism. He depicted Soviet foreign policy as operative on official and unofficial levels. The official level, Kennan believed, would constitute: intensive military-industrialization; when opportune, the physical extension of Soviet power; membership of international organizations to counteract Western influence; policies to weaken Western influence in colonial areas; and measures to secure Soviet influence in potential centres of opposition to the West such as Germany or the Middle East (Kennan, 1946, quoted in Etzold and Gaddis, 1978, pp. 55–7). The unofficial level was seen as a 'concealed Comintern', the secret support structure for official policy conducted by Communist parties (ibid., pp. 58–60).

Kennan concluded that, although the Soviet challenge was the 'greatest task our diplomacy has ever faced' it could be met 'without recourse to any general military conflict' (ibid., p. 61) – this on the grounds that Soviet power was 'highly sensitive to [the] logic of force' and would 'easily withdraw ... and usually does ... when strong resistance is encountered at any point' (Kennan, ibid., p. 61). The importance of the 'Long Telegram' was that its analysis confirmed the redundancy of the *quid pro quo* approach' hitherto held by the Truman administration. Kennan did not offer an alternative strategy but did advocate that 'our public is educated to realities of [the] Russian situation' and that the Western powers pursue 'cohesion, firmness and vigour' (Kennan, ibid., p. 62). Secretary of State Byrnes began the process in February 1946 warning that the USA would not accept unilateral challenges to the status quo while Churchill's 'Iron Curtain' speech at Fulton in March 1946 dramatically depicted the consequences of Moscow policies. Truman made no further concessions to the Soviet Union and the policy of firmness was adopted across the board. The problem for Washington was to find the means to support the new policy stance. Demobilization reduced American armed forces from 12 million in 1945 to 1.6 million in 1947 (Gaddis, 1982, p. 23). Defence expenditure fell in a corresponding manner from 81.6 billion dollars in fiscal year 1945 to 13.1 billion dollars in fiscal year 1947 (ibid., appendix one). The Republican Congressional victory in 1946 ensured fiscal prudence and budgetary control. The divergence between Washington's policy objectives and the means at its disposal worsened with the European postwar economic crisis. The Bretton Woods system had proven incapable of dealing with the strains of war, dislocation, debt and reconstruction in Western Europe. Import needs not only for reconstruction but survival generated European deficits that exceeded reserves (see Spero, 1980, p. 34). In February 1947 the British government informed the State Department that, due to economic difficulties, it would cease all military and economic aid to Greece and Turkey on 31 March. Truman sought to take on the British role but needed Congressional support to do so. He decided to 'shock' Congress into action by depicting the world as being divided into two conflicting ideologies, totalitarianism versus freedom. Truman declared 'it must be the policy of the United States to support free peoples who are resisting attempted subjugation by armed minorities or by outside pressures' (Truman, 1947, quoted in Bernstein and Matusow, 1966, p. 255). The rhetoric of the Truman Doctrine was, however, at odds with the policy reality which endorsed intervention in Greece but not China.

The Joint Strategic Survey Committee called for a selective policy concentrating American assistance on key countries designated by criteria of risk and value. The Committee considered which countries should receive aid on the basis of 'their importance to United States security and the urgency of their need in combination' (Joint Strategic Survey Committee, 1947, quoted in Etzold and Gaddis, 1978, p. 83). The Committee rank ordered 16 countries with Britain, France, Germany, Italy, Greece and Turkey constituting the first six (ibid., p. 83). The plan envisaged was 'to assist the nation aided to achieve, or retain a sound economy, to maintain the armed forces necessary for its continued independence and to be of real assistance to the United States in case of ideological warfare' (ibid., p. 83). Kennan advised the Secretary of State in a similar vein warning that the 'present "bi-polarity" will, in the long run, be beyond our resources' (Kennan, 1947, PPS 13, quoted in Etzold and Gaddis, 1978, p. 91). He believed it was 'imperative therefore that we economise with our limited resources and that we apply them where we feel that they will do the most good' (Kennan, 1949, quoted in Gaddis, 1982, p. 31). Kennan thought 'our best answer to this is to strengthen in every way the local forces of resistance, and persuade others to bear a greater part of the burden of opposing communism' (Kennan, 1946, quoted in Etzold and Gaddis, 1978, p. 91). He advo-cated a 'particularist' approach to foreign policy and a rejection of 'uni-versalism' as the basis of American security, believing that 'security can be obtained, nonetheless, through a careful balancing of power, inter-ests and antagonisms' (Gaddis, 1978, p. 26).

The early phases of what became known as the strategy of contain-ment were directed, as Kennan hoped, to the restoration of the balance of power in Europe and Asia. Policies to secure a pro-Western Japan, including a non-punitive peace treaty, were adopted in 1949. Policies for recovery in Western Europe were initiated in 1947 when Secretary of State Marshall announced the European Recovery Programme (ERP). The Truman administration had moved from Roosevelt's universalist prescription to a 'strong point' defence using economic means to secure vital interests. The second phase of containment, however, departed from Kennan's counsel for positive as well as negative induce-ments to the Soviet Union (see Gaddis, 1982, p. 71) as emphasis was placed upon strategic means. Policies to create the North Atlantic Treaty Organization (NATO) and the West German state and to build the hydrogen bomb were seen by Kennan as cementing and militariz-ing the divide with Moscow. The Truman administration, in contrast, saw the policies as necessary to sustain the strategy of containment and to enhance Western security. The Czech coup of 1948 and the Berlin blockade, which took relations between East and West to 'the edge of war' (Yergin, 1980, p. 378), spurred West European calls for NATO. The Alliance and Washington's commitment to the new German Federal Republic structured American interests and security understandings for the Cold War.

The Western and Eastern spheres of Europe developed under the direction of their respective core powers and the structure of the bloc system became mutually reinforcing. The two spheres were, however, different: 'one empire arose ... by invitation, the other by imposition' (Gaddis, 1998, p. 52). It was the West Europeans who sought more than economic aid and what is 'significant, then is not simply that the West Europeans invited the United States to construct a sphere of influence and include them within it; it is also that the Americans encouraged the Europeans to share the responsibility for determining how it would function ...' (ibid., p. 51). In this manner Washington's understanding of security had developed from Roosevelt's view that America's security depended upon the structure of the postwar order, to the Truman administration's recognition of the need to restore the European balance of power, to finally a direct American defence commitment to Western Europe. This process was soon, however, overshadowed by another element, the nuclear arms race. The pursuit of credible nuclear deterrent strategies not only reinforced the existing East–West divide but, moreover, created new dynamics of conflict.

## The nuclear arms race

In response to the Soviet atomic test of 1949, Mao's victory in China and Washington's own decision to develop thermonuclear weapons, a new strategic analysis, NSC68, was commissioned in 1950. It was to set the parameters of United States strategic policy. NSC68 recognized the bipolar structure of the postwar order and its endemic conflict. Conflict was seen as 'zero sum' – 'in the context of the present polarization of power a defeat of free institutions anywhere is a defeat everywhere' (NSC68, quoted in Etzold and Gaddis, 1978, p. 389). NSC68 endorsed containment as a means short of war to 'block [the] further expansion of Soviet power' but only when supported by 'superior aggregate military strength, in being and readily mobilizable ...' (NSC68, ibid., p. 402). The analysis, nevertheless, believed that the existing policy of containment had failed by allowing a relative decline of military power vis-à-vis the Soviet Union, and partly as a consequence a diplomatic impasse had resulted. The strategic review recommended an increase in military power supported by an expanded American economy. NSC68 called for an expansion of air, ground, sea and atomic forces. It was believed that 'for the moment our atomic retaliatory capability is probably adequate to deter the Kremlin from a deliberate direct military attack against ourselves or other free peoples' but 'when it calculates that it has a sufficient atomic capability to make a surprise attack on us, nullifying our atomic superiority and creating a military situation decisively in its favour, the Kremlin might be tempted to strike swiftly and with stealth' (NSC68, ibid., p. 416). The review concluded that in the absence of international measures to eliminate nuclear weapons the United States had to increase the number and strength of its atomic weapons and to develop thermonuclear forces in advance of Moscow. NSC68 did not advocate, however, a completely nuclear-centric strategy and sought to avoid the dilemma of having to react 'totally to a limited extension of Soviet control or of not reacting at all' by having sufficient forces in being 'to thwart such an expansion locally' (NSC68, ibid., p. 428). The proposal was to have 'the military power to deter, if possible, Soviet expansion, and to defeat, if necessary, aggressive Soviet or Soviet-directed actions of a limited or total character' (NSC68, ibid., p. 432). With the outbreak of the Korean War in June 1950 the case for Presidential approval of NSC68 (formally given in September) was cemented. The war was not, however, a simple defeat of Communism but an inconclusive affair which lost public support over its three-year duration. The Eisenhower administration drew upon those 'lessons' and chose to favour nuclear deterrence as the cornerstone of its strategy rather than the more comprehensive approach of NSC68. The 'New Look' of 1953 emphasized the policy of nuclear deterrence. Local defences were to be retained but reinforced by a deterrent of massive retaliatory power. Secretary of State John Foster Dulles saw local defences as important to deal with indirect aggression and to demonstrate commitment but 'the main reliance must be on the power of the free community to retaliate with great force by mobile means at places of its own choice' (Dulles, 1954, p. 359). Dulles did not believe that this meant 'turning every local war into a world war' but 'the essential thing is that a potential aggressor should know in advance that he can and will be made to suffer for his aggression more than he can possibly gain from it' (Dulles, 1954, pp. 358–9). With the deployment of American nuclear forces, including tactical weapons, in Europe, the retaliatory force was given visible presence in the front line of the Cold War. The decision which would 'trigger' the force was left deliberately vague but clearly lay in Moscow's hands. It was, however, this very imprecision and related questions of credibility which led to demands that the 'New Look' be revised.

Critics of the strategy were soon to argue that once a Soviet retaliatory force had been created Washington's threats to use nuclear forces over territorial disputes other than a direct threat to its homeland would carry little credibility. The credibility question of how far deterrence could be 'extended' was seen as especially acute in areas of ill-defined commitment, the so-called 'Gray areas'. Kissinger looked for a new strategy in which American nuclear forces deterred the Soviet Union while other forces were available for employment. Kissinger believed limited war 'capabilities should enable us to confront the opponent with contingencies from which he can only extract himself by all out war while deterring him from this step by a superior retaliatory capacity' (Kissinger, 1957, p. 144). The notion of a 'ladder of force' became fashionable with rungs rising from political and economic aid to capabilities for general war at the top. At the same time the meaning of deterrent strategies was questioned. It was argued that a retaliatory force could only act as such if it could survive a Soviet first strike and deliver an unacceptable second strike.

The implications of the strategic revisions of the New Look called for by Kissinger et al. were an expanded defence budget and a restructuring of the American strategic nuclear force. Eisenhower presided over the beginnings of the latter with the development of the Minuteman intercontinental ballistic missile (ICBM) housed in bunkers and the Polaris submarine-launched ballistic missile (SLBM). It was the Presidential election of 1960 that led to the adoption of flexible response as official strategy with John F. Kennedy's campaign pledging to end the alleged post-Sputnik 'missile gap' and to redress the nation's inability to fight limited wars (see Gaddis, 1982, pp. 198–236). The new Kennedy administration endorsed 'survivability' as the basis of its deterrent force, increasing orders for Polaris and Minutemen while enhancing capabilities for intervention in the Third World and limited warfare. The new approach did not, however, end crises with the Soviet Union.

Soviet strategic policy had been constrained by technology and geography. Moscow's deterrent force was effectively a counter-deterrent targeting Western Europe until it had the means to effectively threaten the United States itself. This cemented the Cold War impasse in Europe and made Western European governments critically sensitive to issues of American credibility and linkage. Moscow sought credibility for its deterrent force and the launch of Sputnik in 1957, the world's first satellite, demonstrated rocket technology which could directly target the United States homelands. Khrushchev's claims to have a force of ICBMs spread public concern in the United States and provided the backdrop to the 1960 elections. In reality the Soviet position was relatively weak. In this context the deployment of medium- and intermediate-range nuclear missiles on Cuba in 1962 can be seen as a means to enhance Soviet credibility and defend the Cuban revolution. The post-Sputnik deployment of similar American missiles in Britain, Italy and Turkey can further be seen as setting a strategic precedent. The consequent crisis as Washington demanded the Soviet weapons be removed marked the zenith of Cold War superpower confrontation. The direct collision over Cuba led to a new era of nuclear diplomacy in which the political accommodation of rivalry came to encompass superpower military confrontation.

## Détente

The era of détente was, as we have seen, viewed by Moscow as a means to confirm its primacy in Eastern Europe. Similarly in nuclear terms détente became a vehicle to assert Moscow's parity with the West. The Soviet acquisition of a second strike (survivable) nuclear force in the mid-1960s led to Washington's acceptance of strategic parity and consequent recognition of Mutually Assured Destruction (MAD). Stability in the strategic balance of forces then became of prime importance to both superpowers and the Strategic Arms Limitation Talks (SALT) integral to its attainment.

The wider political and territorial implications of the central balance, however, remained problematic. Just as past strategists had sought to link nuclear force to conflicts in the world system, Kissinger and Nixon sought a linkage between stability in the central balance and conflict in the Third World. The Nixon administration sought to replace containment by confrontation with containment through negotiation. The basis of this strategy was the belief that a combination of self-interest and necessity would lead the Soviet Union and China into a new relationship with the West. The process was to be the 'politics of linkage', by which issues became interrelated and the outcome the 'net'. 'The Russian bear had to be caught in a dense web of agreements it would have neither the interest nor the possibility of breaking out of' (Hoffmann, 1978, p. 46). American policy-makers looked to linkages between strategic arms negotiations, European security, trade, agricultural agreements and policy in the Third World. The failure to realize such a comprehensive 'net' was to lead to accusations that the Soviet Union was violating the rules of détente and, with the advent of the Reagan administration, a return to the 'colder' policies of confrontation. The problems of linkage stemmed from Soviet rejection and American expectation. The 'twin pillars of resistance to Soviet expansion and a willingness to negotiate on concrete issues' were a major challenge for the Nixon administration when 'the bitter divisions of Vietnam and the ugly suspicions of Watergate produced a domestic climate ill-suited for any thoughtful discussion' (Kissinger, 1982, p. 983). In addition to the problems of securing domestic support, Washington had to secure Moscow's cooperation in linkage. The Soviet

Union's selective response to détente, embracing arms control and trade but not acquiescence in the Third World, left the United States with a dilemma. To 'punish' Moscow the logic was to de-link, to withdraw from another element of détente, but could Washington simply abandon an area of overriding interest such as arms control or jeopardize détente as a process? The choice for the Nixon administration was 'between a fragmented progression and regression' (Hoffmann, 1978, p. 60). Kissinger chose the former which was to create a complex pattern of superpower relations, combining cooperation in the central balance with competition in regional and Third World power balances. A series of crises in the Third World, together with Soviet intervention, fatally undermined this policy, weakened the credibility of détente and facilitated a return to Cold War confrontation (see Halliday, 1989).

## The role of the United Nations in Cold War conflict resolution

The United Nations was the international institution entrusted after the Second World War with the task of conflict resolution in the international system. It was empowered by its Charter to undertake a number of roles ranging from the pacific settlement of disputes to collective security. The Security Council was entrusted with 'primary responsibility for the maintenance of international peace and security ...' (Article 24.1). The Security Council was to work with the Military Staff Committee to formulate plans for the regulation of armaments. Under Chapter Six of the Charter the Security Council could investigate any dispute 'or any situation which might lead to international friction or give rise to a dispute, in order to determine whether the continuance of the dispute or situation is likely to endanger the maintenance of international peace and security' (Article 34). The Charter looked to a solution of disputes first by 'negotiation, enquiry, mediation, conciliation, arbitration, judicial settlement, resort to regional agencies as arrangements, or other peaceful means of their own choice' (Article 33.1). If the Security Council determined the existence of any threat to the peace, breach of the peace or act of aggression it could decide what measures to take under articles 41 and 42 of the Charter. Article 41 empowered the Security Council to take economic sanctions, sever diplomatic relations and curtail communications should it deem this necessary to give effect to its decisions. Should the Security Council consider that such measures would be or have been inadequate 'it may take such action by air, sea, or land forces as may be necessary to maintain or

restore international peace and security' (Article 42). The Charter envisaged that all members of the United Nations would make available
armed forces for the Security Council and their strategic employment
would be planned by the Military Staff Committee.

In practice the above provisions proved difficult to implement under
the conditions of the Cold War. The regulation of armaments, the
control of atomic power and disarmament all fell victim to the
East–West confrontation. The pursuit of credible strategies of deterrence,
alliances and deployment of forces were far more important to the
superpowers than the principles of the United Nations. The Military
Staff Committee was formed but was soon grounded by the division
between East and West. On 2 July 1948 the Committee reported that it
could not make any further progress. The Security Council was also
unable to fulfil its Charter roles. The permanent members of the Security
Council held veto powers over non-procedural actions. A single negative
vote effectively ended Security Council action on any issue whatever the
threat to international peace and security. By the end of 1966 the veto
had been used 109 times (Goodrich, 1972, p. 33). The capability of the
United Nations to exercise its collective security functions was therefore
severely curtailed. The one exception was Korea in 1950. The Security
Council without the Soviet Union, absent due to Moscow's boycott of
the United Nations in relation to Chinese representation, decided that
the North Korean invasion was a breach of the peace. The Security
Council in a subsequent meeting recommended that members furnish
such assistance as necessary to repel the North Korean attack and restore
peace (Nicholas, 1979, p. 51). The consequent deployment of forces
under a United Nations flag was threatened with the return of the Soviet
Union to the Security Council. The United States' response was to
sustain the Korean operation through the General Assembly under the
'Uniting for Peace' resolution (ibid., p. 52). For the rest of the Cold War
neither superpower dared absent itself from the Security Council and
immobilism resulted. The United Nations was denied any influence in
crises within the superpowers' spheres of influence or in conflicts that
they were to deem vital to their interests. The negative effects of the
Cold War spread throughout the organization.

The issues that arose in the organisation were not all Cold War
problems in origin. Some did arise directly from the confrontation
between East and West: Azerbaijan, Greece, East European questions, above all Korea. Others had different causes, arising in quite
other areas of the world from the centre of East–West confrontation:

Indonesia, Palestine, Kashmir. Yet all, whatever their origin, came to be seen in the UN through Cold War eyes. All were fought and manoeuvred, partly at least, as episodes within the wider struggle between the two great ideological camps.

(Luard, 1982, p. 93)

One important contribution that the United Nations developed in the face of Cold War adversity was its peacekeeping role. While the origins of peacekeeping may be traced to truce supervision and observer missions (UN, 1990, p. 9) the dispatch of United Nations forces to Egypt during the Suez crisis of 1956 set the precedents for such operations. The United Nations Emergency Force (UNEF) was dispatched to Egypt with Cairo's consent. The troops were voluntarily offered by member states not party to the dispute to ensure their impartiality. The force was deployed after a ceasefire had been agreed and, while its functions were more than those of an observer corps, it was not an instrument of enforcement. UNEF was in practice a 'buffer' between the local protagonists facilitating a de-escalation of tension and the commencement of negotiations. On this basis peacekeeping developed to become an instrument available to the international community to assist in conflict resolution. Peacekeeping, like other UN measures, remained subject to the vicissitudes of superpower politics affecting both its initiation and maintenance. Peacekeeping also faced a challenge when it was applied to crises involving intra-state conflict rather than inter-state conflict. The difficulties of applying the principles of classical peacekeeping in such conflicts were amply demonstrated in the Congo crisis of 1960–64. It was one thing to secure consent and a ceasefire from states but quite another to secure compliance from factions seeking secession and separatism from the state. When the United Nations could not maintain order the resort to force to impose its authority became compelling. As peacekeeping drifted into peace-enforcement in the Congo, Moscow questioned the legitimacy of the mission. Enforcement meant an end to strict impartiality and the United Nations became a key player in the conflict. This heralded problems for the United Nations peacekeeping in ethnic conflicts and civil wars which have become all too evident in the post-Cold War order.

## Transition in the European order

The Cold War structure of European order began to unravel in the late 1980s with the advent of Gorbachev's new Soviet strategic policies. The end of the Cold War in Europe was signalled by the superpower resolution of strategic divisions. Agreements in arms control ended prolonged disputes over intermediate-range nuclear forces (INF), strategic nuclear forces and conventional forces. The INF agreement of 1987 was followed by the momentous decision to limit conventional forces in Europe (CFE) in 1990 and the commencement of the Strategic Arms Reduction Treaty (START) in 1991. All three agreements contributed to the stabilization and normalization of the European order. The threat of war was diminished and the prospects for further arms reductions positively outlined. The dramatic 'thaw' followed Gorbachev's reform programme and need to transform Soviet defence expenditure. Gorbachev had inherited a Soviet economy in serious decline. Growth rates had fallen close to stagnation, output in key industries had declined, agricultural output failed to meet targets, and foreign debt had increased as had price inflation. Structural weaknesses included 'the inflexibility of the central planning system which rewarded gross output rather than productivity and management techniques' (Crockatt, 1996, p. 31). Against this background the Soviet Union was spending 15–20 per cent of Gross National Product (GNP) on its military budget (see Goldman, 1992, p. 108). Gorbachev's response was built around the programme of perestroika (restructuring) and glasnost (openness). Perestroika was a 'decisive acceleration of the socioeconomic and cultural development of Soviet society which involves radical changes on the way to a qualitatively new state ...' (Gorbachev, 1988, p. 50). Glasnost was seen as an essential means to achieve change against the entrenched institutions of the old Soviet system. Gorbachev believed 'it is no longer a question of whether the CPSU Central Committee will continue the policy of glasnost through the press and the other mass media and with the active participation of citizens. We need glasnost as we need air' (Gorbachev, 1988, p. 78). In conjunction with domestic reform Gorbachev adopted 'New Thinking' for Soviet foreign policy. The Soviet leader declared 'it is no longer possible to draft a policy on the premises of the year 1947, the Truman doctrine and Churchill's Fulton speech. It is necessary to think and act in a new way' (Gorbachev, 1988, p. 140). Gorbachev argued that 'nuclear war cannot be a means of achieving political, economic, ideological or any other goals' (ibid., p. 140). He believed security could no longer be attained by military means and saw 'the only way to security is through political decisions and disarmament' (ibid., p. 141). New Thinking could then directly contribute to Soviet reform by contributing resources to the civilian economy and cut the spiralling costs of the arms race. Gorbachev recognized strategic and economic interdependence. He sought Western assistance in the restructuring of the Soviet economy and in arms control to facilitate a redirection of capital to domestic needs. He saw Europe as a 'Common Home', in which 'the requirements of economic development in both parts of Europe, as well as scientific and technological progress, prompt the need for a search for some form of mutually advantageous coopera-tion' (ibid., p. 196). New Thinking further ended the Soviet marriage of ideology and foreign policy.

> Ideological differences should not be transferred to the sphere of interstate relations, nor should foreign policy be subordinate to them, for ideologies may be poles apart, whereas the interest of sur-vival and prevention of war stand universal and supreme.
>
> (Ibid., p. 143)

In the case of Eastern and Central Europe, Gorbachev sought a new relationship. He had made a commitment to the principles of 'absolute independence' of socialist countries and the independence of each Party as a 'sovereign right' (ibid., p. 165) but until the Poles and Hungarians tested Moscow's propensity for intervention it was feared the Brezhnev Doctrine remained in force. When the Soviet Union did not intervene in the transition of these two states the door opened for a far wider transformation of the European order.

Gorbachev could not have envisaged the scale of the changes his poli-cies unleashed as reform led to revolution first in Eastern Europe and the Balkans and then in the Soviet Union itself. The process of change in Eastern and Central Europe was different in each country reflecting their differing domestic politics and relations with Moscow. Gorbachev's liber-alization and the pattern of Soviet change was endorsed to varying degrees by reformist elites and resisted by others. The pattern of change has been well documented (see Stokes, 1993; Mason, 1992; Waller, 1993) but it is important to stress its domestic dynamics:

> In all of these states there was an internal dynamic which led to a situation ripe for radical change. In a way the changes in the Soviet Union made the explosion come earlier but an explosion would have come even without Gorbachev.
>
> (Niklasson, 1994, p. 206)

Issues of political legitimacy, economic crisis and identity varied in intensity and relevance in each of the East European states. In Czechoslovakia the 'velvet revolution' led to the 'velvet divorce'. In the DDR revolution became reunification of the German state. Yet in each case what the Soviets did or rather did not do was a key factor in the revolutions of 1989–90. Without Soviet intervention – without the forceful imposition of the Soviet line – the regimes of Eastern Europe lost a key constituent of their support and were left answerable to a domestic audience which demanded change. The combination of Soviet policy and East European domestic politics was clearly critical to change. It is 'therefore most fruitful to look at the events as an outcome of a dynamic relationship between domestic and external factors' (Niklasson, 1994, p. 206).

In turn the revolutions of Eastern Europe affected Soviet domestic politics. By 1990 the Soviet system was under stress with economic and political dissatisfaction growing. Political transition in Eastern Europe enhanced demands for reform in the Soviet Union, autonomy, secession and, from other quarters, resistance to these changes. On the economic front Gorbachev had failed to secure a positive response from Soviet society.

> The move towards an economy based on market mechanisms and private enterprise came to be seen by reduced reformers as half-hearted and by Soviet consumers as still inadequate to meet growing demands. Industrial efficiency also suffered as administrative changes, severe staff cuts and low morale over the changes made in the economy began to hit home.
>
> (Kennedy-Pipe, 1998, p. 200)

Political discontent grew and was not controlled by a Communist Party weakened by glasnost and the transfer of authority to the Republics. Nationalism became a potent force as the 'medium through which discontent with the centrally planned and politically controlled system could be expressed and the elections to the republican parliaments in March 1990 provided an institutional framework for it' (McAuley, 1992, p. 105). Boris Yeltsin asserted Russian claims to sovereignty, arguing that Russia had suffered the greatest damage from command-administrative systems (see Yeltsin, 1990, p. 410). In the Baltic Republics demands grew for independence and the issue of nationalism threatened to engulf the Union. In 1991 Gorbachev sought to introduce a new Union treaty entailing voluntary association. On the eve of the Treaty's signature conservative hardliners in the Soviet cabinet attempted a *coup d'état* to 'save' the Soviet Union. Ironically the very forces that the coup sought to arrest accelerated with its failure. The Communist Party and the Soviet elite were discredited and the break-up of the Union became inevitable with the Ukraine following the Baltic states in declaring independence. The Communist Party of the Soviet Union was suspended, the KGB disbanded and on 25 December 1991 Gorbachev resigned as Soviet President.

## The new world order

The collapse of the Soviet Union marked the advent of a new world and European order. The bipolar system of world politics ended and with it Cold War understandings of security. This section examines the key features of the new order, the nature of its conflicts and new conceptualizations of security.

The United States is now the sole superpower in the international system. For some observers international politics are now unipolar.

> First, the system is unambiguously unipolar. The United States enjoys a much larger margin of superiority over the next most powerful state or, indeed, all other great powers combined than any leading state in the last two centuries.
>
> (Wohlforth, 1999, p. 7)

For others the existence of a sole superpower does not mean the world is unipolar.

> A unipolar system would have one superpower, no significant major powers, and many minor powers. As a result, the superpower could effectively resolve important international issues alone, and no combination of other states would have the power to prevent it from doing so.
>
> (Huntington, 1999, p. 35)

The contemporary system can also be seen as moving toward multipolarity, certainly in economic terms. The United States may enjoy an unrivalled military-technical pre-eminence but has suffered a relative economic decline since the 1970s which makes Washington sensitive to economic competition. Huntington has suggested that the contemporary international system is 'a strange hybrid, a uni-multipolar system with one superpower and several major powers' (Huntington, 1999, p. 36). The settlement of key international issues, Huntington argues, requires action by the single superpower 'but always with some combination of other major states: the single superpower can, however, veto action on key issues by combinations of other states' (ibid., p. 36). The major powers including the 'German-French condominium in Europe, Russia in Eurasia, China and potentially Japan in East Asia, India in south Asia, Iran in south west Asia, Brazil in Latin America and South Africa and Nigeria in Africa' (ibid., p. 36) are seen as having regional pre-eminence but not the global reach of the United States. In each region Huntington also depicts secondary powers: Britain in relation to France and Germany, Ukraine in relation to Russia, Japan in relation to China, South Korea in relation to Japan, Pakistan in relation to India, Saudi Arabia in relation to Iran and Argentina in relation to Brazil (ibid., p. 36). The interrelationship of the major and secondary regional powers is seen as being critically affected by the United States:

> The principal source of contention between the superpower and the major regional powers is the former's intervention to limit, counter, or shape the actions of the latter. For the secondary regional powers, on the other hand, superpower intervention is a resource that they potentially can mobilize against their region's major power.
>
> (Ibid., p. 46)

The regionalization of security can therefore be seen to have intensified since the Cold War. As the bipolar 'overlay' has been lifted, 'a clear shift is now underway toward primacy for regional military security dynamics' (Buzan, Wæver and Wilde, 1998, p. 70). The consequences of security regionalization have not, however, been uniform. In some regions, such as Western Europe, the military security dilemma has ceased to be of prime importance for local actors but in others, such as the Balkans or the Caucasus, local conflicts both between and within states have intensified. The collapse of Soviet power 'unleashed intense processes of securitization and local conflicts over territory, population, and status' (ibid., p. 67). In contrast relations between the advanced industrial democracies have remained cooperative and stable. Western Europe, Japan and the United States have sustained old patterns of engagement in the post-Cold War order. For some analysts this reflects the nature of Washington's policy, as United States behaviour 'can affect the calculations of other major states and may help to convince them that it is unnecessary to engage in balancing behaviour' (Mastanduno, 1997, p. 60). In other accounts the sustained relevance of inter-state cooperation has transcended the end of the Cold War:

> The Western States are not held together because of external threats or the simple concentration of power. Rather, Western order has

what might be called 'constitutional characteristics' – a structure of institutions and open polities that constrain power and facilitate 'voice opportunities', thereby mitigating the implications of power asymmetries and reducing the opportunities of the state to exit or dominate.

(Ikenberry, 1998, p. 45)

For such states inter-state conflict in the form of war can be argued to be obsolete. Major war 'is going out of fashion; if it is not yet fully obsolete, it is certainly obsolescent' (Mandelbaum, 1998, p. 21). Debellicization may characterize the relations of Japan, the United States and Western Europe but for Mandelbaum it is on 'the policies of and preferences of China and Russia that the obsolescence of major war depends' (ibid., p. 28). The two major powers are seen as neither 'fully or irreversibly democratic', for both 'spheres of influence are not entirely obsolete', and for both 'national prestige is of prime importance' (ibid., p. 29). The issue that Mandelbaum argues has the potential to embroil Russia, China and others in a major war is irredentism but he recognizes that neither is on the 'verge of launching a war of reincorporation' (ibid., p. 30).

## United States security in the new world order

American foreign and defence policy in the post-Cold War era can be summarized as an attempt to preserve the 'unipolar moment'. The 'grand strategy of preserving primacy has spanned the Bush and Clinton administrations, notwithstanding differences in their foreign policy rhetoric' (Mastanduno, 1997, p. 52). While the overall direction of American policy is discernible the means to sustain primacy and the nature of America's new role have not been equally clear.

The transformation of America's security environment from the global confrontation with the Soviet Union to the regionalization of security set Washington new challenges in foreign and defence policy. The United States' relationship to major regional powers can be seen in a number of potential guises: the 'lone superpower', the 'global balancer' or the 'conciliator' (Miller, 1994, pp. 623–4). The Regional Defence Strategy of 1993 outlined some of the problems facing Washington:

Together with our allies, we must preclude hostile non-democratic powers from dominating regions critical to our interests and otherwise work to build on international environment conducive to our values. Yet even as we hope to increasingly rely on collective approaches to solve international problems, we recognize that a collective effort will not always be timely and, in the absence of US leadership, may not gel. Where the stakes so merit, we must have forces to protect our critical interests.

(Cheney, 1993, quoted in Bowen and Dunn, 1996, p. 154)

American regional intervention was also complicated by the dual nature of potential conflicts: 'aggression by parties with interests antithetical to those of the United States; but also the potential for smaller, internal conflicts based on ethnic, tribal, or religious animosities; state sponsored terrorism; and subversion of friendly governments' (Aspin, 1994, quoted in Bowen and Dunn, 1996, p. 162). Domestic politics have also intruded into this calculus of interest. America's domestic concerns rose to the top of the political agenda in the 1990s. With the end of the Cold War, arguments focused on the need to revitalize the 'home front' before embarking on new foreign policy adventures. President Clinton campaigned on domestic issues in 1992 and elevated the importance of trade and economics within foreign policy. The importance of the domestic agenda and the rise of neo-isolationism have denied policy-makers a clear consensus on intervention strategy and defence allocations. Politically costly encounters, such as the Somalian intervention (1992–94), tempered American enthusiasm for participation in further domestic conflagrations. Despite the success of 'Desert Storm' sensitivity over casualties remained a significant factor affecting American deployment of forces. The Clinton administration turned to diplomacy, sanctions and air power in preference to ground forces for operations such as in Bosnia. The level of defence spending and resources to sustain America's post-Cold War policy has also been the subject of debate. The Bush administration's defence review resulted in the 'Base Force', a plan to reduce the American military by some 25 per cent compared to its Cold War predecessor. In 1993 the Clinton administration unveiled the 'Bottom-Up Review' which cut force levels by 15 per cent from the 'Base Force' targets. The two reviews were to leave the United States the ability to fight and win two major regional conflicts (MRCs) on the scale of 'Desert Storm'. The 'two MRC capability' became synonymous with the 'level of military capability viewed as necessary to support the US position as the world's sole remaining superpower' (Khalilzad and Ochmonek, 1997, p. 44). The 'Bottom-Up Review' was criticized by some analysts as failing to cut defence expenditure sufficiently and by others for being driven by budgetary and not strategic concerns. The problem for defence planning in the post-Cold War era 'is that there exists no obvious yardstick against which to measure these capabilities' which has resulted in 'the construction of potential future conflict scenarios against which to judge prudent force levels' (Bowen and Dunn, 1996, p. 72). The Quadrennial Defense Review of May 1997 argued that America's strategic path lay between neo-isolationism and the role of a world policeman.

> In between these competing visions of isolationism and world policeman lies a security strategy that is consistent with our global interests – a national security strategy of engagement. A strategy of engagement presumes the United States will continue to exercise strong leadership in the international community, using all dimensions of its influence to shape the international security environment.
> (Report of the Quadrennial Defense Review, 1997, Section III, p. 1)

The Quadrennial Review endorsed the 1993 Regional Defense Strategy which emphasized coalitions, cooperative multinational approaches that 'distribute the burden of responsibility among like-minded states' (ibid., p. 2). It also, however, recognized America's unique position as the 'only power in the world that can organize effective military responses to large-scale regional threats, the cornerstone of many mutually beneficial alliances and security partnerships, and the foundation of stability in key regions of the world' (ibid., p. 2). The use of American forces though, was to be selective, guided by the 'US national interests at stake – be they vital, important, or humanitarian in nature – and by whether the costs and risks of a particular military involvement are commensurate with those interests' (ibid., p. 2). The stress upon selectivity was underlined with respect to humanitarian crises where the use of the US military was not seen as most appropriate. If the US military was to be dispatched to address a humanitarian catastrophe the Quadrennial Review stated that the mission should be 'clearly defined, the risk to American troops should be minimal, and substantial US military involvement should be confined to the initial period of providing relief until broader international assistance efforts get underway' (ibid., p. 3). Whatever the crisis, however, the Review concluded:

> In all cases where the commitment of US forces is considered, determining whether the associated costs and risks are commensurate

with the US interest at stake should be the central calculus of US decisions. Such decisions should also depend on our ability to define a clear mission, the desired end state of the situation, and the exit strategy for forces committed.

(Ibid., p. 3)

While the use of American forces was to be selective the Quadrennial Review retained the commitment to maintaining capabilities to deter and defeat two MRCs.

If the United States were to forgo its ability to deflect aggression in more than one theater at a time, our standing as a global power, as the security partner of choice, and as the leader of the international community would be called into question.

(Ibid., p. 8)

Indeed the United States remains committed to a 'full spectrum of military operations, from deterring an adversary's aggression or coercion in crisis and conducting concurrent smaller-scale contingency operations, to fighting and winning major theater wars' (Cohen, 1999, p. 6). The maintenance of such forces led President Clinton in 1999 to propose the first substantial increase in defence spending in 15 years (ibid., p. 1). The problem for policy-makers was seen as planning for an uncertain, complex and dynamic security environment.

## Russian security in the new European order

Russia has, since the demise of the Soviet Union, followed an uncharted role, reflecting challenges of identity, and political and economic transition. In a very short time Moscow ceased to be the capital of a superpower with global interests and became the capital of the Russian Federation. Russia as a major Eurasian power now had to define its role and direction in the new international order.

In the immediate post-Soviet period Russian leaders embraced Gorbachev's legacy and pursued reformist policies and a strategy of engagement with the West. Yeltsin and his foreign minister, Kozyrev, proclaimed support for Western values including human rights, liberal democracy and free markets. Moscow sought Western assistance in the reform of the Russian economy and its integration into the world economy. In 1992 and 1993, however, the pro-Western direction of Russian policy became increasingly criticized by a wide spectrum of 'moderates and hard line nationalists, communists, neo-Bolsheviks and so-called Eurasianists' (Buszynski, 1995, pp. 105–6). As the West failed to rejuvenate the Russian economy the position of the 'Atlanticists' became more isolated. Russian politics is more complex though than a simple confrontation between the 'Westernizers and Atlanticists' versus the 'Eurasianists'. Several schools of thought can be identified that 'cut across institutions and that reflect broader alignments within society' (Dawisha and Parrot, 1994, p. 199). In addition to the pragmatic Westernizing approach there are those who argue for a multi-ethnic democratic state but with the assertive foreign policy of a great power, particularly in the 'Near Abroad'; a third tendency holds the view that Russia rests on a defined ethnic base and has a particular responsibility to the 25 million Russians outside the current Federation; a fourth school is isolationist, slavophile and focuses on domestic reconstruction; and a final approach looks to the restoration of the Soviet Union and its wider role (Dawisha and Parrott, 1994, pp. 199–202). The approaches do not correlate exactly with defined political groups; rather it 'is more appropriate to picture the deviations from the New Thinking paradigm as lying on a continuum, with fluid transitions, from moderate to extreme, from authoritarian to fascist, from non-violent to coercive, and from multi-ethnic, multicultural and multilateralist to Russian nationalist, isolationist and xenophobic' (Adomeit, 1995, p. 51).

In 1993 the domestic base for pro-Western policy was eroded by the results of the legislative elections. Zhirinovsky's ultra-nationalist Liberal Democratic Party won 25 per cent of the vote and in total neo-imperial parties won 39.4 per cent of the vote (Wyllie, 1997, p. 60). The popular stress was now upon the restoration of Russia's great power status, the protection of Russian rights and a new Russian assertiveness in the former Soviet Union, the 'Near Abroad'. The Russian leadership moved to adopt policies which reflected the new mood, a 'Russia first' stance.

In 1993 the Russian Foreign and Defence Ministers agreed the 'Basic Principles of the Foreign Policy of the Russian Federation'. The defence of the territorial integrity of the Russian Federation was given top priority followed by relations with the former Soviet Union and security of the region surrounding the borders of Russia (ibid., p. 62). Taken together with the new political emphasis on Russia's 'great power' interests it brought Moscow into conflict with the West over NATO enlargement, made for problematic relations over the Balkan debacle and justified intervention in the 'Near Abroad'.

Russia has political strategic and economic interests in the 'Near Abroad'. The plight of the 25 million ethnic Russians located in the former Soviet Republics has generated political concern in Moscow and fuelled nationalist politics. In some instances the protection of the minorities has become interwoven with military and strategic factors. In the Baltic states Russia delayed the withdrawal of its troops until citizenship issues and the status of strategic installations were resolved. The Crimea's predominantly Russian population's demands for independence from the Ukraine have threatened to worsen disputes between Russia and the Ukraine over control of the Black Sea fleet. The dispersal of this former Soviet strategic force has also been linked to the disposal of Soviet nuclear forces. The Ukraine together with Russia, Belarus and Kazakhstan inherited Soviet strategic nuclear forces, and sought security guarantees in return for its commitment to a non-nuclear status. Conflict with Russia threatened Ukraine's disarmament and the START regime.

Russia has also militarily intervened in the 'Near Abroad' under the title of 'peacekeeping'. The Russian military doctrine of 1993, while acknowledging the possibility of global conventional or nuclear war, gives more emphasis to regional threats and local conflicts (Lepingwell, 1994, p. 73). The doctrine envisaged the protection of 'ethnic Russians' in the 'Near Abroad' and while the final version spoke of 'Russian citizens', the intent was not lost on neighbouring republics (ibid., p. 74). In April 1994 Yeltsin authorized the Russian military to negotiate base rights in the 'Near Abroad' and with the appointment of Yevgeny Primakov as Foreign Minister in 1996 the seal was set on the new policy. Primakov spoke of the need for reintegration of the former Soviet Union, arguing that further economic reform was contingent upon that step. He denied neo-imperialism claiming that this was not just a Russian demand. He declared, however, that Russia must 'more vigorously and effectively' defend its interests, rejected any 'strategic alliance' with its former 'Cold War adversaries' and argued Russia must become an 'international counterweight' to those adversaries (Primakov, 1996, p. 1).

The 'Near Abroad' is precisely the space where Russia could 'defend its interests' with minimal Western interference. Russian forces have been deployed in a number of former Soviet republics. In Georgia, where conflict erupted between Georgians, Abkazians and Ossetians upon independence, the Russian role has been far from neutral (Lepingwell, 1994, p. 76). The intervention rewarded Russia with base rights and Georgian membership of the CIS. In Armenia Russia is looked to as a counter against a possible Turkish intervention on behalf of Azerbaijan in the war over Nagorno-Karabakh. In Tajikistan Russian forces intervened first in the civil war and then to support the government against fresh guerrilla invasions. In Moldova the Russian 14th Army under Lebed played a significant role in supporting the virtual secession of the Russian and Ukrainian peoples on the Trans-Dniester region. Russian motives in these interventions varied but overall 'Russians increasingly believe that post-Soviet Eurasian geopolitics have left little choice for them – either the Russian Federation will shape and stabilise its "outer" geopolitical space, or the events in the near abroad will determine Russia's own development through waves of refugees, political upheaval, regional conflicts and instability' (Shashenkov, 1994, p. 49).

Political instability and conflict has struck the Russian Federation. The autonomous Republic of Chechnya, which first declared independence in October 1991, rejected the 1992 Russian Federal Treaty. Conflict between Moscow and Grozny grew and following the shift to the right in Russian politics in 1993 it escalated to war. Moscow opposed Chechen independence for the precedent it could set for the wider Federation, for the threat it posed to Russia's position in the Caucasus and for the threat it posed to Russia's interests in the oil and gas reserves of the region (Buszynski, 1995, pp. 114–18; Lapidus, 1998, pp. 8–17). Moscow armed the Chechen opposition but when it failed to oust President Dudayev a direct Russian invasion commenced. The 1994 campaign was far from the 'brief and successful surgical strike promised by its advocates' and turned into ' a massive, brutal and protracted war that devastated the republic of Chechnya, weakened Yeltsin's political standing at home and exposed the military and political weakness of the Russian state' (Lapidus, 1998, p. 21). The 1996 ceasefire, negotiated by Lebed following the defeat of Russian forces in Grozny, deferred a decision on the status of Chechnya for five years. In 1999, however, violence flared again with Russian forces striking at Chechnya and Dagestan. The military intervention was prompted by Russian accusations that Chechen terrorists had bombed Moscow apartments and Islamist forces had mounted an incursion into Dagestan. As the Russian offensive intensified it became intertwined with the political battle to be Yeltsin's successor.

Russia's claim to be a great power needs to be set against the struggle in Chechnya, the continuing economic crisis and political instability. These weaknesses are significant and when combined with Russia's status as a Eurasian power with strategic nuclear forces pose a real challenge for the European if not the world order.

## The new European order

The collapse of the Soviet Union marked the advent of a new European order. The idea of a predominant threat to security which had pre-vailed throughout the Cold War gave way to the notion of risks: risks of instability caused by political, economic or societal insecurity within states which could spread outwards in the European space challenging order. The structures developed and sustained by Moscow imploded with the demise of the Soviet formal and informal empires. The states of Eastern and Central Europe then looked to the institutions of the West for economic, military and political security. The same institu-tions became central to the accommodation of a reunified Germany in the new Europe.

West Germany's political elites had looked to the process of European integration as a means to compensate for the state's semi-sovereignty in the Cold War. For security and defence Bonn similarly looked to another forum, NATO. At the same time West Germany's legitimacy, acceptability and predictability was secured through the Europeanization of its national interests. The institutional impact upon West Germany 'restructured and ultimately remolded German interests, so that, in the eyes of German political elites, institutional memberships were not merely instruments of policy but also normative frameworks for policy making' (Anderson and Goodman, 1993, pp. 23–4). The reunification of Germany in October 1990 was conducted within these parameters. The emergence of Germany as the core power in Europe was accompanied by a decision to 'limit its autonomy and to function as a unit of the EU' (Schwarz, 1994, p. 84). The reassertion of Germany's European identity through the policies of Chancellor Kohl and Franco-German cooperation was cemented by the Maastricht Treaty. German policy-makers 'sought to allay the concerns of EC partners by embed-ding the nation in a more capable, powerful union' (Anderson and Goodman, 1993, p. 56). At the same time the new European Union offered Germany a means to advance its economic and security inter-ests. While Germany remains a net contributor to the EU budget with the 'completion of the internal market, together with the opening of the economies of the Central and East European Countries (CEEC), the opportunities for an export-oriented economy like the FRG are very high' (Bulmer and Paterson, 1996, p. 16). The Maastricht Treaty, more-over, established both an internal security field and an external security role. Germany was now afforded new means to stabilize its frontiers and pursue security initiatives. The Maastricht Treaty identified the Western

European Union (WEU) as the body responsible for its decisions, which had defence implications. This Europeanization of security, however, challenged NATO and the transatlantic basis of defence deemed essential during the Cold War. The relationship of NATO to the WEU and the EU consequently became problematized and NATO's future role became a question for both the United States and European governments. The relevance of institutions was not, however, in question. The EU, NATO, the WEU, the CSCE/OSCE and the UN were and are seen by states as integral to stability in the new Europe. International 'regimes and organizations were significant not because they controlled state policies but because they were useful to states, and in the process constrained the choices that governments could make' (Keohane and Nye, 1993, p. 15). In order to gauge the contribution of international institutions to European security we need to assess both the potential for state cooperation and the empirical record of institutions in conflict management in the new Europe.

Contemporary analyses of security have differed in their interpretation of the new order. Mearsheimer has taken a pessimistic view based upon neorealist reasoning. Anticipating the departure of the superpowers from Central Europe in 1990 Mearsheimer envisaged the transformation of Europe from a bipolar to a multipolar system and the removal of the superpower nuclear arsenals (Mearsheimer, 1990). As a consequence 'the prospects for major crises and war in Europe are likely to increase markedly' (ibid., p. 6). Mearsheimer argued that the distribution and character of military power are the root causes of war and peace. He believed the absence of war since 1945 was the consequence of three factors: 'the bipolar distribution of military power on the continent; the rough military equality between the two states comprising the two poles in Europe, the United States and the Soviet Union; and the fact that each superpower was armed with a large nuclear arsenal (ibid., p. 7). For Mearsheimer these factors had a stabilizing and pacifying effect upon international relations which is in 'a state of relentless security competition, with the possibility of war always in the background' (Mearsheimer, 1994, quoted in Brown et al., 1998, p. 334). Cooperation between states is seen as limited 'mainly because it is constrained by the dominating logic of security competition, which no amount of cooperation can eliminate' (ibid., p. 334). The consequences for state behaviour are seen as 'little room for trust', as each state seeks 'to guarantee its own survival' and attempts to 'maximize their relative power positions ...' (ibid., pp. 336–7). The issue of relative gains is seen in particular to constrain security cooperation.

In contrast others have taken a different view of the new strategic environment and the potential for state cooperation. The passing of the Cold War can be seen to have ended not just the bipolar structure of international relations but the military domination of security. In the place of Cold War polarity a new agenda emerged with some military elements but 'most of it was concerned with non-traditional security issues ranging from fears of instability in the global trading and financial systems, through a bewildering array of supposed threats to national and religious identities, to alarmist predictions about the effects of various environmental pollutants' (Buzan, 2000, p. 7). The transformation of international order and security overtook prevailing understandings of strategy and invited new analyses. Approaches which stress the distribution of capabilities or are based upon a materialist understanding have been challenged by social constructivist analyses. Social constructivist approaches stress that there is a 'process of securitization (and desecuritization) by which human collectivities determine what is (or is not) to be understood, and treated, as an existential threat' (ibid., p. 9). In this vein of understanding, attitudes and agendas are critically important to security. In short, how insecurity is conceptualized is important to security itself. The approach facilitates an understanding of the new multi-issue and multi-level security agenda. It enables the focus of enquiry to move beyond states to societies and individuals. It does not exclude the classic concern with the distribution of power in the international system but places it within the processes of securitization and admits the importance of domestic politics to analyses.

In Western and Central Europe in the post-Cold War era there is little evidence, if any, of mutual military threats within the region. Instead, the states concerned have a shared 'commitment to political means of conflict resolution and a displacement of security and rivalry to other sectors' (Buzan, Wæver and Wilde, 1998, p. 62). It has been argued that this can be seen as part of the 'two worlds' perspective in which one world is 'defined by a postmodern security community of powerful advanced industrial democracies' and the other world 'comprises a mixture of modern and postmodern states [where] relations amongst and within these states classical realist rules still obtain, and war is a useable and used instrument of policy' (Buzan, 2000, p. 9). The two worlds are represented in Europe with the Balkans and the Caucasus striking examples of the zones of conflict in contrast to the security community of the European Union. The geographical divide is not, however, exact and conflict 'within' such as in Northern Ireland punctures a simplistic map of zones of peace and conflict. Nevertheless the approach captures much of the nature of the new Europe.

The status of international institutions can be seen to be significantly higher for states seeking to cooperatively manage their security interests. As we shall see the European Union has assumed a new significance for its member states, actual and potential, as the hub of the new European order. NATO has remained relevant to its members, actual and potential, as a security regime. The OSCE has become a means to promote the norms and values of the liberal order endorsed by the core powers of Western Europe. In this context the institutionalization of order is striking. The classical challenge for international institutions, however, to bring order to the 'realist world' still remains. In the 'two worlds' approach the 'central security issue' is 'how the zone of peace and the zone of conflict relate to each other ...' (ibid., p. 10). The interface between the two is dynamic and subject to a number of possible relationships:

> Will the weaker, but perhaps more aggressive, zone of conflict begin to penetrate and impinge upon the zone of peace through threats of terrorism, long-range weapons of mass destruction, migration, disease, debt repudiation, and such like? Will the unquestionably more powerful zone of peace seek to penetrate and influence the zone of conflict, using the levers of geo-economics, and occasionally more robust forms of intervention, to manipulate state-making in the zone of conflict? Will the postmodern world try to absorb and remake parts of the zone of conflict, as NATO and the EU seem to have decided to do in the Balkans? Will it try to insulate itself by constructing buffer zones in Mexico, Central Europe, Turkey and North Africa, and trying to stay out of the more chaotic parts of the zone of conflict? Or will it try to engage with the whole, pushing towards a new world order in its own image?
>
> (Ibid., pp. 10–11)

The answers to these questions are not yet fully evident but in Europe a number of strategies have been enacted by the Western security community. Strategies of integration and incorporation have been promoted by institutional enlargement, actual and potential. Both NATO and the EU have begun processes of enlargement which have an impact upon potential members in the short and medium term. Arms control regimes have been sustained in conventional and nuclear fields with Russia invited to be NATO's 'partner'. In the Balkans intervention both military and political has included strategies for state building. The OSCE has been seen to be a means to set the parameters of the new order and the vehicle to inculcate its values. In short the European security architecture has been at the forefront of strategies of engagement with zones of conflict, actual and potential.

## Conclusion

This book seeks to contribute to the analysis of international institutions as security providers. It looks to place the role of institutions against the strategic environment of the new European order and the policies of key powers in the regional system. The nature of security politics in the new Europe has, though, gone beyond the traditional military security dilemma of states. The end of the Cold War broadened understandings of security to include economic, political, societal and environmental factors and made more explicit levels of conflict in international politics. The challenge for security providers has consequently shifted from the predominant military threat of the Cold War past to the multiple risks of the new order.

Our purpose is to assess the competence of the European security architecture. The focus is upon the political and military dimensions of security within which we include the politics of intra-state conflict. The challenge for the United Nations, the European Union, the Organization for Security and Cooperation in Europe and the North Atlantic Treaty Organization is not just to mediate and manage inter-state conflict but intra-state conflict. The problem of responding to substate and ethnic violence adds new questions on the effectiveness of international institutions to those traditionally posed in state-centric terms. We do not see the debate on state cooperation as redundant but as being supplemented by a new agenda which tests cooperation, cohesion and competence. The issues of inter-state conflict have been recast in a new international order which affords greater space for international institutions. The structure of this order has been outlined above and the detailed relationship between European states and the role of the new security architecture is pursued in Chapter 5. The demise of the Cold War has at the same time released new intra-state conflicts which can be as challenging to institutions as superpower overlay was inhibiting. Freed from the constraints of the Cold War institutions have been confronted by daunting new challenges to their competences and effectiveness as security providers. In Chapter 6 we analyse the role of international institutions in the former Yugoslavia concentrating upon the impact of intra-state forces. To support these analyses we first take forward our examination of conflict in the international system.

# 3
# Conflict and Its Management

> We live in a world where no one is 'in charge'. No one organisa-
> tion or institution has the legitimacy, power, authority, or intel-
> ligence to act alone on important public issues and still make
> substantial headway against the problems that threaten us all.
>
> (Bryson and Crosby, 1992, p. xi)

The post-Cold War international order contains a mixture of both inter-
state and intra-state tensions, sometimes intertwined, which may and
have evolved into overt conflict. The purpose of this chapter is to note
the changing conflict paradigm, namely the increasing salience of substate conflict, to investigate its nature and to evaluate the methods
employed to address it. The chapter will note the puncturing of the
optimism of the immediate post-Cold War period with the emergence,
or re-emergence, of ethno-political conflict. The chapter will analyse the
nature of such conflict, noting its structural components and the permissive environment in which it erupts. The second part of the chapter
will look at the 'old' and 'new' diplomatic strategies employed in efforts
to manage, transform and resolve such conflicts. The premise of the
chapter is that the 'new' diplomacy remains constrained by old thinking
or 'strategic disorientation' (Crocker, in Hampson, 1996, p. vii) on the
part of many of its executors and thus is limited in its capacity to resolve
the complexities of some contemporary conflict scenarios.

  The end of the Cold War, an unanticipated event, seemed to promise
a world of opportunity for all. Perhaps it was the suddenness of the collapse of bipolarity itself which heightened the optimism and raised
expectations that a new world order would emerge wherein liberty,
equality and justice would constitute the norms of human behaviour.
In this new world order, cooperation would replace competition and

the most unexpected but most welcome 'peace dividend' would assist in realizing

> a world based on a shared commitment among nations large and small to a set of principles that undergird our relations – peaceful settlement of disputes, solidarity against aggression, reduced and controlled arsenals, and just treatment for all peoples.
> (President George Bush, 13 April 1991, cited in Snow, 1996, p. 461)

Delivered from the seemingly ubiquitous Soviet 'threat', institutional security providers rushed to confirm their presence in the pantheon of protection. The then UN Secretary-General Boutros-Ghali, announced that the time had come for the maturation of the UN Charter thereby delivering 'a UN capable of maintaining international peace and security'. (Boutros-Ghali, 1992, p. 1). NATO leaders proclaimed the organization's intention to play its part in the creation and maintenance of 'a stable security environment in Europe ... in which *no* country will be able to intimidate or coerce any European nation' (NATO, 1991d). Likewise the CSCE, changing its name to the OSCE, announced that 'a new era of democracy, peace and unity in Europe' had begun (CSCE, 1990).

In the light of hindsight, it is easy to dismiss, if not deride, such hopes for a new Age of Enlightenment. International order and security seem as distant as ever while conflict remains a perennial feature of our human geography. This is hardly a surprising situation. Attempts to eradicate conflict denote both a failure to understand the dynamic of the phenomenon and an overestimation of human capacity. Recognizing that the erasure of conflict was proving more difficult than anticipated, European security providers seem to have surrendered initial ambitious goals and settled for the management of conflict. It is clear that the potential of transforming conflict, that is enhancing its functional aspects at the expense of its dysfunctional features, is the task that the European security providers have set themselves in the wake of the old world order. Such efforts have met with varying degrees of success or failure. On the whole, however, it would appear that some conflicts have proven rather resistant to rectification. Attempts to manage conflicts in the present post-Cold War international system often seem markedly similar to those made throughout the bipolar era.

## Managing conflict in the Cold War era

During the Cold War era when the primary form of conflict had an inter-state character, the central method for addressing conflict was through 'narrow, containment-oriented strategies of coercion and crisis-management' (Bloomfield, 1997, p. 5) as we have seen in Chapter 1. Such strategies were discharged through the prevailing balance of power between the United States and the former Soviet Union, underpinned by their mutual efforts at containment of one another's influence, actual or perceived (Organski, 1968). The threat or actual deployment of coercive force was the foundation upon which the balance of power diplomacy rested. Most especially in the nuclear age, the concept of a general war was rendered obsolete and so it was strategies of deterrence that underpinned the system. The balance of power preserved the international order and, most importantly, preserved the status of the superpowers within the hierarchy of states. As Mayall (1992, p. 19) notes: 'if war has been the midwife of history, the Cold War was its taxidermist.' The international system was characterized by a 'stable equilibrium' (Reynolds, 1971, p. 202) and managed by the 'enemy partners' (Aron, 1966, chapter 18). Challenges to the prevailing order, such as those emanating from Hungary in 1956 and Czechoslovakia in 1968, the call for a New International Economic Order (1971), and Poland in 1981 were rebuffed, though arguably not always permanently. That is not to claim that the system was in a state of constant and pervasive stasis; as Sheehan notes, systemic stability was not synonymous with the absence of disturbance or change:

> Stability exists not at the level of particular interest relations, but at the level of the system as a whole, where the changes occurring are within tolerable limits, that is, not threatening the overall equilibrium.
>
> (Sheehan, 1996, p. 79)

Inter-state competition for prestige and influence continued, both covertly and, via proxy wars, more overtly, but not to the extent that the stability of the system was imperilled. Superpower détente afforded the core states the opportunity to codify their competition and thereby to place it within permissible limits:

> The cornerstone of the whole edifice depended upon the workings of sophisticated realism: both the United States and the Soviet Union were able to make clear if imperfect calculations of their interests while nuclear weapons both lent their world a measure of homogeneity denied in public utterances and ensured a measure of prudence.
>
> (Hall, 1996, p. 162)

In addition, efforts at arms control such as the Non-Proliferation Treaty from this period created a regime to reinforce the norm of safe competitiveness. While 'rogue' states such as Iraq and North Korea have demonstrated the weakness of voluntary participation in the regime on the whole it remains true that

> virtually every nonproliferation initiative has turned out to be much more effective than expected when it was proposed or designed, and nonproliferation success has been cheaper than expected.
> (Graham and Mullins, cited in Ruggie, 1996, p. 74).

## The salience of intra-state conflict

### A typology of conflict within the current international system

Conflict remains rooted in the present international system albeit often in a changed paradigmatic form. There are still instances of ongoing conflict and tension between states but conflicts within states have risen in salience. Recognizing this reality, Boutros Boutros-Ghali observed that 'a culture of death' prevails (cited in Kegley and Wittkopf, 1999, p. 348). The statistics proffered by various academic and organizational sources testify to the accuracy of this observation. Inter-state and intra-state conflicts have caused death and destruction on an almost unimaginable scale. Attempts to quantify such loss advance differing grand totals that may partly be explained by the calculators' use of diverse methods and methodology. One person's 'low intensity conflict' may well be another's 'high intensity conflict' (see Richardson, 1960b, Singer and Small, 1972, SIPRI, 1997, Weiss and Collins, 1996, respectively, for contending definitions and contrasting perspectives on this issue). Undeniably, however, the high costs of conflict remain and, particularly with the pervasive presence of intra-state conflict, are increasingly being borne by civilians. Gurr and Harff (1994, pp. 351–2) noted that, during the period 1993–94, there were approximately 26.7 million refugees from major intra-state ethnic conflicts. Sivard (1996, p. 17) pointed out that 'more than 90 per cent of all casualties are non-combatants'. In summation, ethno-political conflicts 'have caused more misery and loss of human life than has any other type of local, regional, or international conflict in the five decades since the end of World War II' (Gurr and Harff, 1994, pp. 6–7).

The ubiquity of conflict has been matched by a broad range of classification systems that purport to critically understand it. The most simple classification system rests on a distinction between inter-state conflicts and those located at the substate level and uses the identity of the protagonists as the primary definitional method. In terms of deeper classification, emphasis has been placed on intra-state conflict. Singer (1996, pp. 43–7) divides such conflicts into two subgroupings – firstly, 'civil' conflicts in which 'an insurgent or revolutionary group within the recognised territorial boundaries of the state' is a principal actor and, secondly, 'increasingly complex intra-state wars' in postcolonial states wherein the protagonists are 'culturally defined groups whose members identify with one another and with the group on the basis of shared racial, ethnic, linguistic, religious, or kinship characteristics'. Modifying Singer's typology, Holsti advances a more detailed classification system. Using the dichotomy of international and non-international conflict, he categorizes international conflict prior to 1989 according to the source of the conflict – territory, nation-state making, economics, ideology and 'human sympathy'. Holsti concludes that inter-state conflict over territorial and economic interests has become less prominent but conflicts fuelled by the remaining three elements have increased in prominence. Turning to non-international conflict, Holsti devised four categories of such activity: state versus state wars and interventionist wars which have rendered a high death toll; wars of national liberation; 'internal wars based on ideological goals'; and 'state-nation wars including armed resistance by ethnic, language and/or religious groups, often with the purpose of secession or separation from the state' (Holsti, 1996). Miall et al. (1999) have amended the classification systems of Singer and Holsti respectively, producing a highly useful, clear typology of conflict. Initially dividing conflict into one of two types, inter-state or non-interstate, the authors further divide non-interstate conflict into three types according to source: conflict fuelled by revolutionary/ideological impulses; conflict deriving from issues of identity and secession; and conflict stemming from factionalism between political or criminal groups and their power competitions (Miall et al., 1999, pp. 30–2). Although Miall *et al.* have dismissed Holsti's category of 'decolonizing wars', it is clear that one could apply their factional conflict type to some contemporary post-communist societies, stemming arguably from the retreat of an imperial power.

This chapter intends to concentrate on intra-state conflicts that arise from issues of identity and secession. While the above-cited typologies prove helpful in advancing an understanding of the diversity and complexity of contemporary conflict, it should be remembered that the clear-cut nature of categorization contrasts with the more confusing empirical evidence. Conflicts, by their very character, are not static affairs, rather they often are organic phenomena in which the passage of time effects changes in the cast of actors, the stage-setting of their activities and the demands which fuel their script. Thus a conflict may well originate over identity issues but may evolve into an ideologically driven conflict. Likewise, the composition of political elites and their degree of cohesion may be subject to change throughout the lifecycle of a conflict and, in particular, despite Miall et al.'s distinction, there may well be a fusion of political and criminal elements within elites. In addition, it should be noted that intranational conflicts may well have an international structural dimension. The protracted social conflict in Cyprus, for example, displays a regional aspect, namely Greek–Turkish relations, and the various multilateral attempts at its resolution have been adversely affected by the prevailing climate of this bilateral relationship. The intercommunal conflict in Northern Ireland likewise has a regional dimension in the form of the Anglo-Irish inter-state relationship which has had an impact on strategies for the resolution of this conflict. Typologies, then, are useful guides when addressing conflicts but they have their limitations. The pursuit of taxonomical clarity should not diminish an appreciation of the complexity of conflicts.

Throughout the inter-bloc confrontation of the Cold War, inter-state conflict remained the focus of attention. Conflicts and disputes within states, many at the 'periphery' of the more economically developed and increasingly integrated systemic 'core', were permitted to rage until dissipation, zones of exclusion from the 'long peace' (Gaddis, 1987). Other such intra-state conflicts, notably those in areas deemed strategically significant, variously defined, to the superpowers found themselves the recipients of patron assistance which served to 'manage' the conflict, if management may be defined as ensuring that systemic stability was not threatened. Such management strategies generally were unconcerned with the suffering of the indigenous people per se and indeed often, through the exacerbation of inter-communal antagonisms, served to increase it. In the wake of the Cold War, intra-state conflict has risen to prominence upon the international agenda; as Weiss comments, 'eighty-two armed conflicts broke out in the half decade following the collapse of the Berlin Wall, and seventy-nine were intra-state wars' (Weiss, in Pieterse, 1998, p. 26). Saddam Hussein's brief foray into Kuwait in 1990 appears to have marked the end of 'classical-style military aggressions' (Holsti, 1996, p. 16). Admittedly, there remain situations of inter-state tensions which rise or fall largely according to the barometer of domestic politics such as India and Pakistan, China and Taiwan, Ecuador and Peru,

Ethiopia and Eritrea, but such incidents of latent or sporadic conflict fail to match the urgency and ferocity of conflicts within states. Following the Cold War, many intra-state conflicts have reasserted themselves in international consciousness while others have arisen or been resurrected in the territories of the former Soviet Union and former Yugoslavia respectively. In a plethora of geographical locations the battle to inherit the right to rule rages – Angola, Afghanistan, Azerbaijan, Armenia, Ethiopia, Georgia, Liberia, Rwanda, Somalia, Sri Lanka, Sudan and Tajikistan. Some, such as the wars in the former Yugoslavia, appear to have abated, although whether this will prove permanent or temporary depends largely on the durability of the 'peace' accords. In keeping with the diversity of their geographical sites, such intra-state conflicts have been furnished with an array of labels. They are variously and contemporaneously described as 'new internal wars' (Snow, 1996), 'wars of a third kind' (Holsti, 1996), 'new wars' (Kaldor, 1999) and somewhat quaintly if disingenuously 'teacup wars' (Gelb, 1994). The rise in salience of such wars has been attributed to the collapse of bipolarity:

> The end of the Cold War has 'unfrozen' those aspects of international, regional, and intranational conflicts which had been contained within the dynamics of East–West relations. The most important consequences of these changes and the major dilemma to be faced in the post-Cold War international system is that the management of these conflicts has become increasingly complex.
>
> (Hoffmann, 1992, p. 262)

> More than anything else, it is the uncertainties following the passing of the older order that allow conflict to break out with such abandon at the end of the millennium.
>
> (Zartman and Rasmussen, 1997, p. 6)

In this transitional period wherein our environment is 'still not a world fully understood' confused individuals seek out security via a retreat into the sanctity of 'blood and belonging' (Boutros-Ghali, 1995, p. 24; Ignatieff, 1993). Such monocausal explanations of contemporary intra-state conflict, while pleasingly simple, are insufficient despite their repeated airing in the popular media. Gurr and Harff note that intra-state conflict is not a post-Cold War phenomenon. Rather ethno-political conflict may be understood as 'a continuation of a trend that began as early as the 1960s' (1994, p. 13). The ethnic dimension should be regarded as an aspect rather than a structural factor of intra-state conflict. Intra-state conflicts emerge within failed and failing states and it is the nature of such states that must be scrutinized so that 'the *political* mediation' of the causal issues of the conflict can be examined (Pieterse, 1998, p. 6; see also Holsti, 1996; Snow, 1996; Brown, 1996). Holsti (1996) notes that the most salient feature of such states is their deficiency in both vertical and horizontal legitimacy. The absence of vertical legitimacy is expressed via a popular challenge to the state and its institutions while the absence of horizontal legitimacy is visible in the lack of consensus over the composition and political function of the civic community (Holsti, 1996, p. 84). Thus within the civic community there is a lack of allegiance to the state and a withholding of voluntary recognition and respect of its authority. The civic community itself is subject to internal antagonisms, particularly latent insider–outsider perceptions. Such nascent tensions may evolve into overt conflict when a permissive environment arises, that is when they are exacerbated by economic and political factors. In multi-ethnic communities, conflict may erupt if one or more ethnic groups are or perceive themselves to be excluded from economic opportunities and from full and effective participation in the political process. Such objective issues of the conflict thus are overlaid by the subjective perceptions of the contending parties and this blend of objective and subjective material shapes the conflict. In a time of economic difficulty, allegiance to the state may well erode completely for some groups within the civic community if the state is believed to be failing in its function as the impartial allocator of resources (Holsti, 1999, p. 109). It should be noted that such a belief might arise during the processes of democratization, particularly during the transition to a market economy when the 'revolution of rising expectations' meets the reality of expectation non-fulfilment (Rostow, 1960). Notions of 'relative deprivation' may add fuel to already simmering inter-communal tensions (Gurr, 1970). Thus the Western 'solution' to less developed states may well aid their implosion. Political discrimination may also erode legitimacy when minority ethnic groups are wholly excluded from or vastly under-represented within the institutions of the state. If the state should respond to initial challenges from minority groups via coercion from certain branches of the state, notably the security forces and the judiciary, then clearly the minorities' sense of alienation will increase as their fragile loyalty to the state and the social contract with the rest of the civic community collapses entirely. Thus a re-bonding of ethnic ties may well be a reaction to economic and political developments rather than their causation (Snow, 1996, p. 104). As Nash explains:

The stronger and more competent the state, the less relevant are ethnic factors to the political process; the weaker and more incompetent the state, the more politically relevant are ethnic movements.

(Nash, 1989, p. 59)

This is the structural reality of failing and failed states. It should be noted that Holsti regards state weakness as 'a variable rather than a constant' thereby holding out the prospect of addressing such situations and rendering healthy polities from the debris of decay and implosion' (Holsti, 1996, p. 90). The context of a legitimacy-deficient state rather than the ethnically heterogeneous composition of its people creates the climate for ethno-political conflict. This should be clear given that 'of the more than 180 states in existence today, fewer than 20 are ethnically homogeneous, in the sense that ethnic minorities account for less than 5 per cent of the population' (Brown, 1996, p. 15). Research on 'groups at risk' by Gurr emphasizes that ethnic cleavage is not the sole source of disorder within the contemporary international system. 'At risk' status may equally arise from threats against religious groups and frontier peoples for instance. 'Otherness', therefore, is not necessarily a synonym for ethnic difference. Likewise, 'otherness' requires the environment of a weak state to become an active fault-line. Within Titoist Yugoslavia, for example, the state retained sufficient legitimacy to ensure that the ethnic peoples within its territory lived peaceably together, 'shared the same language, social organisation and political structure and intermarried freely' (Eibl-Eibesfeldt and Salter, 1998, p. 401).

Another contributor to the activation of the ethnic fault-line is irresponsible leadership. Political elites often mobilize popular prejudice in order to secure their own support bases. Such instrumentalism occasions forms of ethnic conflict 'at its most cynical and brutal' (Snow, 1996, p. 104). Recent examples such as the leadership strategies of Croatia's Tudjman and Serbia's Milošević bear witness to the veracity of this point. An ethnic group which is regionally concentrated and is, or believes itself to be, subject to pervasive discrimination will prove a ready audience for the ambitions of callous leaders preaching exclusionary creeds . The use of the mass media to convey stereotypical images of 'others' and to peddle propaganda of in-group righteousness and worth serves to confirm, consolidate and exacerbate inter-group antagonisms while protecting the positions of the political elite (Brown, 1996, p. 18; Gurr and Harff, 1994, pp. 83–4).

## Bipolarity, contingency and complementarity: writings on conflict management

The literature within the field of conflict management can be divided into two approaches, namely that which argues in favour of political settlements based on negotiation and that which argues that the resolution of a conflict requires a much more integrative approach. The former school of thought is represented in the work of Bercovitch (1984) and Zartman and Touval (1985). It posits that a political settlement can be achieved through the intervention of a third party with the ability to ensure that the protagonists make mutual concessions. The mediator therefore is not a neutral figure but a player in the power-game:

> Leverage or mediator's power enhance the mediator's ability to influence the outcome. The mediator's task is primarily one of persuasion, and persuasion is best achieved ... not when a mediator is unbiased or impartial, but when he [*sic*] possesses resources which either or both parties value ... Clearly if a mediator can bring to bear resources such as power, influence and persuasion, he [*sic*] can move the parties in the desired direction and achieve some success.
>
> (Bercovitch, 1986, pp. 164–5)

Conflict is regarded by this school as stemming from the objective dimension in that power-interests are in competition. Thus the structural dimensions of the conflict are given emphasis. The second approach to be found in the literature is offered by the human needs school (Burton, 1987, 1990a, 1990b; Azar, 1983, 1985, 1990). In this perspective conflict arises not from a dispute of material interests but from a clash of needs. Economic and political discriminatory policies and practices thus mask a subterranean conflict of ontological, universal needs such as identity, recognition and security. Protracted social conflicts stem from the denial of such needs:

> We are led to the hypothesis that the source of protracted social conflict is the denial of those elements required in the development of all peoples and societies, and whose pursuit is a compelling need in all. These are security, distinctive identity, social recognition of identity, and effective participation in the processes that determine conditions of security and identity ... The real source of conflict is the denial of those human needs that are common to all and whose pursuit is an ontological drive in all.
>
> (Azar and Burton, 1986, p. 29)

The non-negotiable nature of these needs does not render conflict resolution impossible but has implications for the methods of address and redress that should be used. In particular, the emphasis is placed upon the subjective interrelationship of the contending parties. Resolution can be attained, it is argued, because the universality of human needs provides a common basis for an integrative path for the contending parties to follow. The task of the intervenor is to help the protagonists discover this path by the 'facilitation of breakthroughs to a conflict situation through problem-solving workshops' (Azar and Moon, 1986, p. 401). While the needs school criticizes the bargaining school for its view of conflict as unidimensional and thus its inability to deliver rooted and integrated settlements to conflicts, the latter argues that the resolutionists must look at the structural distribution of power between protagonists and third-party intervenors if they are to achieve progress in settling a conflict. The neglect of power relationships and their view of third-party intervention as neutral has led Bercovitch to claim that 'the specifications of the problem-solving model may amount to exploration of the parameters of human optimism' (Bercovitch, 1984, p. 147).

The dichotomy of the bargaining and the resolution approach which is apparent in the literature on conflict management has been criticized by some authors, notably Fisher and Keashly (1991) and Bloomfield (1997). These critics are united in their belief that the two approaches should not be viewed as mutually exclusive when addressing conflicts through third-party intervention. Fisher and Keashly advance a contingency model which notes the evolutionary pathway of conflict through a series of stages in the inter-disputants' relationship: from discussion to polarization to segregation and then to destruction. The authors argue that the type of third-party intervention that will prove apposite will be dependent upon the place of the conflicting parties along this continuum. Bloomfield (1997) accepts that the dualism between the bargaining approach and the resolution approach is unfortunate and is not reflected in the empirical reality of conflict. Thus he is appreciative of the appearance of the contingency model. He is not, however, uncritical of it. Using the protracted inter-communal struggle in Northern Ireland since 1968, Bloomfield critiques the contingency model on two significant points. Firstly, he notes that the model is premised upon the 'assumption of a one-dimensional – that is, temporal – profile of conflict'. Looking at the evolution of the conflict scenario in Northern Ireland, Bloomfield rejects this assumption noting that the conflict did not move sequentially through the cited stages of escalation. The Northern Ireland conflict has not proven to be linear.

Rather it has moved back and forth throughout the continuum and at times has displayed the characteristics of the various stages simultaneously (Bloomfield, 1997, p. 86). Bloomfield's second criticism of the contingency model is based on its 'over-simplified view of intra-party cohesion' (ibid.). Again, looking at the players in the Northern Ireland conflict, Bloomfield notes that 'a more accurate characterization of a disputing party, especially in a protracted or complex social conflict, might be a collection of constituencies' (ibid., p. 87). Thus while appreciating Fisher and Keashly's view that the bargaining and resolution approaches should not be regarded as incompatible, Bloomfield advances his own complementarity model of conflict management. This model is based on empirically tested knowledge that the structural and subjective or cultural dimensions of conflict are inherently interwoven and so attempts at resolution must encapsulate this multidimensional reality of conflict. Using the example of Northern Ireland's conflict, Bloomfield notes that its structural dimension is reflected 'in the objective political issue of territorial sovereignty'. Its cultural dimension can be easily seen in the presence of 'two communities with mutually exclusive solutions to that territorial issue, who are effectively distinct cultural groups' (ibid., p. 92) In the protracted social conflict within Northern Ireland then:

> ... the objective political issue is swathed inseparably in layers of subjective concern related to matters of cultural identity and cultural security in a society dominated by mutual opposition, mistrust and fear.
>
> (Ibid., p. 93)

Given this diagnosis of the conflict situation, Bloomfield argues that strategies for its management and resolution must incorporate both structural and cultural initiatives. The reconstitution of inclusive political practices and processes should be accompanied by attempts to regenerate a healthy civic society. This dual-track approach can presently be seen in the democratization programme of the United Nations and other international institutions dealing with conflict management. As we will see later, making a diagnosis of need and realizing a positive prognosis for ailing states and their peoples are not synonymous.

## Addressing intra-state conflict

Following the Cold War, the UN and many regional security organizations expressed a willingness to combat intra-state conflicts with a new diplomatic arsenal (see Chapter 4). In essence, the emphasis was to be on prevention rather than reaction. Unfortunately, this shift to a 'new diplomacy' has not truly occurred and the new diplomatic initiatives have been taken within an unchanged perceptual context of conflict and its causation. The security providers can be seen to be wedded to using inapposite strategies for dealing with the predominant form of conflict in contemporary Europe. Despite their attempts to adapt to the new risk environment, denoted by changed remits and institutional augmentation, security institutions hold residual perceptions of inter-state conflict and to this end still tend to rely upon traditional diplomatic practices in the new security environment.

The traditional methods of diplomacy centre on arbitration and mediation as the chief methods for the management of conflict as stipulated in Article 33 of the UN Charter. Arbitration occurs when parties to a dispute request external assistance in the search for a settlement. The arbitrator, commonly either an arbitral tribunal or international court, has the authority to impose a settlement on the contending parties. The parties have agreed to accept the settlement by virtue of their recourse to external intervention and thus they abide by the ruling or award. Examples of the arbitration process may be found in the workings of organizations such as the WTO and NAFTA for example. A second form of international arbitration is the judicial settlement of an international court. Such international courts at present are the UN's International Court of Justice and the three EU courts of Justice, of First Instance and of Human Rights respectively. It has not been customary for deep-seated international conflicts to be submitted to the arbitration process. Given the sensitivity of state sovereignty, it is hardly surprising that states have proven unwilling to surrender such control to the arbitrator. Furthermore, arbitration is an inappropriate process for the resolution of intra-state conflict. It has been termed 'a power-dominated process' which focuses upon contesting interests and cannot delve deeply enough into the causation of a conflict based on a clash of human needs in the subjective-cultural realm of conflict. Even if the contending parties agreed to submit to the arbitration process and even if an award was made the durability of such a 'settlement' would be extremely dubious. A 'settlement' which did not reconcile the competing demands for recognition and respect of security and identity could not endure in the long term. Such needs would reassert themselves and the conflict would re-emerge (Burton and Dukes, 1990, p. 111).

Mediation has become the *sine qua non* response of Western policy-makers in situations of post-Cold War conflict (Etzioni, 1995). Mediators are external parties invited into a conflict situation to assist the contending parties in the search for a mutually satisfying settlement of their differences. In contrast to arbitrators, mediators do not possess an overt enforcement capability; rather the mediation process is consensual. Some, but not all, mediators adopt a more passive role in that they create a climate for the indigenous parties themselves to map out possible trajectories from their conflict map. Again there are mediators who adopt a low-profile in their work, such as Senator George Mitchell in the current Northern Ireland peace process, while others, notably Henry Kissinger from the past and Richard Holbrooke in the present, assume a higher level of visibility. Some mediators are neutral figures but others are not impartial, notably those representing governmental or institutional interests. As noted earlier, the bargaining school of conflict management argues that this level on interest augurs well for a settlement to the conflict though the resolution school would view the mediator as more a facilitator than a player in the power game. Fundamentally, the mediator is an agent of change who seeks to assist the contending parties by helping them to reconceptualize their conflict so that an accommodation may be reached. Given this aim, there is a variety of strategies which may be employed, many dependent upon the conflict context, still others dependent upon the nature of the mediator, leading one commentator to observe:

> The variables are so many that it would be an exercise in futility to describe typical mediator behaviour with respect to sequence, timing, or the use or non-use of the various functions theoretically available.
>
> (Simkin, 1971, p. 118)

Nevertheless, there have been attempts to categorize both mediators and mediation. Mediation strategies have been classified by Zartman and Touval (1985) under three headings: communication, formulation and manipulation. In each category they have a detailed list of activities which span the gamut of mediator behaviour but it has been noted that such behaviour will be determined by context: 'mediators try to vary their behaviour to reflect the conflict at hand' (Bercovitch, 1996, p. 137).

Whomsoever the mediator and whatsoever strategy deployed, there is a consensus that the essence of successful mediation is knowing when to intervene. Preventive diplomacy stresses that such intervention should occur before a latent conflict escalates to the threshold of overt action. In practice, however, as the international responses to the wars in the former Yugoslavia attest, in an era of diminished strategic importance, intervention occurs when conflict has exploded and gone into a stage of abatement. This abatement may reflect the point at which the conflict is 'ripe for resolution' (Zartman, 1985). At this time, the warring parties have reached a position of a 'hurting stalemate' in which they are each locked into a position from where the potential unilateral benefits are outweighed by the costs each would accrue in trying to secure them. At this stage, the room for manoeuvre for a third party is greater and the chances of a successful settlement of the conflict are greater. It should be noted, however, that the attainment of this situation might not inevitably evolve into a durable and positive peace. A stalemate may arrive without the requisite amount of hurt. In Cyprus, for example, the intervention by the UN has sustained the stalemate but it is arguable that it has also sustained a level of violence which is acceptable to the conflict parties and has therefore provided a disincentive for meaningful political negotiation and has precluded the attainment of a durable, inclusive peace settlement:

> Above all other factors contributing to the current impasse, the greatest impediment to resolution is the absence of a hurting stalemate. Neither Cypriot community is sufficiently dissatisfied with the status quo to make the difficult compromises necessary for resolving the conflict.
>
> (Mandell, 1992, p. 221)

## The need for a 'new diplomacy'

The primary function of diplomacy has been defined as

> not just the management of order, but the management of change, and the maintenance by continued persuasion of order in the midst of change.
>
> (Watson, 1984, p. 223)

If diplomacy is to successfully execute this task in the post-Cold War world, it undoubtedly needs to be modernized. The presence of both conflicts between and conflicts within states creates a challenging remit for security providers. Traditional diplomatic strategies and practices cannot be simply grafted onto the prevailing order as the structural basis of inter-communal conflicts militates against their settlement by such means. While the international system remains underpinned by the doctrine of state sovereignty, the principle of non-interference has been subject to challenge. Politico-strategic methods, developed and deployed in a statist world, cannot be used to meaningfully address the ontological needs of substate groups and, ultimately, of their individual constituents. The contemporary 'new wars' (Kaldor, 1999) differ from 'old wars' not only in their etiology but also in their aims and their prosecution. Their aims are no longer based upon issues of national prestige or national security but are concerned with 'statehood, governance, and the role and status of nations and communities within states' (Holsti, 1996, p. 21). The prosecution of contemporary intra-state wars is different in that there are 'no declarations of war, no seasons of campaigning, and … [rarely] end with peace treaties' (ibid., p. 20). Thus what Luttwak has described as 'post-heroic warfare' is fundamentally different from the Clausewitzian model of war. Combatants from a mixture of regular and irregular forces, which lack both an internal hierarchical order and a clearly designated command and control centre, carry out the conflict. The rules of the game bear no relation to the strictures of the Geneva Convention. 'Legitimate' targets are most generously defined and commonly include the entirety of the civilian population. Military 'strategies' include the systematic rape of women and 'ethnic cleansing'. Snow correctly notes that such conflicts can accurately be described using von Moltke's assessment of the American Civil War: 'two armed mobs chasing one another across the countryside, from which nothing can be learned' (Snow, 1996, p. 110). In such a context of asymmetrical conflict, it is apparent that diplomacy based upon symmetrical inter-state relations is inappropriate. In inter-state conflict, the parties are easily identifiable, the interests can be readily defined and articulated and the national governments concerned can be legitimately regarded as the rightful authorities with whom to negotiate. In intra-state conflicts, where states have either imploded or are well on the way to such collapse, there are no such certainties. Nevertheless, the international community continues to practise a diplomacy that belongs to the inter-state conflict environment. Miall et al. note the incongruity of this situation:

> It is ironic that the task of managing such [intra-state] conflict has fallen primarily to international institutions which are still based on precisely the system of sovereignty and non-interference that the new conflicts undermine; it is not surprising that the international community struggles to find effective means of response.
>
> (Miall et al., 1999, p. 34)

In its search for 'effective means of response' to intra-state conflicts, the international community has turned its attention to preventative diplomacy and conflict prevention, thereby colliding with 'the talisman of sovereignty' (Helman and Ratner, 1992/93, p. 9). The inter-state system was traditionally based upon the right of the state to hold jurisdiction over its territory. Under Article 2(7) of the UN Charter, intervention is prohibited 'in matters which are essentially within the domestic jurisdiction of any state' unless the state invited such intervention or a Security Council resolution ordered it under Chapter VII. Boutros-Ghali (1992), stressing the increasingly interdependent nature of the international system, declared that 'the time of absolute and exclusive sovereignty … has passed; its theory was never matched by reality'. Thus there have been tentative moves away from the 'myth of sovereignty and independence' when viewing contemporary conflicts within the international system (Azar and Burton, 1986, p. 31). In the interests of good governance the international community has proven willing to abrogate state sovereignty principally upon the grounds of 'international security' or as a reflexive action to the 'humanitarian impulse'. However, such remedial action has not been equitably discharged, making clear that 'hard' sovereignty remains a political reality for more powerful states within the international system. In theory, then, the abrogation of state sovereignty accords with the reconceptualization of security and, most specifically, the refocusing of attention onto people rather than states as the primary security recipient. In practice, however, security providers remain perceptually and behaviourally imprisoned in '… the world of state sovereignty [which] is a world for strategic minds' (Pieterse, 1998, p. 14).

Throughout the Cold War, intra-state conflicts failed to rise to the top of the international agenda but were considered, when at all, as the responsibility of the superpower in whose 'sphere' they arose. Outside-sphere conflicts which occurred in territory with no strategic or prestige implications were ignored. In the present international political climate, intra-state conflicts are deemed to be the responsibility of all as they represent threats to 'international security'. Nevertheless, it would seem apparent that some are more threatening than others, as there is an evident apartheid of address on the part of the more powerful states. One of the criteria for international intervention involves the conflict being presented as a source of contagion for the surrounding region, which may later infect the entire international political system. This was clearly articulated during the wars in the former Yugoslavia:

> You may well have the entire Balkans involved … it could draw in Greece and Turkey … the United States has a stake in preventing the world from going up in flames.
>
> (US Secretary of State Warren, cited in Berdal, 1993, pp. 36–37)

Neighbouring states are frequently portrayed as the passive victims of nearby intra-state conflicts, especially those who end up host to a great exodus of refugees. It should be noted, however, that neighbouring states might act as exacerbators of the original conflict, particularly if ethnic kin are present across common state borders, and may launch 'opportunistic interventions' (Brown, 1996, p. 24). Arguably, the behaviour of Greece and Turkey concerning the conflict in Cyprus acts as an illustration of the exacerbating effect of external agents on intra-state conflicts. Buzan's work on regional security complexes is most useful on this point. States which 'are locked into geographical proximity' and which have a history of mutual distrust may follow policies fuelled by fear and insecurity and thus add an extra layer to the associated intra-state conflict. Buzan's diagnosis of the Indo-Pakistani dispute over Kashmir proves equally valid when applied to the Greek–Turkish dispute over Cyprus as 'this dispute ties into the domestic instabilities of both states, and symbolises the structural political threat they pose to each other' (Buzan, 1983, p. 107). Thus when an intra-state conflict has a structural component located at the regional or intra-state level, the prospect of its resolution may prove more elusive.

Another rationale for intervention by the 'international community' is the much-vaunted 'humanitarian impulse'. In this scenario, the international community is subject to the dictates of decency and must respond actively to systematic and widespread human rights violations. This impulse would appear to be context-dependent, however, particularly if the so-called 'CNN effect' is in play. Human rights abuses in Algeria, Sierra Leone and Sri Lanka, for example, seem not to tap the same international vein of ethical responsibility as the Kosovo crisis. Media coverage of the plight of the Kosovar Albanian refugees led to a growing public demand in the West that 'something' had to be done. The exact nature of the action to be taken is less ably articulated but Freedman (2000, p. 338) notes that when a government has no clear policy 'the impact of striking images and a groundswell of opinion can shape the responses of policy makers'. Snow notes that the decision on whether or not to intervene reflects an incongruity of threats and interests. If no major international power, especially the United States, perceives interests, especially those of an economic nature, in the territory then 'there is certainly not much worth fighting over' (Snow, 1996, p. 22). Also, if a centre of conflict should be seen as falling within the 'sphere of influence' of a great power, such as the Chechnyan conflict, the costs of intervention are deemed in excess of the benefits to be accrued. In short, then, intercommunal conflicts in under-developed areas which are bereft of economic resources and/or vital raw materials command little international attention, still less address:

> We need to appreciate that geopolitics rules the roost when it comes to the enforcement of human rights and humanitarian intervention. This means, among other things, that the overwhelming number of instances will involve the flow of force from North to South, and that strong states are definitely off-limits ...
>
> (Falk, 1995, p. 8)

## Contemporary conflict 'management'

If the major powers do detect interests, then intervention will take place. Generally, intervention, ranging from economic and diplomatic sanctions to the imposition or enforcement of peace, has taken on a punitive nature, as it remains rooted within a Cold War paradigm of appropriate responses to conflict. Such efforts at conflict 'management' have been criticized as detrimental to the resolution of conflict, as they permit 'no room for reconciliation between perpetrator and victim but for a clean slate after punishment has been delivered' (Galtung, 1996, p. 269). The ultimate method of management has included the launching of sustained and pervasive bombing raids over the territory of the recalcitrant. The result of this arguable attachment to retribution rather than rapprochement is a world order in which the international community isolates those very parties which are essential to the resolution of conflict. There is a tendency on the part of the international community to assume that with the deployment of sufficient coercion and vilification, the offending parties will be ousted by their respective domestic populace and peace can be restored. One thinks of the tenacity of leaders such as Saddam and Milosevic to disprove this thesis. Nevertheless, when dealing with inter-state conflict, the use of force has proven successful to an extent. In a case of a clear-cut violation of state sovereignty, such as the invasion of Kuwait by Iraq in 1991, there is generally a high level of international consensus that force may be legitimately used as measure of last resort. Thus if there is a clear justification for intervention and the intervention is based on a clearly articulated mandate and set of political objectives, then force may prove successful in altering an opponent's behaviour. In the case of inter-communal conflicts, the use of force against a protagonist may prove less acceptable to the wider international community. The deployment of force in such cases is problematic as it fails to appreciate the breadth of involvement by the populace within these conflicts due to the leadership's instrumental use of ethnicity as a rationale for the conflict. In addition, the use of force depends upon a clear conception of 'them', that is, those who are to be punished. In reality, it is very difficult to identify 'them', as NATO operations demonstrated in the Kosovo crisis when they mistakenly targeted Serbian civilians, Kosovar refugees and, arguably, the embassy of the People's Republic of China. When using the humanitarian imperative, rather than the principle of non-aggression, as legitimization for such a policy, the political objectives of military action are less easy to articulate. Freedman (2000, p. 337) notes that NATO's air strikes against Serbia in 1999 demonstrated the importance of the 'normative dimension' of intervention: 'The Kosovo War, more than most, was framed in terms of competing moralities – intervention against atrocities versus non-interference in internal affairs – and competing immoralities – strategic bombing versus ethnic cleansing.' Therein lay 'the moral paradox of the Kosovo War, for it was always easier to proclaim the morality of the ends pursued than of the means deployed' (ibid., p. 341).

Coercive strategies of conflict management may temporarily halt an intra-state conflict but they provide no grounds for constructive and enduring political accommodation. The anachronistic cognitive framework wherein such management methods are rooted is filled with the depiction of conflict solutions as win–lose and zero sum games. However, such 'parlour-game cleverness' fails to appreciate the existentialist basis of inter-communal conflicts (Galtung, 1996, p. 96). The symptoms of the conflict may be addressed, however inappropriately, but there is no attempt to tackle its structural or subjective causes.

Given this reality, there is little cause for wonder at the repercussions of such 'management' strategies. Following the attainment of 'settlements', the European security providers are finding it difficult to ensure that such 'settlements' take root within the indigenous communities and consequently have left themselves open to criticism for their 'functional imperialism' (Griffiths et al., 1995, 113, cited in Pieterse, 1998, p. 8) that they now discharge in such 'protectorates' as Bosnia.

## Conflict resolution

Such conflict management strategies are no substitute for conflict resolution. Conflict resolution refers to the initiation and maintenance of long-term diplomatic processes, which are cognizant of the complementary structural and subjective dimensions of protracted inter-communal conflict. Even then conflict resolution should not be interpreted as the permanent solution of conflict. Conflict resolution demands a new diplomacy, which recognizes the 'decentralization' of post-Clausewitzian conflict (Natsios, 1995, p. 339). Most especially, there is a fundamental need to incorporate contending parties into the diplomatic process rather than exiling them from it on the grounds of their past behaviour. Such an inclusive forum with full and free participation for all the endogenous actors can provide a space for the protagonists to examine their interrelationship and move towards a sustainable political accommodation between them. Participation will contribute over the longer term to the reduction of polarization between the protagonists. The primary stage of the resolution process is to create an environment in which all parties can contribute to the process of conflict transformation wherein the perceptions of the 'enemy' and self-fulfilling prophecies regarding its behaviour can be altered. In a protracted conflict, a vicious cycle evolves in which each of the parties expects the 'other' to behave in a negative and detrimental fashion towards them. This expectation will frequently rest upon historical myths or communal narratives and will have been sustained through stereotyping. The aim of conflict resolution is to replace such negative attitudes and associations with 'positive relationships [based upon] satisfaction, co-operation, empathy and interdependence between parties' (Zartman and Rasmussen (eds), 1997, p. 11).

A durable settlement must be an integrative agreement rather than a compromise, which is a short-lived form of 'premature resolution' (Sherman, 1987, p. 39). The contending parties of an inter-communal dispute simply cannot compromise on such existential concerns as identity, recognition and security. Intervenors who press for a compromise solution sacrifice sustainability and substance for immediate gratification as 'compromises are more likely to unravel over time because they are typically closer to the parties' limits' (Sherman, 1987, p. 69). Integrative agreements not only last but they also represent an organic process for the peaceful settlement of future issues of conflict. An integrative agreement is necessarily preceded by a positive and cooperative environment for the addressing and redressing of the causes of conflict. In this transformative space the actors have reconceptualized the 'other', thoroughly explored the map of their conflict and overcome 'conflict rigidification' (Sherman, 1987, p. 40) to reach a mutually satisfactory outcome. This positive experience will encourage repeat performances in the future as, from the initiation of the process, there must be instilled in the parties an understanding that conflict transformation constitutes 'a never ending process' because 'We are all in conflicts. And they in us' (Galtung, 1996, p. 90).

The difficulties in pursuing such an inclusive strategy of conflict res-olution should not be under-estimated. Deep-rooted and pervasive pro-tracted communal conflicts are complex in their causation and their sustaining dynamics. A culture of suspicion and distrust is endemic and representative of generations of mutual fear. Translating the theo-ries and mechanisms of resolution into practice is a daunting task for all security providers and one which raises continual challenges.

## Post-conflict peace-building

Having secured a peace agreement, it is imperative that the peace should be won: as Hampson (1996, p. 221) observes, '[a] negotiated peace agreement is little more than a road map to the peace process'. Winning the peace and securing a ceasefire are not synonymous as the Cyprus situation attests. The task for security providers is to prevent a return to overt political violence. In effect, then, it is 'what we might call the challenge of "Clausewitz in reverse" – the continuation of the politics of war into the ensuing peace' (Miall et al., 1999, p. 188). The mediating parties must ensure that the agreement is not stillborn but is brought to maturity through an effective implementation phase. A positive peace environment must be created through taking 'action to identify and support structures, which will tend to strengthen and solidify peace in order to avoid a relapse into conflict' (Boutros-Ghali, 1992, p. 11). The indigenous peoples must be given 'a sense of confidence and well-being' (ibid., p. 32) through the creation of an inclusive polity and attendant healthy political culture. There are many functions which have to be undertaken to render such a post-conflict environment. These include the disarming of the protagonists, the return of displaced peoples, the holding and monitoring of elec-tions, the creation of inclusive organs of the state and the creation of a pluralistic political culture in which human rights are protected and promoted. In short, the new polity must be such that all citizens per-ceive themselves to be stakeholders in its existence. The United Nations uses the term 'democratization' to describe this post-conflict remit for the intervening parties. Democratization involves a multi-sectoral approach to reconstruction in that it encompasses both the cultural and the structural dimensions of conflict. The transformation of the conflict environment requires both 'light' and 'deep' prevention.

The former type of preventive action is to be found in missions of long-term duration, diplomatic intervention and mediation by private actors. The latter sort of prevention focuses upon the underlying foundation of conflict and is demonstrated by efforts to build 'domestic, regional or international capacity to manage conflict' (Miall et al., 1999, p. 97). The focus is upon the creation of 'domestic peace constituencies' (Lederach, 1995; Miall et al., 1999, p. 18). The involvement of the indigenous peoples is essential if the 'legacy of bitterness that hampers conflict resolution' is to be erased (Zartman, 1989, p. 269). To this end the formation or extension of cross-community initiatives at the grassroots level is especially important. Such activities may help to establish new social networks which can assist in the reconceptualization of inter-communal relationships by deconstructing stereotypical images of 'otherness' and 'we-ness'. In the protracted social conflict within Northern Ireland, for example, one witnesses what has been termed 'the pursuit of civic Republicanism and Loyalism' (Stewart, 1999, p. vi) which, combined with change in the structural dimension of the conflict, has led to the rejection of paramilitarism and the acceptance of liberal-democratic modes of behaviour. The attempt to introduce or strengthen forms of identity which can be accommodated within the reconstituted polity is not without difficulty. Often those who define themselves primarily through a fundamental structural cause of the conflict reject efforts to change their perception of self. In Northern Ireland, this is true of those who now claim their purity through titles such as *Continuity* IRA and *Real* IRA. Equally, on the Loyalist side of the conflict, such groups as the Loyalist Volunteer Force and the Red Hand Defenders refuse to surrender their identity with the present constitutional status of the province. In terms of parties to the peace process, it is crucial that such groups are marginalized and limited in their ability to exploit the difficulties facing those focused upon resolution. Bloomfield (1997) has noted that attempts to change attitudes within the perceptual realm of the protagonists have been a regular feature of the Northern Ireland conflict, especially in the early and mid-1970s. However, as such efforts were somewhat incoherent and lacking a strategic element, their influence at the macro-level of the conflict was diminished. It was not until a more strategic approach was adopted, especially at the structural level with the establishment of the Central Community Relations Unit in 1987 and the Community Relations Council in 1990, that such initiatives were given a greater chance of efficacy. This reconstitution of civic society on the basis of trust, tolerance and mutual respect is fundamental to the successful operation of democratic political arrangements; as Parrott points out, 'without key components of civil society, government structures that are formally democratic cannot be expected to operate in a fashion that is substantially democratic' (Parrott, 1997, p. 24).

Thus transformation in the structural dimension of the conflict too is imperative if the parties are to be given the opportunity to build mutual trust and confidence. Changes in the organs of the state to enhance their representativeness and fairness are required. Transformation of the police force in the post-conflict phases is a primary requirement. In both Kosovo and Northern Ireland steps have been taken to move towards a more socially acceptable police service. Under the auspices of the OSCE Kosovo Mission, the Kosovo Police Service School has been established to recruit and train a service which will prove equally acceptable to the indigenous Kosovar Albanian and Serbian communities (Bloed, 2000, p. 61). In Northern Ireland the Patten Commission on Policing has delivered its report detailing how the Royal Ulster Constabulary should be reformed so that it 'can enjoy widespread support from, and is seen as an integral part of the community as a whole' (Belfast Agreement, 1998, Section 9, Annex A). Another important confidence-building measure is the disarming of paramilitary groups within the conflict environment. This can prove to be a difficult issue as the current phase of the Northern Ireland peace process attests.

The holding and monitoring of free and fair elections to establish pluralistic political institutions is another important element in the transition to a post-conflict situation. Commonly in divided societies these institutions are based upon a consociational or power-sharing model to ensure representativeness and impartiality. Such arrangements have been defined as 'the participation of the representatives of all significant groups in the government of the country and a high degree of autonomy for these groups' (Lijphart, 1991, p. 494). Underpinning consociational arrangements is the principle of proportionality which

> serves as an effective conflict-regulating practice insofar as it reduces the degree and scope of competition for governmental power, administrative positions, and scarce resources ...
>
> (Nordlinger, 1972, p. 23)

Such arrangements have been established in Northern Ireland through the Belfast Agreement of 1998. Strand One of this agreement provides for proportional electoral representation, a minority veto and cross-community decision-making. A power-sharing apparatus also has been established in Bosnia via its constitution in the Dayton Agreement of 1995. As in Northern Ireland, steps have been taken to decentralize political power and an ethnic key has been used to ensure that all the ethnic groups within the state have fair representation, can vote for a three-member presidency and have the opportunity to participate in cross-community decision-making.

Within the economic dimension too there is a need for structural change to tackle the socio-economic differentials between the contending parties. Within the Northern Ireland conflict environment programmes of economic regeneration have been established, notably 'Policy Appraisal and Fair Treatment' (PAFT) in the 1990s and the current 'New Targeting Social Need' (New TSN) which aims to concentrate resources on communities which are economically marginalized. In addition, the Department of Economic Development (DED) has issued a Strategy Report detailing a development programme until 2010 which aims to attract foreign private investment to the country (DED, 1999). Within Bosnia, international economic institutions, notably the World Bank, the International Monetary Fund, the European Bank for Reconstruction and Development and the European Commission, are heavily engaged in such 'deep' prevention measures. Linkage between their financial assistance and good governance is the norm but, as Woodward (1995) highlights, these same institutions via their economic programmes helped to create a conflict-permissible environment in the FRY through the consequent cuts in public services, reduction in work opportunities and the attendant inter-republic contest for a reduced federal budget.

Given the pervasive remit of post-conflict peace-building, it is evident that the intervening parties must accept the sustained nature of their involvement:

> Building a peace constituency in settings of protracted conflicts must be understood in its long-term implications. Put simply, this principle suggests that peace-making endeavours are not exclusively nor perhaps primarily a series of events or products, like achieving direct negotiations, ceasefires, and the signing of accords: rather, they are embedded in the development and transformation of relationships over time.
>
> (Lederach, 1995, p. 214)

The longevity of engagement is demonstrated by the continued presence, with an indefinite leave of stay, of international institutions in

Bosnia. Initially these organizations were to stay only until September 1996 at which point they would have transferred their remits to indigenous state authorities, institutions and groups. The international institutions involved have legitimized their extended stay on the grounds that '... true signs of ethnic conciliation are still sorely missing' (OHR, 1996, paras 83 and 84). This raises a number of difficult questions concerning the democratization project as a whole. Firstly, if democratization is a continuum of transition, what are the criteria for measuring a society's progress towards the destination of a market-economy liberal democratic polity? If democratic elections are held and monitored, as they were in Bosnia in September 1996, is it acceptable for the international community to remain because it does not appreciate the result? Secondly, there is the nature of the processes of democratization and the telos of such a polity; as Miall *et al.* (1997, p. 115) insightfully note, 'we need to be sensitive to the charge that imposing these particular methods may amount to westernization, especially when conditionality is imposed'. The question asked is '*Quis custodiet custodies*?' In addition there is criticism that such a degree of semi-permanent international involvement has undermined the chance of creating 'viable institutions of self-government' in Bosnia (Chandler, 1999, p. 2).

In terms of the security providers themselves, this level of engagement has raised issues of both 'overstretch' in terms of their capabilities and resources and of 'mission creep' in terms of their open-ended mandates. The raising of such crucial issues must be addressed by the international institutions themselves if they are to avoid their efforts, however well-meaning, from resembling the toils of Sisyphus:

> It is important to set clear and realistic peacekeeping mandates that are sensitive to local conditions and to limit external intervention to functional areas where the need is compelling and mandates can be properly executed. Otherwise third-party efforts to develop local governance structures will be counter-productive and ultimately self-defeating.
>
> (Hampson, 1996, p. 233).

## Conclusion

This chapter has addressed the residual presence of inter-state disputes and the increased salience of intra-state conflict within the contemporary international system. The nature of protracted communal conflict has been noted and attention drawn to its causation and its pervasiveness. Contending theories of conflict management and resolution have been reviewed and their clarity has been contrasted with the difficulties inherent in the implementation process. In the present international order, which is characterized by elements of continuity and change, security institutions have endeavoured to develop strategies to manage and resolve the variety of challenges they face. Such changed institutional remits and efforts at resolution will be addressed in the following chapter.

# 4
# The New European Security Architecture

## Introduction

A significant feature of the new European order is its degree of institutionalization. International institutions have been important anchors of stability in the transition of the European system from its Cold War structures. Institutions have provided bases of order in a rapidly changing political environment. The pattern of institutionalization, already established in Western Europe, was extended to the East in the wake of the Cold War. Institutions have sustained their relevance by adapting to the new political conditions, broadening their auspices and developing new roles. NATO, the EU, the WEU and the CSCE/OSCE have all sought to respond to the end of the Cold War by trying to incorporate the wider Europe in their policy design or by implementing pan-European roles. This chapter will trace this process and the recent evolution of the European Security architecture. It will also include consideration of the United Nations given its relevance to crisis management in the Balkans. The emphasis will be upon the manner in which each institution has defined its security competences, role and strategies with regard to political and military stability in the new Europe. The resources available to each institution for security management will be assessed and, critically, the nature of each institution's decision-making process. Finally the chapter will seek to ascertain the degree to which the security architecture can be considered a cohesive entity.

## NATO

The North Atlantic Treaty was signed in Washington on 4 April 1949 by Belgium, Canada, Denmark, France, Iceland, Italy, Luxembourg, the

Netherlands, Norway, Portugal, the United Kingdom and the United States. The Treaty was created within the framework of Article 51 of the UN charter and established an alliance for collective defence. Article 3 of the Treaty committed the Parties 'separately and jointly, by means of continuous and effective self-help and mutual aid, [to] maintain and develop their individual and collective capacity to resist armed attack' (NATO, *Handbook*, 1995a, p. 231). The Treaty provides for consultation 'whenever, in the opinion of any of them, the territorial integrity, political independence or security of any of the Parties is threatened' (Article 4, ibid.). This provided a transatlantic forum to review events both inside and outside the NATO area which could affect the security of Alliance members. The cornerstone of the Alliance is Article 5, which states:

> The Parties agree that an armed attack against one or more of them in Europe or North America shall be considered an attack against them all and consequently they agree that, if such an armed attack occurs, each of them, in exercise of the right of individual or collective self-defence recognized by Article 51 of the Charter of the United Nations will assist the Party or Parties so attacked by taking forthwith, individually and in concert with the other Parties, such action as it deems necessary, including the use of armed force, to restore and maintain the security of the North Atlantic area.
>
> Any such armed attack and all measures taken as a result thereof shall immediately be reported to the Security Council. Such measures shall be terminated when the Security Council has taken the measure necessary to restore and maintain international peace and security.
>
> (Ibid., p. 232)

While Article 5 does not specify the action to be taken, it nonetheless makes action to restore security an imperative of membership. By this means American power was wedded to Europe and the basic deterrent value of the Alliance established.

Article 6 denotes the area to which the Treaty applies:

> For the purpose of Article 5, an armed attack on one or more or the Parties is deemed to include an armed attack: – on the territory of any of the Parties in Europe or North America, on the Algerian Departments of France [inapplicable from 3 July 1962], on the territory of Turkey or on the Islands under the jurisdiction of any of the

Parties in the North Atlantic area north of the Tropic of Cancer; – on the forces, vessels, or aircraft of any of the Parties, when in or over these territories or any other area in Europe in which occupation forces of any of the Parties were stationed on the date when the Treaty entered into force or the Mediterranean Sea or the North Atlantic area north of the Tropic of Cancer.

(Ibid.)

The organizational basis of the Treaty was established by Article 9 of the Treaty. It created the North Atlantic Council which was authorized to establish subsidiary bodies including a defence committee. The North Atlantic Council is the supreme decision-making body of NATO. It consists of permanent representatives (ambassadors) of all member states who meet on a regular basis. The Council can also convene as a decision-making body at heads of state and foreign minister level in summit meetings. The North Atlantic Council and its key supporting committees – the Defence Planning Committee (DPC) and the Nuclear Planning Group (NPG) – are chaired by the Secretary-General. Decisions in the North Atlantic Council are taken on the basis of unanimity and consent. There is no voting or decision by majority. This places the onus upon consultation, political cooperation and shared thinking on strategic issues. Consequently NATO has developed a complex network of committees to serve its Council. The work of the Council is supported by a number of subordinate bodies including the Senior Political Committee consisting of Deputy Permanent Representatives with specialist and ad hoc committees in turn providing inputs into the decision-making process. This structure also supports the DPC and the NPG involving all member states except France (see NATO, *Handbook*, 1998, p. 40). The international staff also serves the Council and is organized into a number divisions (ibid., p. 218). Under the authority of the Council, the DPC and the NPG a Military Committee consisting of the Chiefs of Staff of each member state (except for France) meets on a regular basis to provide advice and direction on military policy. From 1951 the Alliance has been committed to an Integrated Military Structure (IMS) which has subsumed a series of military commands for the North Atlantic area. Member governments (except for France since 1966) assign forces to the IMS. Forces have been identified for different degrees of readiness but 'in general, most NATO forces remain under full national command until being assigned to the Alliance for a specific operation decided upon at the political level' (ibid., p. 249). In 1994 the Military Committee launched its Long

Term Study to re-evaluate the IMS in light of changes to NATO and the strategic environment since the end of the Cold War. The new command structure, agreed in 1997, reduced the number of headquarters from 65 to 20 and with new command and control concepts was designed to enhance flexibility and greater emphasis upon the regional level. The Supreme Allied Commander Europe (SACEUR) retains overall responsibility for defence planning for Allied Command Europe (ACE) but now has two subordinate Regional Commands: Allied Forces North Europe and Allied Forces South Europe.

NATO is clearly more than a classical alliance operating upon intergovernmental lines. Its decision-making procedures are long established and complex. National inputs meet international coordination procedures and layers of political and military committees. The procedure is not without tension, limitation or division, as we shall see, when sensitive security matters are at stake but it is more than a simple coalition of like-minded states. It is a politico-military organization which has become embedded in the formulation of security policy among its member states. The British Strategic Defence Review of 1998 declared:

> We are a major European state and a leading member of the European Union. Our economic and political future is as part of Europe. Our security is indivisible from that of our European partners and allies. We therefore have a fundamental interest in the security and stability of the continent as a whole and in the effectiveness of NATO as a collective political and military instrument to underpin these interests. This in turn depends on the transatlantic relationship and the continued engagement in Europe of the United States.
>
> (*British Strategic Defence Review*, 1998, chapter 2, p. 18)

The changing nature of European security and NATO's breadth of functions are also seen to underline its future relevance to member states.

> While NATO's high degree of organizational and institutional development sets it off from other alliances, increasing political and economic integration suggest that future security efforts by states will be more multilateral in nature and show greater institutional development than in the past. To the degree that the security needs of increasingly interdependent states are seen as in a broad, multilevel perspective that encompasses political, economic, social and domestic dimensions, alliances like NATO are likely to endure, especially

as publics are increasingly unwilling to support unilateral security measures whose costs cannot be spread.

(McCalla, 1996, p. 472)

### NATO's adaptation to the new Europe

The end of the Cold War challenged NATO's *raison d'être*. The Alliance responded by attempting to adapt to the new security environment, stressing its political role, changing its military posture and looking to new understandings of security. The London Declaration of the NATO Heads of State and Government in July 1990 confirmed that the Alliance 'must and will adapt' (North Atlantic Council, 1990, p. 3). The Declaration looked to NATO to remain a defensive alliance but recognized that 'security and stability do not lie solely in the military dimension, and we intend to enhance the political component of our Alliance as provided for by Article 2 of our Treaty' (ibid.). A new relationship with former adversaries in Eastern Europe was sought: 'the Atlantic Community must reach out to the countries of the East which were our adversaries in the Cold War, and extend to them the hand of friendship' (ibid.). To that end the member states of the Warsaw Pact were invited to commence regular diplomatic and military contact. The Declaration further identified the objective of pursuing conventional arms control through the CSCE framework which would permit the restructuring of NATO's forces. NATO looked to the institutionalization of the CSCE, to 'provide a forum for wider political dialogue in a more united Europe' (ibid., p. 7). In June 1991 the North Atlantic Council looked to reinforce the 'CSCE's potential for conflict prevention, crisis management and the peaceful settlement of disputes by appropriate means ...' (North Atlantic Council, 1991a, p. 28). The CSCE was seen, together with the process of European integration, as the basis of a 'network of interlocking institutions and relationships, constituting a comprehensive architecture ...' (ibid.). NATO, nevertheless, sought to underline its particular importance declaring that a 'transformed Atlantic Alliance constitutes an essential element in the new architecture' (North Atlantic Council, 1991b, p. 31). In the face of perceived potential competition with other security providers NATO published its 'Core Security Functions' and declared that member states had confirmed that their rights and obligations under the Washington Treaty remained unchanged (see North Atlantic Council, 1991c, p. 30). The Alliance did, however, seek to sustain its process of change and in November 1991 adopted a New Strategic Concept.

## NATO's New Strategic Concept 1991

NATO's New Strategic Concept was founded upon the changing security environment that had developed since 1989.The end of the Cold War, the end of the division of Europe, reform and change in the Soviet Union and arms control were seen to have transformed the security of the Western allies. The 'monolithic, massive and potentially immediate threat which was the principal concern of the Alliance in its forty years has disappeared' (North Atlantic Council, 1991d, p. 4). NATO envisaged security challenges nonetheless but 'risks' rather than 'threats':

> Risks to Allied security are less likely to result from calculated aggression against the territory of the Allies, but rather from the adverse consequences of instabilities that may arise from the serious economic, social, and political difficulties, including ethnic rivalries and territorial disputes, which are faced by many countries in central and eastern Europe. The tensions which may result, as long as they remain limited, should not directly threaten the security and territorial integrity of members of the Alliance. They could, however, lead to crises inimical to European stability and even to armed conflicts, which could involve outside powers or spill over into NATO countries, having a direct effect on the security of the Alliance.
>
> (Ibid.)

The process of change in the Soviet Union was also seen as uncertain and 'cannot be seen in isolation from the fact that its conventional forces are significantly larger than those of any other European State and its large nuclear arsenal comparable only with that of the United States' (ibid.).

Despite the changes to European security the Strategic Concept asserted that the 'new environment does not change the purpose or the security functions of the Alliance' but offered 'new opportunities for the Alliance to frame its strategy within a broad approach to security' (ibid., p. 5). Allied security policy was to adopt three mutually reinforcing elements, 'dialogue, cooperation, and the maintenance of a collective defence capability' (ibid., p. 7). The objectives of the strategy were to 'reduce the risks of conflict arising out of misunderstanding or design; to build increased mutual understanding and confidence among all European states; to help manage crises affecting the security of the Allies; and to expand the opportunities for a genuine partnership among all European countries in dealing with common security problems' (ibid., p. 7). The Alliance believed the new security environment in Europe had multiplied the opportunities for dialogue with the Soviet Union and Eastern Europe. NATO saw its arms control and disarmament policy as integral to its strategy for dialogue and cooperation. In addition the New Concept looked to regular diplomatic contact to 'increase transparency and predictability in security affairs' (ibid., p. 7). The policy of cooperation was 'built upon a common recognition among Alliance members that the persistence of new political, economic or social divisions across the continent could lead to future instability, and such divisions must thus be diminished' (ibid., p. 8). The Strategic Concept endorsed the ideas of conflict prevention and crisis management. It saw the success of the Alliance in preventing war as dependent upon the effectiveness of preventive diplomacy and successful management of crises.

> The success of Alliance policy will require a coherent approach determined by the Alliance's political authorities choosing and coordinating appropriate crisis management measures as required from a range of political and other measures, including those in the military field. Close control by the political authorities of the Alliance will be applied from the outset and at all stages. Appropriate consultation and decision making procedures are essential to this end.
>
> (Ibid., p. 8)

The Strategic Concept did not further define the strategy of crisis management but placed it within the framework of collective defence. The concept stated that the 'maintenance of an adequate military capability and clear preparedness to act collectively in the common defence remain central to the Alliance's security objectives' (ibid.). A commitment was made to retain a mixture of nuclear and conventional forces although at a significantly reduced level. Nuclear weapons were seen to make a 'unique contribution in rendering the risks of any aggression incalculable and unacceptable' (ibid., p. 10). The alliance was also to maintain the forces 'necessary to provide a wide range of conventional response options' (ibid., p. 9). The Strategic Concept, however, ended the comprehensive linear in-place defence in the central region and looked instead to flexibility, mobility and an assured capability for augmentation. NATO forces were to consist of immediate and rapid reaction elements which could be reinforced to a level in proportion to potential threats 'including the possibility – albeit unlikely, but one that prudence dictates should not be ruled out – of a major conflict' (ibid., p. 13).

The Soviet Union collapsed in December 1991 shortly after the proclamation of the New Strategic Concept and with its demise threatened NATO's new rationale. What need was there now for a collective defence organization? Could NATO hold together without the residual threat from the Soviet system? If 'traditional collective defence was no longer necessary, what should cooperation be aimed at?' (Wijk, 1997, p. 51). The answers to these questions lay in part in the new strategic environment and in part in the Alliance's continuing capacity to adapt. The new environment placed fresh challenges upon NATO. Security for the Allies was moving from the era of territorial defence to a wider concept including political, social and economic dimensions. The geographical basis of security was changing too and the relevance of non-Article 5 missions was growing in importance. The transformation of the Alliance from the understandings of the 1991 Strategic Concept was greatly influenced by its involvement in the crises affecting the former Yugoslavia. The pull of this 'out of area' operation led NATO to evaluate its contribution to peace support, its relationship to other international institutions, and ultimately its conceptualization of security.

The process of change within the Alliance was not, however, without difficulty or disagreement. For some there was a 'growing consensus among the Allies – almost dictated by the circumstances – on NATO's competence to undertake humanitarian and peacekeeping operations on behalf of the United Nations and the CSCE, thus transcending the hypothetical situations contemplated in Article 5' (Andò, 1993, pp. 5–6). For the others, such as the former West German Chancellor Helmut Schmidt, there was a clear need for public debate before 'fundamentally broadening or reshaping the aims of the Alliance and concern amongst the Allies that the North Atlantic Treaty does not provide "for actions beyond the territory of the NATO member states without specific UN backing"' (Schmidt, 1999, p. 23). The problem for NATO can be seen in political terms. Changing the missions of the Alliance raises questions not only of legitimacy but of political commitment.

> NATO's dilemma is that the greatest political commitment exists for the least probable threat (Article 5 security threat), and the least commitment for the most probable threat (non-Article 5 regional crisis).
>
> (Wijk, 1998, pp. 16–17)

NATO's strategic evolution proceeded nevertheless, though the political context within which Alliance decisions have been taken needs to be placed against the pressures for change. The stimuli for Alliance change have been generated by both the new security environment and the changing roles of the other elements of the security architecture. The institutionalization of the CSCE and the development of its 'mandate' role led NATO in June 1992 to support on a 'case-by-case basis' peacekeeping under its auspices. In December 1992 this undertaking was extended by the North Atlantic Council to operations under the authority of the United Nations. While this development boded well for the concept of 'interlocking institutions', the enhancement of the EU's security role, and in particular the potential revitalization of the WEU, challenged NATO's monopoly of security provision. The pattern of NATO's consequent evolution necessitated responses to the emergent European Security and Defence Identity (ESDI) as well as UN and CSCE/OSCE initiatives.

## The United Nations

As the Cold War ended the United Nations found a new lease of life. Between 1988 and 1992 the UN mounted 13 operations, equal to its record for the entire Cold War. The use of the veto dramatically declined (see Roberts, 1994, p. 96) and the organization's response to the Iraqi invasion of Kuwait in 1990 set a new sense of purpose. The Security Council, with the exception of Yemen, supported Resolution 660 which declared the invasion a threat to international peace and demanded an Iraqi withdrawal. Of greater significance all permanent members except China, who abstained, endorsed the key Resolution 678 which authorized member states to 'use all necessary means to uphold and implement resolution 660 and all subsequent resolutions and to restore international peace and security in the area ...' (Hiro, 1992, p. 538). The coalition use of force to liberate Kuwait heralded the 'new world order' through it is arguable that the ceasefire Resolution 687 was of equal importance. The resolution 'represents a major effort by the UN to control the future behaviour of a country' (Johnstone, 1994, p. 9). The resolution was indicative of a change in attitudes towards intervention as well as an easing of constraints upon Security Council action. United Nations action with regard to the crisis in Somalia underlined the new approach. In December 1992 the Security Council under Resolution 794 authorized the Secretary-General and member states to use 'all necessary means' to establish a secure environment for humanitarian relief in Somalia. Resolution 794 was the first to establish a humanitarian operation under Chapter VII of the Charter and without explicit consent from the parties to the conflict (see Mayall, 1996, p. 111). State sovereignty as an 'in principle' obstacle to intervention was clearly declining in significance. Sir David Hanney reported that:

> Article 2.7 of the Charter which says you cannot intervene in internal affairs meant that there were no-go areas. That has rather changed now ... the United Nations is doing things that would have been absolutely off-limits some years ago.
> (House of Commons Foreign Affairs Committee, 1992–93)

The Secretary-General's report *An Agenda for Peace* in 1992 captured much of the new thinking. Boutros-Ghali saw the United Nations as a 'central instrument for the prevention and resolution of conflicts and for the preservation of peace' (Boutros-Ghali, 1995, p. 43). He identified four key roles for the world organization. The first role was preventive diplomacy, 'to prevent disputes from arising between parties, to prevent existing disputes from escalating into conflicts and to limit the spread of the latter when they occur' (ibid., p. 45). The second role was peacemaking, 'action to bring hostile parties to agreement, essentially through such peaceful means as those foreseen in Chapter VI of the Charter of the United Nations' (ibid., p. 45). The third role was peacekeeping, 'the deployment of a United Nations presence in the field, hitherto with the consent of all the parties concerned, normally involving United Nations military and/or police personnel and frequently civilians as well' (ibid., p. 45). The fourth role was post-conflict peace-building, 'action to identify and support structures which will tend to strengthen and solidify peace in order to avoid a relapse into conflict' (ibid., p. 46). In addition Boutros-Ghali saw the need to bring into being the peace-enforcement units. He saw the need for forces to restore and maintain ceasefires which can 'on occasion exceed the mission of peacekeeping forces and the expectations of peacekeeping force contributors' (ibid., p. 56). Such troops would be more heavily armed than peacekeepers but would not constitute the forces envisaged under Article 43 of the Charter to respond to outright aggression. The Secretary-General was suggesting gradations of response and did not see a 'dividing line between peacemaking and peacekeeping' (ibid., p. 57).

The hopes and aspirations of the new United Nations have, however, met new challenges which, while not as stultifying as the inertia of Cold War politics, have provided nonetheless very real constraints upon the realization of objectives. The majority of post-Cold War conflicts have been within states rather than between states, a 'dramatic proliferation of ethnic, religious and similar types of conflicts' (Kühne, 1994, p. 41). Some of the conflicts have or have generated inter-state dimensions but the focus of conflict is firmly intra-state. Of the eleven UN peacekeeping operations established between 1992 and the end of 1994 all but two related to intra-state conflict compared to only one of five in 1988 (Boutros-Ghali, 1995, pp. 7–8). The 'new breed of intra-state conflicts have certain characteristics that present the United Nations peacekeepers with challenges not encountered since the Congo operation of the early 1960s' (ibid., p. 8). The conflicts are often marked by a breakdown in governance, fought by militias or guerrillas, without clear front lines and with civilians as the principal victims and often the main targets (ibid., p. 9). The challenge for the United Nations is that its intervention must 'extend beyond military and humanitarian tasks and must include the promotion of national reconciliation and the re-establishment of effective government' (ibid., p. 19). The tasks inherent in such missions are multi-faceted and in stark contrast to classical peacekeeping and interposition roles. United Nations peacekeepers now often find themselves in the midst of violence with little protection from ceasefires or the norms of consent. Traditionally UN 'peacekeepers worked with the legal consent and practical cooperation of all sides to the conflict and acted with impartiality and without prejudice to the rights and claims of any side' (Tharoor, 1995, p. 126). In ethnic, intra-state conflict the lines of 'conflict as well as the parties fighting each other are fragmented and in flux ... [and] there is a constantly shifting mixture of systematic and erratic violence' (Kühne, 1994, p. 44). In this anarchic environment 'the sacrosanct principle of consensus is very much reduced in its reliability as an operational basis for peacekeeping' (ibid., p. 44). In Bosnia the UN Protection Force (UNPROFOR) did not enjoy the benefit of a lasting agreement between the protagonists to enable it to perform its mission, ad hoc agreements were, moreover, frequently violated and the peacekeepers faced routine obstruction by all asides (Tharoor, 1995, p. 126). In the absence of consent and consensus the peacekeeping forces face a basic dilemma: the risk of operational irrelevance or the use of force. Enforcing cooperation in the absence of consensus is understandable but carries with it risks: risks to the peacekeepers themselves who may not be equipped for such a role, risks to the mandate if enforcement ends the peacekeepers' perceived impartiality, and risks to the future of peacekeeping as it becomes associated with military intervention (see Roberts, 1994, p. 105). The interrelationship between consent, peacekeeping and the use of force is sensitive and complex. Peacekeeping has been defined as 'operations carried out with the consent of the belligerent parties in support of efforts to achieve or maintain peace in order to promote security and sustain life in areas of potential or actual conflict' (Dobbie, 1994, p. 22). Peace enforcement in contrast is seen as 'operations carried out to restore peace between belligerent parties who do not all consent to intervention and who may be engaged in combat activities' (ibid., p. 122). Between the two are a range of possible gradations summarized by terms such as 'robust peacekeeping', 'enlarged peacekeeping' or 'wider peacekeeping'. Charles Dobbie has argued that peacekeepers can use force but it needs to be supported by consent.

> Peacekeeping with consent, however, does not exclude significant applications of force. Indeed, the use of force is facilitated by consent and should not necessarily be equated to the non-consensual category of peace-enforcement.
>
> (Ibid., p. 121)

Consent is seen as the dividing line between enforcement and peacekeeping including the concept of 'wider peacekeeping'. Dobbie argues consent can be seen at two levels: the tactical (field operations) level where it is derived from 'local events and the many influences that shape prevailing popular opinion', and the operational (theatre) level when it is derived from 'formal agreements and its boundary is consequently relatively clear cut and stable' (ibid., p. 124). If force has to be used at the tactical level of consent it is arguable that it 'does not necessarily equate to breaching the divide as a whole' (ibid., p. 124). If peacekeepers use force at the local level 'stability may be retained if the operational boundary to the consent divide is preserved intact ...' (ibid., p. 136). The principle of impartiality is also seen to guide the use of force in 'wider peacekeeping'. Dobbie contrasts the impartial use of force to protect a humanitarian convoy against whoever might choose to attack it and the 'pre-emptive bombing of a particular faction because it was that faction [which] would clearly abandon impartiality since it would constitute a deliberate attack to the detriment of one party to the conflict and the advantage of the others' (ibid., p. 137).

For some observers the relationship of military and non-military means in response to intra-state conflict is not a matter of choice, but 'rather of how to mix, coordinate and sequence military and non-military means in the prevention and management of ethnic and similar conflicts' (Kühne, 1994, p. 47). The role of the military is seen as critical to the protection of UN personnel and humanitarian missions, to the deterrence of attacks on safe areas and for disarming the protagonists (ibid., p. 47). The challenge for the military and the mission is to sustain such efforts over time recognizing there is 'no war to win but only a peace process to sustain or wreck' (ibid., p. 48). The use of force entails the risks of escalation, it can jeopardize negotiation and challenge the impartiality of the UN force. Preparation and planning of such missions is critical as is adaptation on the ground to the specific conflict. In practice it is not surprising that intra-state conflicts have produced for the UN 'a crisis of mandate (over the tasks it has been called upon to perform), a crisis of method (over the manner in which it has attempted to fulfil these tasks), and a crisis of means (over the resources needed to execute them)' (Tharoor, 1995, p. 124).

The scale of the United Nations post-Cold War activity has posed challenges for the organization's resource base. This has led in the case of UNPROFOR to a new relationship between the UN and NATO. NATO's provision of air power in support of UNPROFOR raised issues of 'command and control that are unprecedented in UN peacekeeping ...' (ibid., p. 129). While the 'dual key' arrangement between the two organizations resolved procedural matters it did not resolve the deeper issue of 'competing credibilities'. Differences between the UN and NATO over the use of air power in Bosnia 'inevitably called into question the degree to which the United Nations can, in these circumstances, expect to control the military environment within which its forces function' (ibid., p. 125).

The new peacekeeping is also expensive. In the period 1990 to 1995 the cost of peacekeeping increased by a factor of eight (Baehr and Gordenker, 1999, p. 91). The United Nations has not, however, been funded in relation to its new activities. Boutros-Ghali reported that 'a chasm has developed between the tasks entrusted to this organization and the financial means provided to it' (Boutros-Ghali, 1995, p. 66). Contributions to peacekeeping costs are based upon the regular UN scale of assessments but at a differential rate with the permanent members of the Security Council paying more and less developed countries paying less. Since the 1960s problems have resulted from members of the Security Council refusing to pay for peacekeeping missions. The Soviet Union refused to pay for UNEF and argued that its costs should be met by Egypt's aggressors. France and the Soviet Union refused to support the UN in the Congo and the United States under the Goldberg resolution reserved its right of exemption from collective financial responsibility in the future as a response. In 1985 the Reagan administration cut United States' contributions to the regular UN budget from 25 per cent to 20 per cent. Congressional opposition to UN policies and programmes then blocked financial contributions and the United States debt to the UN amounted to more than one billion dollars by 1988 (Baehr and Gordenker, 1999, p. 63). In 1993 Congress sought to decrease the United States' share of peacekeeping costs from 30 per cent to 25 per cent creating new financial pressures on the world organization. Late or non-payment from the United States and other key member states has left the United Nations in a vulnerable position. Finance is a major constraint upon the development of peace-keeping and renewal of missions. The failure of member states to pay their assessed contributions 'calls into question the credibility of those who have willed the ends but not the means – and who then criticize the United Nations for its failures' (Boutros-Ghali, 1995, p. 36).

## The OSCE within the European security architecture

The origins of the Conference on Security and Cooperation in Europe lie in the brief period of détente between East and West during the early to mid-1970s. Established by the Helsinki Final Act of 1975, it had 35 signatories including all European states (except Albania but including the Soviet Union), Canada and the United States. During the bipolar years, the CSCE acted as a permanent forum for the discussion of a wide variety of issues related to any of the three 'baskets' of the Final Act but its capacity to achieve substantive change was limited by the hostile international environment. Embodying a Europe which stretched from Vancouver to Vladivostock, this pan-European institution proved unable to progress beyond the *quid pro quo* of a recognition of geo-political realities for the rhetorical endorsement of human rights.

The end of the Cold War liberated the CSCE from the shackles of the East–West stalemate. Like many of its counterparts, the CSCE reviewed its remit in light of the changed European landscape. The commence-ment of this process of regeneration may be traced to the Second Meeting of the Conference of the Human Dimension in Copenhagen, 5–29 June 1990. At this conference, the primacy of a liberal democratic polity was accepted (Buergenthal, 1990, p. 217). Later that same year, the CSCE formally proclaimed a new era for Europe and itself in the 'Charter of Paris for a New Europe' (November 1990). This charter announced that 'a new era of democracy, peace and unity in Europe' had started. To secure its place within this new terrain, the CSCE undertook to institutionalize and consolidate its processes.

## The organizational structure of the OSCE

The Paris Charter facilitated the establishment of the following bodies: a Council of Foreign Ministers; a Committee of Senior Officials (CSO); an Office for Free Elections (OFE) (in January 1992, the OFE became the ODIHR, the Office for Democratic Institutions and Human Rights); a Conflict Prevention Centre (CPC); and an Administrative Secretariat. The Paris Charter also made reference to the OSCE Parliamentary Assembly which was established later in the Madrid Declaration of 1991.

The CSCE continued its path of institutional augmentation at both the Helsinki Review Conference of 1992 and the Budapest Review Meeting of 1994. At the former gathering, CSCE procedures were strengthened with the establishment of the post of High Commissioner for National Minorities (HCNM) and the Forum for Security Cooperation respectively. In addition, an armoury of measures related to conflict prevention and crisis management was unveiled. At the Budapest meeting, the CSCE officially changed its name to the Organization for Security and Cooperation in Europe (OSCE) to be effective from 1 January 1995 and consolidated the roles of the Chairman in Office (CIO) and the Office for Democratic Institutions and Human Rights respectively.

The functions of the OSCE can be listed as: a framework for norm-setting in relation to international law, human rights, democracy and market economics; a forum for arms control; a mechanism for monitoring human rights; a forum for pan-European multilateral diplomacy; and a framework for early warning, conflict prevention and conflict resolution. From 1994 the latter activity has become the prime concern of the OSCE as it has sought to move firmly into the realm of implementation.

## The OSCE and conflict prevention and management

Following the Cold War, the rise in salience of intra-state conflict seemed like a natural invitation to the OSCE to practise what it preached in its indivisible definition of security. Indivisible security contends that the security of one state is inextricably linked to the security of all others. As Niels Petersen, Chairman in Office (CIO) in 1997, put it, 'security is now more than ever indivisible. The consequences of risks to security cannot be isolated to one country' (Petersen, 1997, p. 4). Consequently, intra-state conflict is regarded as a matter of legitimate concern to the international community rather than a local issue for the sovereign state concerned. The very nature of such struggles, which are frequently centred upon zero sum perceptions of ethnicity and identity and have a wide and variable cast of sub-state actors, often militates against their expeditious diplomatic settlement. Continued, long-term involvement is necessary to foster observance and acceptance of the conditions of peace. Through the office of the HCNM and its mission capacity, the OSCE attempts to apply 'soft diplomatic pressure' on protagonists. Both the CIO and the HCNM may facilitate early-action processes in potential conflict spots. The CIO may undertake the mission personally or delegate personal representatives to do so. The HCNM can act as a channel of communication between the contending parties. OSCE missions broadly fall into any one of three categories: information-gathering, rapporteur or sanctions support.

Frequently, the OSCE mission works in cooperation with other international actors. For example, the OSCE mission to Albania works with the Council of Europe, the North Atlantic Council and the European Union to support the democratization process, while in Bosnia-Hercegovina, the OSCE has worked closely with IFOR and subsequently SFOR, the Council of Europe, the UNHCR and NATO.

The option of peacekeeping, enshrined in the 1992 Helsinki Document, is based on the traditional interpretation of the concept. As a regional organization under Article 52 of the UN Charter the OSCE may deploy a peacekeeping force but only with the consent of the warring parties and in the context of a ceasefire in place. As noted, the nature of contemporary intra-state conflict generally does not afford such conditions, limiting the likelihood of a potential OSCE intervention.

## The role of great powers and the OSCE in practice

The inclusion of Russia within the OSCE is often noted as one of its most significant assets. Western diplomats have hoped that the OSCE can moderate Russian policy in the 'Near Abroad' but Moscow has instead looked to the institution to legitimize its role in the region. The empirical evidence forces one to conclude that membership appears not to have had much effect upon Russian behaviour in Chechnya.

Russian armed intervention in the Chechnyan conflict clearly violated the OSCE commitment towards the peaceful resolution of such disputes and the other member states of the OSCE failed to bring effective institutional pressure to bear on their wayward member. Mechanisms such as the Vienna Mechanism for Consultation and Cooperation on Unusual Military Activities could have been utilized by any of the OSCE member states prior to the Russian invasion but it was not. Likewise the OSCE member states could have utilized the Vienna Human Dimension Mechanism to collect data on human rights violations before the outbreak of overt conflict but they failed to do so. Neither did any of the OSCE member states employ the Moscow Human Dimension mechanism to despatch a fact-finding mission to Moscow or Chechnya. Such failures highlight the weakness of the OSCE when a major power is involved in a conflict.

The OSCE did eventually succeed in sending a mission to Chechnya but the mission was of short-term duration and failed to influence the situation. The Russian offensive in 1999 reinforced the past lessons about the 'power' of the OSCE in this context.

### OSCE decision-making constraints

The OSCE's decision-making procedure rests upon the principle of consensus. This principle can act as a major internal constraint and has severe consequences for OSCE efficacy in preventive diplomacy. Although the principle has been modified in order to allow 'consensus minus one' in the case of 'clear, gross and uncorrected violation of CSCE commitments' and 'consensus minus two' in the 'context of the directed conciliation procedure' (Hyde-Price, 1998, p. 24), the organization remains basically wedded to the need for consensus for its decision-making. In the case of high-tension areas where a potentially overt conflict looms, it is desirable that the OSCE should have the ability to take decisions promptly and undertake action rapidly and having to secure consensus may militate against this, thus there have been discussions about changing the voting rules. The case for reforming the principle of consensus was strengthened by the conflict in the former Yugoslavia. Given its consensus ruling, the OSCE could act in the crisis only when it has suspended Yugoslavia's state membership – a cumbersome and time-consuming process. Consequentially, there have been calls for the OSCE to reconsider the consensus principle. It has been suggested that in respect to peacekeeping operations the OSCE should adopt the technique of a 'coalition of the able and the willing' wherein member states could declare their willingness to participate in such a peacekeeping force prior to its despatch. Another approach which could prove viable is that of the 'consensus-minus-the-parties' whereby member states could 'opt-out' of the decision-making process upon a specific matter. The OSCE Parliamentary Assembly has joined the chorus requesting reformation of the consensus ruling. It has advanced the concept of 'approximate consensus' in which a 90 per cent endorsement by the membership's financial contributors would be sufficient to endorse a decision. Using such a decision-making process would ensure that no one member state could veto an OSCE decision.

### The OSCE and the new European security architecture

At the Budapest Summit in 1994 Russia proposed that the CSCE be turned into an international organization with a legally binding charter and a central role in directing other European security structures. Russian proposals would have effectively subordinated NATO to the OSCE and given, for example, the CIS priority for security in its region. Moscow would also have in effect secured a veto, similar to its United Nations position, over the European security architecture. The summit instead decided to look for 'a genuine security partnership among all participating states' and made a commitment to draft a 'Common and Comprehensive Security Model for Europe for the Twenty-First Century'. The OSCE was to enhance cooperation with the United Nations, European 'and other regional and transatlantic organizations while avoiding duplication of effort' (CSCE Budapest Decisions, 1994, p. 3). It was clear that the OSCE decision sought to 'filter' issues before reference to the UN as participating states were 'to make every effort to achieve pacific settlement of local disputes before referring them to the United Nations Security Council' (CSCE Budapest Decisions, 1994, p. 4). The discussion of the Common and Comprehensive Security Model gave rise to the 'Platform for Cooperative Security' intended to outline the scope and technicalities of cooperation between the OSCE and other security providers. The 1997 Copenhagen OSCE Ministerial sought to facilitate this cohesion of international institutions with the 'Common Concept for the Development of Cooperation between Mutually Reinforcing Institutions'. Ministers recognized that security in the OSCE area required cooperation and coordination among participating states and relevant organizations of which they were also members. The OSCE set criteria for cooperation including adherence to: the Helsinki Final Act, the Charter of Paris, the Helsinki Document 1992, the Budapest Document 1994, the OSCE code of conduct on politico-military aspects of security, the Lisbon Declaration on a Common and Comprehensive Security Model, and transparency as per the Vienna documents (OSCE Ministerial Council, 1997, p. 17). The Ministerial looked for cooperation which would 'avoid duplication and ensure efficient use of available responses' (ibid., p. 18). The Oslo OSCE ministerial took the issue further and stressed that cooperation with other institutions would be flexible, pragmatic and non-hierarchical (OSCE Ministerial, 1998, p. 5).

The OSCE Istanbul Summit in 1999 agreed to adopt the Platform for Cooperative Security. Its objectives were to attain political and operational coherence among the bodies dealing with security in the OSCE area both for specific crises and in formulating responses to new risks and challenges (OSCE, 1999, p. 5). The summit did not seek to create a 'hierarchy of organizations or a permanent division of labour among them' (ibid., p. 5). Instead 'we offer the OSCE, when appropriate, as a flexible coordinating framework to foster cooperation, through which various organizations can reinforce each other drawing on their particular strengths' (ibid., p. 5). The summit also proposed to develop cooperation with other institutions by

> regular contacts, including meetings; a continuous framework for dialogue; increased transparency and practical cooperation, including the identification of liaison officers or points of contact; cross-representation at appropriate meetings; and other contacts intended to increase understanding of each organization's conflict prevention tools.
>
> (Ibid., p. 15)

The OSCE also envisaged enhanced cooperation with other organizations in the field of operations through 'regular information exchanges and meetings, joint needs assessment missions, secondment of experts by other organizations to the OSCE, appointment of liaison officers, development of common projects and field operations and joint training efforts' (ibid., p. 15).

These pragmatic proposals reflected the political realities of the OSCE membership's divisions and the pattern of institutional development in the European security architecture which currently prevents a predetermined division of responsibilities. As we shall see, each of the key institutions in the security architecture has sought to develop and broaden their competences making a 'dovetailed' approach or 'blueprint' for security responsibilities difficult to attain. Pragmatism can be positive, however, and in the case of Bosnia institutional cooperation was successful in the post-Dayton era. The NATO-led Implementation Force (IFOR) and its successor SFOR collaborated closely with the OSCE and other international institutions including United Nations agencies to implement the Paris Peace Agreement. The challenge for the security architecture is to be equally cohesive in conflict prevention.

## The European Union

The end of the Cold War was accompanied by a 'deepening' of integration in the European Community. The transition from Community to Union at Maastricht marked an intensification of the process of Eurogovernance (see Carr and Massey, 1999). Indeed Wæver has argued that the 'primary relevance of the European Community as regards security is not ... its expression in narrowly-defined security structures like the WEU or Eurocorps, but the general political and symbolic importance of the Community as such, the strength of the process of integration' (Wæver, 1996, p. 229). The European Union can be seen as a 'hub' or 'core' of the European order whose influence emanates outwards in 'concentric circles' 'taken in conjunction with the graduated system of agreements with European States outside the community, the whole of Europe up to the boundaries of the former Soviet Union can be seen as a core–periphery structure' (Miall, 1993, p. 106). As the general political and economic significance of the EU has grown it has sought means to focus its influence in external relations. It is precisely because the Union has such political significance but to date relatively ineffectual instruments for external policy that advocates of reform such as Jacques Delors and Jacques Santer have called for change. This section examines the Union's Common Foreign and Security Policy (CFSP) and its defence implications. It will examine the development of the EU's external security policy and its consequences for the other institutions in the European security architecture.

### The Common Foreign and Security Policy

The Maastricht Treaty on European Union in 1992 committed its signatories to implement a 'common foreign and security including the eventual framing of a common defence policy, which might in time lead to a common defence' (Title I, Article 3). CFSP was presented as a new policy (Petersen and Bomberg, 1999, p. 229) but it drew upon the conventions and record of the process known as European Political Cooperation (EPC).

EPC was essentially the attempt to coordinate foreign policy by the members of the European Community and it was developed following summits in a series of 'Reports'. EPC was grounded outside of the 'community method' on an intergovernmental basis. Just as in NATO and the OSCE consensus was required among member states for decision-making. The process was launched by the Hague EC Summit in 1969 and consolidated by the Luxembourg 'Report' of 1970. Foreign ministers were to meet biannually supported by a Political Committee of senior officers from member foreign ministries meeting four times a year, in turn supported by a number of 'working groups'. In practice the Political Committee met on a far more regular basis and the Copenhagen 'Report' of 1973 lifted all restrictions on its activities. Attempts to limit the life of the Working Groups to prevent a transnational policy base emerging independent of state control failed and EPC increasingly became supplanted by a network of committees (see Nuttall, 1992). The Commission became 'fully associated' with EPC under the London Report of 1981 but it remained under the existing policy framework. The Single European Act (SEA) of 1987 provided a legal base for this framework confirming past precedent and recognizing the European Council of Heads of State and Government as the most senior body in EPC decision-making. Finally in the Luxembourg and Hague Council meetings in 1987 defence policy was seen as an integral part of any future European Union. The Hague EC Council of Ministers saw the revitalization of the Western European Union (WEU) as an important contributor to the process of European unification. The relaunch of the WEU, the European alliance which NATO had left in the shadows, signalled a first commitment to European security cooperation. The context was at first heightened superpower tension but rapidly became the revolutionary conditions of 1989–90. Franco-German interests (discussed in Chapter 2) led to the formal inclusion of defence and the WEU in proposals for European Political Union (EPU) to complement Economic and Monetary Union (EMU).

## Maastricht

The record of EPC was an extensive network of working groups and committees bringing together the foreign ministries of member states into a complex multilateral system. The output of this network was in contrast more modest. The Community's response to the Iraqi invasion of Kuwait in 1990 illustrates some of the difficulties. While the Community supported sanctions against Iraq and a freeze on Iraqi assets as the likelihood of an Allied military intervention increased divergences among member states grew. Britain steadfastly supported the United States and looked for a full reversal of Iraqi policy by all necessary means including force. In contrast France pursued an independent line up to the brink indulging in bilateral diplomacy with Baghdad without reference to allies. In the German case the 'emphasis given to the constitutional prohibitions on the use of German troops beyond their own borders showed not only a reluctance to be diverted from their domestic concerns but also perhaps a reluctance to contemplate the implications of once more becoming an "ordinary" state, which would include the preparedness to use force if and when the need arises' (Matthews, 1993, p. 273). For Jacques Delors the Gulf crisis provided an 'object lesson – if one were needed – on the limitations of the European Community' (Delors, 1991). 'Once it became obvious that the situation would have to be resolved by armed combat, the Community had neither the institutional machinery nor the military force which would have allowed it to act as a community' (ibid.). Delors saw the need for urgent reform and all 'provisions relating to external aspects – foreign policy, security, economic relations and development cooperation should be brought together in one title of the treaty' (ibid.). Member states were not, however, in agreement; while Belgium, Germany and the Netherlands wanted to end EPC separation from the Community, Britain, Denmark and France did not.

France proposed a three-pillar design in which foreign policy and interior affairs would be kept outside the Community and centred on the European Council. This was 'designed to restrict definitively, through qualitative institutional breaks, the Commission and Parliament's prerogatives in foreign and interior policy' (Moravcsik, 1999, pp. 449–50). France, supported by Germany, however, wanted to make greater use of Qualified Majority Voting (QMV) for the implementation of decisions taken by unanimity but Britain, Denmark and Ireland opposed the proposal (ibid.). On the issue of defence policy different alignments resulted from those states keen to maintain a strong 'Atlanticist' basis for security led by Britain and those favouring a 'Europeanist' future led by France seeking the rapid integration of the WEU into the EU. Between the two lay gradations of opinion on the actual and potential role of the WEU. The consequences of the negotiation were a series of compromises which permeated the Maastricht Treaty.

The Maastricht Treaty made CFSP one of the 'three pillars of the EU' under the auspices of the European Council. Like EPC, the CFSP structure was intergovernmental outside of the European Community 'pillar' but as in the past the Commission was to be 'fully associated' (Article J. 0.9). The European Council was to 'define the principles of and general guidelines for common foreign and security policy' (Article J. 8.1). Decision-making was to proceed on the basis of unanimity as in EPC but when the Council has decided on a joint action it can 'when adopting the joint action and at any stage during its development, define those matters on which decisions are to be taken by a qualified majority' (Article J. 3.2). The Treaty confirmed the role of the Presidency and the Political Committee as developed under EPC (Articles J. 5, 1, 2 and 3, Article J. 8.5). Following EPC precedent the stress was upon consultation, cooperation and coordination. The innovation of 'joint action' still required consensus and was clearly reserved for those 'areas in which member states have important interests in common' (Article J. 1.3).

On defence issues the Treaty 'requests' not 'instructs' (Forster and Wallace, 1997, p. 426) the WEU 'which is an integral part of the development of the Union, to elaborate and implement decisions and actions of the Union which have defence implications' (Article, J. 4.2). The Treaty made clear that issues having defence implications would not be dealt with under the procedures for adopting joint actions including QMV, and explicitly recognized the obligation of certain members under the North Atlantic Treaty (Article J. 4.4). At Maastricht the nine member states of the WEU who were also members of the EU agreed to develop a 'genuine' ESDI and a greater European responsibility on defence matters 'through a gradual process involving successive phases' (Maastricht Declaration on Western European Union). The member states agreed to strengthen the role of the WEU, 'in the longer term perspective of a common defence, compatible with that of the Atlantic Alliance' (ibid.). The WEU was to be 'developed as the defence component of the European Union and as a means to strengthen the European pillar of the Atlantic Alliance' (ibid.). The WEU was given in effect a pivotal role between the EU and NATO and committed itself to closer working links with both organizations. The WEU also adopted a series of commitments to enhance its operational capability with respect to a planning cell, closer military cooperation, meetings of Chiefs of Staff and military units. The WEU Council and Secretariat were transferred from London to Brussels and new members were invited to join.

Following the Maastricht Treaty the development of the European security identity took two related pathways: the CFSP process was formally reviewed in the 1997 Amsterdam Treaty and the WEU role was progressively defined in relation to the auspices of NATO and the EU.

## The 1997 Amsterdam Treaty

The political background to the Amsterdam Treaty was basically similar to the period preceding Maastricht. The President of the Commission, Jacques Santer, was critical of the record of CFSP. He questioned the political will of member states to work together, the adequacy of the intergovernmental 'pillar' and the unanimity rule (Santer, 1995). The Commission proposed, with the support of some member states, an introduction of QMV to some foreign policy areas excluding defence which would 'be subjected to a formula better suited to the nature of the subject – unanimity when the vital interests of a member state may be called into question' (ibid., p. 8). Britain, Portugal and Greece led the opposition to an extension of QMV while France sustained its position on the need for the second pillar to remain intergovernmental. France, Germany and the Commission advocated the integration of the WEU into the EU while the British maintained their opposition to the possible subordination of the WEU to the European Council. The consequent Treaty, like its predecessor, was therefore a compromise.

The Amsterdam Treaty confirmed that the 'Union shall define and implement a common foreign and security policy' (Article II.1). The Union was to pursue this objective by 'defining the principles of and general guidelines for the common foreign and security policy: deciding on common strategies; adopting joint actions; adopting common positions; [and] strengthening systematic cooperation between member states in the conduct of policy' (Article 12). The role of the European Council as the determining body in CFSP matters was restated (Articles 13, 14, 15, 23). So too was the principle of unanimity: 'decisions under this Title shall be taken by the Council acting unanimously' (Article 23.1). However, abstentions 'shall not prevent the adoption of such decisions' and abstentions may be qualified by a formal declaration which means a member state will 'not be obliged to apply the decision, but shall accept that the decision commits the Union' (Article 23.1). The member state concerned is to refrain from any action likely to impede Union action based on that decision but if members qualifying their abstention in this way represent more than one third of the votes under QMV rules the decision will not be adopted.

It has been argued that this is not necessarily a constructive step forward but a counterproductive measure upgrading dissent to 'a formal act of dissociation from a decision taken by the Union but also combined with an automatic opt-out possibility as regards any action taken' (Monar, 1997, p. 419). The Treaty does enhance the use of QMV compared to Maastricht by stating the 'Council shall act by a qualified majority: when adopting joint actions, common positions or taking any other decision on the basis of a common strategy: when adopting any decision implementing a joint action or a common position' (Article 23.2). As Monar points out, the key qualification to QMV is the phrase on the 'basis of a common strategy', i.e. on the basis of an agreed decision (ibid., p. 420). QMV remains therefore focused on the implementation of agreed positions taken on the basis of unanimity and can still be arrested by the following provision:

> If a member of the Council declares that, for important and stated reasons of national policy, it intends to oppose the adoption of a decision to be taken by qualified majority a vote shall not be taken. The Council may, acting by a qualified majority, request that the matter be referred to the European Council for decision by unanimity.
>
> (Article 23.2)

The Treaty did make an innovation with regard to the appointment of a High Representative for CFSP and a new planning unit. The Presidency of the Council was to be 'assisted by the Secretary General of the Council who shall exercise the function of High Representative for the common foreign and security policy' (Article 18.3). The High Representative was to assist the Council 'through contributing to the formulation, preparation and implementation of policy decisions, and, when appropriate and acting on behalf of the Council at the request of the Presidency, through conducting political dialogue with third parties' (Article 26). In a Declaration added to the Treaty a Policy Planning and Early Warning Unit (PPEWU) was to be established under the authority of the Security General (High Representative). The PPEWU's effectiveness will depend though on the degree to which it receives confidential information 'yet it is still up to each member state to decide how much information will be made available and when' (Monar, 1997, p. 417).

The Amsterdam Treaty did not alter the relationship of the EU and WEU. The WEU was seen as an integral part of the development of the European Union. The Union was to 'foster close institutional relations with the WEU with a view to the possibility of the integration of the WEU into the Union...' but only 'should the European Council so decide' (Article 17.1). The EU relationship with the WEU was, moreover, not to prejudice the defence policy of member states who see their common defence realized under the North Atlantic Treaty. The Amsterdam Treaty did, however, introduce the idea that the WEU would provide the Union with an operational capability, notably for 'humanitarian and rescue tasks, peacekeeping tasks and tasks of combat forces in crisis management, including peacemaking' (Article 17.2). While the use of WEU military forces would require a unanimous decision of the Council the delineation of the 'Petersberg tasks' (see below) became important for the future division of roles in the European architecture.

## The WEU

The reactivation of the WEU at Maastricht was followed by its adaptation in terms of membership, role and relationship to NATO. The WEU invited members of the EU to accede or become 'observers'. Similarly European members of NATO were invited to become 'associate members' of the WEU. Central and Eastern European states which had or were about to conclude 'Europe Agreements' with the EU were granted 'Associate Partnerships'. The WEU Petersberg Declaration of 1992 envisaged that, apart from contributing to the common defence in accordance with Article 5 of the Washington Treaty and Article V of the modified Brussels Treaty, the WEU could contribute to the peacekeeping roles of the UN or CSCE. It was stated that military units of WEU member states acting under its authority could be employed for: 'humanitarian and rescue tasks; peacekeeping tasks; tasks of combat forces in crisis management, including peace making' (WEU, 1992, p. 6). To prepare for WEU missions a Planning Cell was created which was soon recognized to be in need of additional capacities in the area of intelligence and crisis management (WEU, 1994, p. 9). To support the WEU, member states designated which of their forces were 'answerable to WEU' (FAWEU). In 1994 such forces consisted of: the Belgian, French, German, Luxembourg and Spanish Eurocorps; the Multinational Division consisting of Belgian, British, Dutch and German units; and the UK–Netherlands amphibious force. The WEU also recognized its deficiencies with regard to operational capabilities, information-gathering, resources, decision-making and command and control (ibid., pp. 8–9). In this respect its relationship with NATO was of fundamental importance as the North Atlantic Alliance held the resources vital to the development of the WEU.

At its Brussels Summit in January 1994 the North Atlantic Council welcomed the ESDI and supported the strengthening of the European pillar of the Alliance through the Western European Union. The summit agreed that 'in future contingencies, NATO and the WEU will consult, including as necessary through Joint Council meetings, on how to address such contingencies' (North Atlantic Council, 1994, pp. 2–3). NATO declared its willingness to

> ... stand ready to make collective assets of the Alliance available, on the basis of consultations in the North Atlantic Council, for WEU operations undertaken by the European Allies in pursuit of their Common Foreign and Security Policy. We support the development of separable but not separate capabilities which could respond to European requirements and contribute to Alliance security.
>
> (Ibid., 1994)

To implement this process the internal Alliance military and political structures required adaptation. The NATO summit looked to the concept of Combined Joint Task Forces (CJTF) as a means to facilitate both peacekeeping and cooperation with the WEU. The North Atlantic Council formally endorsed the concept in Berlin in 1996 but its development and implementation were still to follow. A CJTF has been defined as a 'deployable multinational, multi-service formation generated and tailored for specific contingency operations' (Cragg, 1996, p. 7). The Berlin Summit saw that by taking full 'advantage of the approved CJTF concept... [the ESDI] will be grounded on sound military principles and supported by appropriate military planning and permit the creation of militarily coherent and effective forces capable of operating under the political control and strategic direction of the WEU' (North Atlantic Council, 1996, p. 31). NATO envisaged the identification of 'separable but not separate' assets for WEU missions including headquarters, 'double hatting' appropriate personnel in the NATO Command Structure and military planning for illustrative WEU missions (ibid.). The CJTF concept therefore allowed the WEU to conduct operations without having to duplicate the capabilities held by NATO. For the WEU it meant dependence on NATO but the reality was that 'European military capabilities are so limited that the WEU would only be capable of undertaking military operations of a certain magnitude if it could rely on NATO assets and capabilities' (Cutileiro, 1997). For NATO the sharing of assets was meant to 'ensure as far as possible that Europe's CFSP effectively complements rather than competes with the transatlantic security structures' (Schake et al., 1999, p. 22). The implementation of the CJTF concept had technical difficulties (see Cragg, 1996; Silva, 1998) and political challenges. The position of states with NATO membership but not EU membership was exemplified by Turkey whose concern was that Ankara would not enjoy the same influence in WEU-led operations as full WEU members (Wijk, 1997, p. 138). French support for CJTFs was balanced by residual concern with the IMS and the potential for NATO control of WEU-led missions (see Grant, 1996). Paris looked for maximum autonomy for non-Article 5 WEU missions drawing on NATO assets and feared that 'NATO logistics support or information could culminate in practice in a right of veto, a right to inspect, and indirect NATO control over WEU actions' (Dumoulin, 1995). While President Chirac led France back to participation in NATO's decision-making bodies which 'respected national sovereignty' he made clear that greater reintegration required the further Europeanization of NATO. The French Defence Minister stated, 'we have a clear picture: the NATO chain of command must be able to function in a European mode to ensure that, when the time comes, we are in a position to use the means necessary for the command of an operation under European control' (Millon, 1996, p. 13). Paris looked to a European Deputy SACEUR to be given author-ity to command European missions and for Europeans to be given command of two regional European commands (Wijk, 1997, p. 135). The United States rejected the latter proposal and insisted an American command AFSOUTH in Naples. The role of the Deputy SACEUR was, however, agreed and the Madrid Declaration on Euro-Atlantic Security and Cooperation endorsed

> the decisions taken with regard to European command arrange-ments within NATO to prepare, support, command and conduct WEU-led operations using NATO assets and capabilities (including provisional terms of reference for Deputy SACEUR covering his ESDI-related responsibilities both permanent and during crises and operations), the arrangements for the identification of NATO assets and capabilities that could support WEU-led operations, and arrangements for NATO–WEU consultation in the context of such operations.
>
> (North Atlantic Council, 1997, p. 3)

By 1998 the relationship between the EU, WEU and NATO had come to mean a series of political and pragmatic understandings. Collective defence was NATO's acknowledged responsibility and in turn the EU and WEU had limited their ambitions to the Petersberg tasks. NATO had sought to make its strategic resources accessible and flexible for non-Article 5 missions to be conducted either by itself or by the WEU on behalf of the EU. The ESDI was therefore to be developed through

NATO and CFSP was to complement the transatlantic basis of security. While the implementation of these understandings required development and refinement the pattern of institutional interrelationships appeared to have been settled. The Anglo-French declaration on European Defence in Saint Malo in December 1998, however, reopened the debate with its call for the European Union to

> have the capacity for autonomous action, backed up by credible military forces, the means to decide to use them, and a readiness to do so, in order to respond to international crises.
>
> (Foreign and Commonwealth Office, 1998)

### The Common European Policy on Security and Defence

The Saint Malo Declaration looked to a 'full and rapid implementation of the Amsterdam provisions on CFSP'. Collective defence commitments under the Washington Treaty were to be maintained but:

> In order for the European Union to take decisions and approve military action where the alliance as a whole is not engaged, the Union must be given appropriate structures and a capacity for analysis of situations, sources of intelligence, and a capability for relevant strategic planning, without unnecessary duplication, taking account of the existing assets of the WEU and the evolution of its relations with the EU. In this regard, the European Union will also need to have recourse to suitable military means (European capabilities pre-designated within NATO's European pillar or national or multinational European means outside the NATO framework).
>
> (Foreign and Commonwealth Office, 1998)

The British Prime Minister, Tony Blair, stressed the enduring value of NATO but believed 'Europeans should not expect the United States to have to play a part in every disorder in our backyard' (Blair, 1999, p. 3). He explained that the Anglo-French initiative was to go beyond the 1996 Berlin agreement to give 'Europe a genuine capacity to act, and act quickly, in cases where the Alliance as a whole is not militarily engaged' (ibid.). The Prime Minister believed 'Europe's foreign policy voice in the world is unacceptably muted and ineffective, given our economic weight and strategic interests' (Blair, 1998, p. 3). Robin Cook, the Foreign Secretary, explained that Britain had taken the initiative because 'Bosnia, Albania and Kosovo have all shown that crisis management requires a joined up approach which brings together the economic, financial and humanitarian resources of the European Union with the military assets of the European countries in NATO' (Cook, 1999, p. 6). The Foreign Secretary stressed that to undertake the Petersberg tasks the EU needed to develop: a more coherent and urgent capacity for crisis management; better 'transmission between the European Union which is where we agree on our Common Foreign Policy and NATO ...; and improved military capabilities' (ibid., p. 7). Kosovo was seen to have exposed a number of problems for Europe including 'projecting effective military assets from immobile standing armies (ibid., p. 7) and for George Robertson the fact that 80 per cent of air power in the conflict was provided by the USA was a lesson that 'Europe should do better' (Robertson, 1999, p. 2).

The British initiative secured French, German and, after clarification of NATO's role, United States support. Deputy Secretary of State Strobe Talbott warned European leaders not to seek an 'autonomous defence capability' (*International Herald Tribune*, 26 November 1999). The London Anglo-French summit in November 1999 sought to reassure Washington that the EU would only seek to act 'where the alliance as a whole is not engaged' (*The Times*, 26 November 1999). Robin Cook suggested that in 'any developing crisis, there would be parallel discussions in NATO and the EU ... America has a very clear choice if it wants to be involved. There is no decoupling' (*International Herald Tribune*, 26 November 1999). President Chirac also argued that a European rapid deployment force of 50,000–60,000 troops would strengthen NATO (*The Times*, 26 November 1999). The British Foreign Secretary also stressed the point in the House of Commons: 'far from weakening NATO, the improved military responses that we demand will provide resources not just for the European Union but for NATO' (Hansard, 1 December 1999, col. 324). The NATO Washington Summit in April 1999 had taken this approach. It confirmed that a stronger European role would help the Alliance and acknowledged the 'resolve of the European Union to have a capacity for autonomous action so that it can take decisions and approve military action where the alliance as a whole is not engaged' (North Atlantic Council, 1999a, p. 5). The summit looked for a number of issues to be resolved. It wanted effective 'mutual consultation, cooperation and transparency' between NATO and the EU 'building on the mechanisms existing between NATO and the WEU' (ibid.). It attached the 'utmost importance to ensuring the fullest possible involvement of non-EU European Allies in EU-led crisis response operations, building on existing consultation arrangements within the WEU' (ibid., p. 5). The North Atlantic

Council further looked to address: assured EU access to NATO planning capabilities; pre-identified NATO capabilities and common assets for use in EU-led operations; identification of a range of European command options for EU-led operations and further development of the role of DSACEUR; and the further adaptation of NATO's defence planning system to incorporate more comprehensively the availability of forces for EU-led operations (ibid.).

The European Union took its policy on defence forward in the Cologne and Helsinki European Council meetings in 1999. The Cologne Council in June confirmed that the European Union should have the ability to take decisions with regard to the Petersberg tasks, 'backed up by credible military forces, the means to decide to use them, a readiness to do so, in order to respond to international crises without prejudice to actions by NATO' (European Council, 1999a, p. 21). The General Affairs Council was tasked 'to prepare the conditions and the measures necessary to achieve these objectives, including the definition of the modalities for the inclusion of those functions of the WEU which will be necessary for the EU to fulfil its new responsibilities in the area of the Petersberg tasks' (ibid., p. 22). The end of the year 2000 was set as the target date for completion of decisions and by that point 'the WEU as an organisation would have completed its purpose' (ibid.). The Council saw the need for the development of EU decision-making in security and defence policy. It envisaged that this would require: meetings of the General Affairs Council as appropriate including Defence Ministers; a permanent Political and Security Committee in Brussels; an EU Military Committee; an EU Military Staff including a Situation Centre; and a Satellite Centre (ibid., p. 24). The summit saw decision-making being taken within the framework of the CFSP. Depending upon the case, implementation would either use national or multinational assets or NATO assets based upon the principles agreed in NATO's 1996 Berlin Summit. The European Union was further committed to meeting the principles identified at the Washington Summit including the pursuit of satisfactory arrangements for European NATO members who are not EU member states to be fully involved and consideration of ways to involve WEU Associate Partners.

The Helsinki European Council sought to advance preparations for the Common European Policy on Security and Defence. The Council set the target of creating by 2003 a force 50,000–60,000 strong which could be deployed in 60 days and sustained for a year (European Council 1999b, p. 3). The European NATO members who were not members of the EU were to contribute to the improvement of European military capabilities. The summit made clear that the

'Council decides upon policy relevant to Union involvement in all phases and aspects of crisis management, including decisions to carry out Petersberg tasks in accordance with Article 23 of the EU Treaty' (ibid., p. 20). The Cologne proposals for new permanent political and military bodies were confirmed with a Political and Security Committee (PSC) composed of national representatives of senior/ambassadorial level dealing with all aspects of CFSP, and a Military Committee (MC) composed of the Chief of Defence and the Military Staff (MS) who will perform early warning, situation assessment and strategic planning for the Petersberg tasks. In the interim provisional political and military bodies were to be established with the High Representative contributing to the formulation of policy. Measures were advanced for the involvement of non-EU NATO members should they so wish in crisis management. The European Council also sought to enhance and better coordinate its non-military crisis management response tasks. The Council recognized that the Union 'needs to strengthen the responsiveness and efficiency of its resources and tools, as well as their synergy' (ibid., p. 22). An Action Plan was to be developed in which 'member states and the Union should develop a rapid reaction capability by defining a framework and modalities, as well as by pre-identifying personnel, material and financial resources that could be used in response to a request of a lead agency like the UN or the OSCE, or where appropriate in autonomous EU actions' (ibid., p. 23). The summit mandated the ensuing Portuguese Presidency of the Council to take forward institutional developments, proposals for third states' participation in EU military crisis management and principles for consultation with NATO on military issues.

## NATO's 1999 Strategic Concept

As the EU moved to approve means to undertake a new security role NATO adopted a new Strategic Concept in April 1999. The new Strategic Concept incorporated commitments made by the Alliance since the early 1990s to: conflict prevention and crisis management; peace support operations in consultation with the OSCE and UN; mutually reinforcing institutions; and the development of ESDI and a new command structure including the CJTF concept. The implementation of the EU Amsterdam Treaty provisions on CFSP including the progressive framing of a common defence policy was seen as compatible with the common security and defence policy within the framework of the Washington Treaty. The Alliance reaffirmed its 1996 Berlin decisions to make available its assets and capabilities for WEU-led operations and acknowledged the incorporation of the Petersberg tasks into the EU. The increase of the responsibilities and capacities of the European allies was seen to enhance the 'security environment of the Alliance' (North Atlantic Council, 1999b (18), p. 5). The new Concept was to do more, however, than catalogue the recent political evolution of NATO and was to meet current and future security challenges for the Alliance.

The contemporary security environment was seen to have positive and negative features. Positive features were seen as: greater integration in Europe; the emergence of a Euro-Atlantic security structure; and successful arms control. There were also, however, 'complex new risks to Euro-Atlantic peace and stability, including oppression, ethnic conflict, economic distress, the collapse of political order, and the proliferation of weapons of mass destruction' (ibid. (3), p. 1).

The security of the Alliance was seen to be subject to a 'wide variety of military and non-military risks which are multi-directional and often difficult to predict' (ibid. (20), p. 5). The risks included 'uncertainty and instability in and around the Euro-Atlantic area and the possibility of regional crises at the periphery of the Alliance' (ibid. (20), p. 5). In addition the existence and proliferation of weapons of mass destruction was seen as a significant element for Alliance security. Such weapons could pose a direct threat to the territory of the Allies. While non-proliferation regimes were being strengthened NATO acknowledged that the technology to build such weapons was becoming more common. Alliance security was also to take account of the global context.

> Alliance security interests can be affected by other risks of a wider nature, including acts of terrorism, sabotage and organised crime, and by the disruption of the flow of vital resources. The uncontrolled movement of large numbers of people, particularly as a consequence of armed conflicts, can also pose problems for security and stability affecting the Alliance.
>
> (Ibid. (24), p. 6)

The Strategic Concept retained NATO's broad approach to security and commitment to a mutually reinforcing security architecture.

> The Alliance seeks to preserve peace and to reinforce Euro-Atlantic security and stability by: the preservation of the transatlantic link;

the maintenance of effective military capabilities sufficient for deterrence and defence and to fulfil the full range of its missions; the development of the European Security and Defence Identity within the Alliance; an overall capability to manage crises successfully; its continued openness to new members; and the continued pursuit of partnership, cooperation, and dialogue with other nations as part of its cooperative approach to the Euro-Atlantic security, including in the field of arms control and disarmament.

(Ibid. (26), p. 7)

NATO's security functions were listed as: an 'essential transatlantic forum for Allied consultations on any issues that affect their vital interests' (ibid. (10), p. 3), deterrence and defence, crisis management and partnership. Underpinning these functions was a commitment to retain adequate military capabilities for collective defence and non-Article 5 crisis response operations. For collective defence it was envisaged that

the combined military forces of the Alliance must be capable of deterring any potential aggression against it, of stopping an aggressor's advance as far forward as possible should an attack nevertheless occur, and of ensuring the political independence and territorial integrity of its member states.

(Ibid. (41), p. 11)

NATO was also to retain nuclear forces as the supreme guarantee of security. The fundamental purpose of nuclear forces is seen as political, 'to preserve peace and prevent coercion and any kind of war' (ibid. (62), p. 18). The Strategic Concept concluded, however, that the radical changes in the contemporary security environment meant that the circumstances in which 'any use of nuclear weapons might have to be contemplated by them are therefore extremely remote' (ibid. (64), p. 19).

Non-Article 5 missions were seen as highly demanding and 'can place a premium on the same political and military qualities, such as cohesion, multinational training, and extensive prior planning, that would be essential in an Article 5 situation' (ibid. (29), p. 8). NATO looked to work with other international organizations to prevent conflict or to contribute to conflict management. The Alliance was committed to conducting operations in support of other international institutions such as the United Nations or OSCE or on the basis of 'separable but not separate capabilities, operations under the political

control and strategic direction of the WEU or as otherwise agreed'
(ibid. (49), p. 13).

The Strategic Concept looked for interoperable forces which 'must be
held at the required readiness and deployability, and be capable of military success in a wide range of complex joint and combined operations, which may also include Partners and other non-NATO nations'
(ibid. (52), p. 14). The Alliance sought an

> optimum balance between high readiness forces capable of begin-
> ning rapidly, and immediately as necessary, collective defence or
> non-Article 5 crisis response operations; forces at different levels of
> lower readiness to provide the bulk of those required for collective
> defence, for rotation of forces to sustain crisis response operations or
> for further reinforcement of a particular region; and a longer-term
> build-up and augmentation capability for the worst case – but very
> remote – scenario of large scale operations for collective defence.
>
> (Ibid. (54), p. 16)

At the same time NATO's command structure was to be sufficiently
flexible to control multinational and multi-service forces, and operations under the direction of the WEU 'or as otherwise agreed', and to
conduct NATO-led non-Article 5 crisis response operations.

## Conclusion

Since the end of the Cold War the institutions constituting the
European security architecture have undergone an almost continued
process of adaptation. NATO, the UN, the OSCE, the WEU and the EU
have all sought to respond to the new security environment and
develop relevant strategies of engagement. The commitment and
energy devoted by member states to the development of these institutions is indicative of their perceived importance. The end of the
East–West divide in Europe opened the way for international institutions to play a far greater role than before in the management of
conflict. The political space afforded to institutions by changing power
relations in Europe also brought new problems. The end of the Cold
War relationship between NATO and the EU provided a significant
dynamic to the development of the security architecture. The process
of accommodation between the two institutions, first mediated
through the WEU, is ongoing as a new balance between the transatlantic and European Security frameworks is pursued. The relationship

between institutions endowed with resources for intervention – currently NATO (and potentially the EU) – and those with the authority to mandate action – the UN and OSCE – has also been uncertain. The rejection of a hierarchical structure between the organizations, while understandable, leaves inter-institutional cohesion to a case-by-case basis. The emergence of intra-state conflict from the demise of Cold War structures in Europe has set new challenges for international organizations. Security 'providers' have been presented with the need to plan for intervention in substate conflict, to mobilize resources for potentially long-term involvements and to anticipate such crises in order to pursue preventive diplomacy. Security in the new environment poses complex questions for institutions and their members in contrast to the simplicity of the Cold War divide. Inter-state conflict, actual and potential, remains, however, an important element of the European order. It has been eclipsed by the violence of ethnic conflict but arms control and the management of state relations remain highly relevant activities of European conflict management. The ability of international institutions to translate their new security agendas into policy is the subject of the next two chapters.

# 5
# The Management of Inter-State Conflict

The management of inter-state conflict, which for so long has preoccupied debates between neorealists and neoliberals, remains of fundamental importance to the contemporary European order. It is necessary, however, to restate the significance of inter-state conflict as the end of the Cold War has both 'lifted' the East–West confrontation from Europe and led to a new focus on intra-state conflict. The tragedy in the former Yugoslavia became the centre of attention rather than the patterns of conflict and cooperation between states in the new Europe. This chapter seeks to redress this balance and consider the role of international institutions in the maintenance of security and stability between states. The chapter will address the role of international institutions in managing the conflicts of their member states and the 'outreach' of such organizations to stabilize the wider European political space.

## Institutional types and settings

To date we have briefly intimated the differences between those international institutions composed of 'like-minded states' such as NATO or the EU and those with an 'open membership' such as the OSCE. We have suggested that the identities of interest in the former lend themselves to institutional regulation in a manner that is often denied to organizations reflecting more diverse constituencies. A more precise typology of institutions has been offered by Wallander and Keohane in terms of commonality, specificity and differentiation (Wallander and Keohane, 1999, p. 24). Commonality is defined as 'the degree to which expectations about appropriate behaviour are shared by participants' (ibid., p. 24). Specificity 'refers to the degree to which specific and enduring rules exist, governing the practices of officials, obligations of states and legitimate procedures for changing collective policy' (ibid., p. 24). Functional differentiation refers to 'the extent to which the institutions assign different roles to different members' (ibid., p. 24). Wallander and Keohane also suggest that security institutions vary according to their inclusivity or exclusivity. Collective security institutions are seen as inclusive 'since they are designed to deal with threats among members' (ibid., p. 26). Alliances are 'exclusive because they deter and defend against external threats' (ibid., p. 26). Exclusive strategies are seen to be 'better suited to coping with threats, while inclusive strategies appear to be better able to cope with and manage risks' (ibid., p. 26).

The capacity of international institutions to adapt to a changing international environment is seen as a product of institutionalization and 'portability'. Highly institutionalized coalitions of states are seen as more likely to persist, 'since the marginal costs of maintaining existing institutions are smaller than the average costs of new ones' (ibid., p. 33). 'Portability' is defined as 'the ease with which the rules and practices of one institution can be adapted to other situations' (ibid., p. 34). Institutions that 'combine a variety of functions are more likely than narrowly focused institutions to find that some of their rules and practices are more portable: the fact that they have a variety of rules and organizational repertoires means that some of these rules and repertoires are more likely to remain relevant after sudden environmental change occurs' (ibid., p. 34). In this sense NATO has successfully adapted from its Cold War role due to its degree of both institutionalization and portability. For Wallander and Keohane NATO is a hybrid institution combining 'risk-directed management functions with threat-directed power aggregation functions ...' (ibid., p. 34). It is arguable that in some measure NATO always combined these elements, helping to manage the conflicts of its members as well as responding to the Soviet threat. It is in the new Europe, however, that NATO's hybrid role has been clarified, not least in its revisions to the Strategic Concept in 1999. NATO is not yet though a fully inclusive security management institution dealing only with risks. It still retains collective defence functions and, while seeking to engage Moscow in a new partnership, it still provides security insurance for its members. The dual functions of the Alliance – the degree to which it manages the conflicts of its members and its external role – to stabilize the wider Europe will be analysed below.

The security environment is also clearly pertinent to the relevance and functions of international institutions. The security environment is a key to understanding the security dilemma and the significance to states of relative and absolute gains. The European security order has profoundly changed moving from Cold War bipolarity to an 'economic multipolarity conjoined by a military bipolarity that has been eclipsed, for the time being, by the economic and environmental security concerns of the states occupying the European security space' (Sperling and Kirchner, 1998, p. 224). This transition in security has facilitated cooperation among states and heightened the relevance of international institutions. The dramatic decline of military threats has largely resolved the classic security dilemma of states and focused concern instead on political and economic stability.

The two intertwine in a complex manner. Sperling and Kirchner define economic security in three ways:

> First, economic security reflects a concern over the ability of the state to protect the social and economic fabric of a society. Second, economic security involves the ability of a state to act as an effective gatekeeper and to maintain societal integrity. Third, economic security concerns the ability of the state in cooperation with others to foster a stable international economic environment in order to reinforce cooperation in the military sector, as well as to extract the welfare gains of openness.
>
> (Sperling and Kirchner, 1998, p. 230)

The importance of economic and political aspects of security does not replace the military dimension but leads to a wider definition of the overall security agenda. The importance of economic security is 'a reaction against the various dangers of global liberalization – the risks of becoming a loser; the general hazard of system instability, especially financial; and the dark side of trade in the form of criminal activities in drugs, weapons and other banned products ...' (Buzan, Wæver and Wilde, 1998, p. 211). The relationship of the economic, political and military dimensions of security has become particularly complex in the new Europe. The end of superpower overlay has released local military security dynamics (ibid., p. 65) while at the same time the challenge of globalization in economic terms has intensified. The dual challenge to states intensifies the relevance of the European security architecture and in particular the EU.

## Institutions and member states

The impact of international institutions upon their member states and the management of their conflicts is an important element of both 'inclusive' and 'exclusive' organizations. Here we consider the EU, NATO and the OSCE.

## The European Union

The European Union is a highly institutionalized and deeply regulated body. Similar to a regime it establishes common expectations, norms and information and offers protection to its members. Yet it is more than a regime: 'the flexible and dynamic Community is much more centralized and institutionalized than an international regime and receives a much higher level of commitment from its members' (Keohane and Hoffmann, 1991, p. 10). The political process of the EU involves well-established institutions with a growing range of executive, legislative and judicial powers set in a formal procedural framework. The EU 'probably has the most formalized and complex set of decision-making rules of any political system in the world' (Hix, 1999, p. 3). Member states are critical players in the policy process but in the context of 'constant interactions within and between the EU institutions in Brussels, between national governments and Brussels, within the various departments in national governments, in bilateral meetings between governments, and between private interests and government officials in Brussels and at the national level' (ibid., p. 4). The process is multi-centred and reveals the Europeification of policy-making (Andersen and Eliassen, 1993, p. 12). It can be divided into: 'history making decisions' at a super-systemic level, or one that transcends the EU's policy process'; 'policy setting' decisions at a 'systemic level'; and 'policy shaping' decisions at a 'sub-systemic' level which determine policy details or options (Peterson and Bomberg, 1999, pp. 10–28). These approaches do not exclude the role of the state from intergovernmental bargaining in Eurogovernance. Intergovernmentalism varies in intensity between policy sectors as well as between policy stages in both formal and informal guises.

All the Maastricht pillars afford opportunities for intergovernmental bargaining but the second and third covering CFSP and Justice and Home Affairs rest upon intergovernmental cooperation. States, however, have had to accept that they have to share power with one another and the Community institutions in this process (see Kohler-Koch, 1996). States have 'both lost and gained power by pooling sovereignty, by intergovernmental collaboration and accepting the need in the EU for regulation of the single market' (Carr and Massey, 1999, p. 238). The overall consequence is that state conflicts of interest are accommodated within the parameters of the European Union's decision-making process. The expansion of the policy sectors falling under Eurogovernance ensures growing Europeification. This is not to imply that a European policy consensus is emerging but that the EU has considerable impact upon the external relations of its member states. From monetary policy to CFSP and from agricultural policy to social policy, the overarching Union binds together member states but still leaves space for the assertion of differing state preferences. As Hix argues we should see the EU as a fully functioning political system (Hix, 1999). Key stages in the development of this European system may reflect 'Intergovernmentalism, lowest common denominator bargaining and strict limits on the future transfers of sovereignty' (Moravcsik, 1991, p. 25) but they remain European outcomes. Perhaps more importantly the 'drivers' in these outcomes 'consistently reflect issue-specific patterns of asymmetrical interdependence' (Moravcsik, 1999, p. 498). The consequences for institutional theory are that:

> Economic interests and even ideology take precedence over objective geopolitical threats [which] casts doubt on specific variants of Realism, including theories that stress 'security externalities' and 'relative gains-seeking' ... In the EC, we saw, there is little evidence of a stable realist issue hierarchy. National preferences tend instead to vary predictably across issue and countries in accordance with issue-specific, largely economic concerns.
>
> (Moravcsik, 1999, pp. 497–498)

Disputes and conflicts of interest from beef to the single currency are integral to the EU process. Conflicts of interest are resolved by bargaining or accommodated on occasions by selective 'opt-outs' which have raised questions of a 'multi-speed' Europe. At the same time the EU is deeply embedded in the political structures of its member states. The model is of a 'favourable version of intergovernmentalism in the context of a positive-sum game' (Chryssochoou, 1999, p. 25). It can be explained by the EU stress upon regulation rather than redistribution in policy and 'limited encroachment into the traditional areas of state power' (internal and external security) (Hix, 1999, p. 364).

### NATO and its members

Alliances are traditionally analysed in terms of their impact upon adversaries rather than member states. If we examine the role alliances play as managers of their members' interests it is important to distinguish between the coincidence of interest that 'like-minded' states share and the mediation 'effect' of alliances when member states' interests conflict. The latter are of central concern to test the capability of alliances in resolving conflicts.

In a study of 117 mediation attempts in international crises between 1918 and 1988 Gelpi found that the 'most successful mediators in international crises are great powers which are allied to one of the disputants and choose to use coercive mediation tactics to persuade the disputants to settle' (Gelpi, 1999, p. 139). In the case of NATO the United States has played a critical leadership role. The centrality of American power to the *raison d'être* of the Alliance has granted Washington a decisive influence over the strategic policies of its allies. The nature of the NATO decision-making framework, its process of consultation and emphasis upon consensus has facilitated alliance cohesion and Washington's leadership. This can be illustrated with the rebirth of West German military power in the 1950s. The United States after the outbreak of the Korean War looked to Bonn to contribute to Western defence. West German rearmament had profound consequences for the European balance of power not just vis-à-vis the Soviet Union but among the allies. NATO can be seen to have managed this change in power relations without allowing conflicts of interest between allies to threaten its overall strategic rationale. Through 'multilateral command and control systems, transparency, mechanisms to facilitate concessions, the integration of otherwise diverse national personnel, and the enforcement of national commitments, NATO's procedures enabled Germany's allies to accept and manage Germany's rising power and increased role in alliance policies and practices' (Tuschhoff, 1999, p. 141). By these means allies were reassured that German rearmament was not a unilateral policy. The Alliance provided transparency and insurance. Bonn, in turn, was provided with a means to assert influence through an organization which conferred legitimacy. The Allies therefore chose 'multilateral, cooperative strategies instead of unilateral, confrontational ones in reacting to changes in the internal dynamics of NATO' (Tuschhoff, 1999, p. 161). In 1990/91 NATO again provided an institutional means to accommodate German unification. As we have seen, NATO and the EU provided transparency and security to anchor Germany's multilateralism. This was arguably equally important to both Moscow and Western Europe.

A more difficult challenge for NATO has been the management of Greek and Turkish relations. Since the Turkish occupation of Northern Cyprus in 1974, the predominant threat to Greek security was seen to originate in Ankara. Turkish policy is seen as revisionist 'in Cyprus, the Aegean, and Thrace as well as aiming to alter the balance of power and interests in the region' (Ifantis, 1996, pp. 153–4). NATO has not been the framework for the mediation of this conflict. During the Cold War the United States directed its policy towards the containment of the Soviet Union and subordinated its relationships with Greece and Turkey to that end. The principal 'consequence of Washington's preoccupation with Cold War priorities in conducting its relations with Athens and Ankara was to cause American policy-makers in every administration to underestimate (when they did not completely ignore) the importance of any problems in the region that did not pose a clear and immediate threat to the efforts of the United States to maintain a military balance with the Soviet Union (Stearns, 1993, p. 19). Turkey's geostrategic position made it critical to the implementation of American containment strategy. Ankara received the fourth largest share of American military assistance in the period 1946 to 1985 (Evriviades, 1998, p. 35). The allocation of United States military aid to Athens, in a seven to ten ratio compared to Turkey, ensured a regional arms race. In certain interpretations such American policies prevented Washington from acting as a mediator and encouraged Turkish revisionism and conflict in Cyprus. While the United States has called for negotiations between the two allies it has been 'regardless of the motives for and the validity of the Turkish demands' (Coufoudakis, 1996, p. 34).

When the Cold War ended it was reasonable to expect that the strategic relationship between the United States, Greece and Turkey would change. It was further possible to envisage the resolution of regional conflicts with a new role for Washington. It has been the case that the level of US military aid to Ankara has been cut and Washington has adopted a more critical stance on the Turkish government's policy toward its Kurdish minority. The relative 'cooling' of American–Turkish relations has not, however, signalled a fundamental shift of Washington's priorities. Turkey remains important to post-Cold War American foreign policy which we have seen is increasingly influenced by the regionalization of security. Ankara's significance is as a pro-Western state geographically contingent to the Middle East, the Balkans and the newly independent states of the former Soviet Union. The Gulf War and crises in Bosnia, Croatia and Kosovo have further underlined Turkey's strategic position. The Balkan debacle has also highlighted the problems of Turkish–Greek relations and the challenge of regional stability. The post-Cold War regional order has consequently become more complex and difficult for institutions to manage. The United States has pressed for Turkey's inclusion in the EU to underpin its westernization. Greece has opposed Turkish EU membership while the regional security agenda and, above all, the issue of

Cyprus remains unresolved. The Kemalist tradition of pro-westerniza-tion with authoritarianism and a limited engagement with pluralism has posed a further obstacle to Turkish membership of the EU. Differences in domestic politics matter little to a strategic relationship but are 'unacceptable when the prospect is a quite deep integration of economy, law and politics such as that being undertaken by the members of the EU' (Buzan and Diez, 1999, p. 46). The EC rejected the Turkish application for membership in 1989 citing a number of prob-lems, including limited human rights and democratization together with Cyprus, as obstacles. The EU decision in 1996 to engage Turkey in a Customs Union was clearly linked to the invitation to Cyprus to commence negotiations for full membership. The EU and Washington had 'calculated that the benefits of accession to the Island's two ethnic communities, combined with Ankara's desire to eliminate Cyprus as a stumbling block to Turkey's full membership in the EU, would lead to a comprehensive Cyprus solution that would help to formalize Turkey's European status' (Prodromov, 1998, p. 5). The initiative failed and a series of events, not least the 1997 EU decision to exclude Turkey but to include the government of Greek Cyprus in membership negoti-ations, hastened a downward spiral of relations. Turkey launched a partial integration of the Turkish Republic of Northern Cyprus and the Greek Cypriots announced a contract with Russia for surface-to-air mis-siles. At the local level in Cyprus conflict began to worsen. Despite the efforts of the USA, UN, EU and NATO the intensity of the Greek–Turkish conflict proved beyond resolution. The objective became the containment of crisis both within Cyprus and in the wider regional setting.

The contrast between the Alliance's capacity to redress potential insecurity in the German case and the Turkish case is striking. Germany's membership of the Western security community was confirmed by NATO. In comparison NATO does not appear to have the regulatory authority to redress the conflicts of 'warring members'. The difficulty of normalizing relations among such states is even more evident in the case of the OSCE.

## The OSCE

The wide geographical scope of OSCE membership is noted as an asset by some commentators; however, it may also be seen as a deficit. While some people see the OSCE's inclusive approach to membership as con-trasting favourably with that adopted by NATO or the European Union, others have pointed out the drawbacks of such inclusion. They note that the post-Cold War expansion of the OSCE has not only further lessened the arithmetic chances of attaining consensus but that the recent inclusion of some states, notably the former Soviet Central Asian republics, may dilute the community of values that the OSCE seeks to sustain. The prerequisite for admission to the OSCE involves the prospective member state accepting all prior OSCE documents and expressing its commitment to their implementation; however, there is concern that the most recent member states do not share the essentially European tradition associated with the protection and promotion of human rights.

Thus faith in the socialization of new member states, in terms of both elites and populace, into OSCE norms and practices may prove misplaced. In addition, as noted when reviewing the behaviour of Russia in the Chechnya affair (in Chapter 3), socialization would appear to be a relatively shallow experience for some longer-term member states. Russia's perceived state interest in the Near Abroad has, to date, proved a stronger force than its collective interest as expressed via OSCE membership.

Another factor which may adversely affect the operationalism of the OSCE is its stated commitment to territorial integrity. As an organization composed of states and charged to represent their interests, territorial boundaries are seen to be integral to international order. At the Lisbon summit meeting of December 1996, at which the Common and Comprehensive Security Model was approved, the OSCE reaffirmed its respect for the inviolability of national borders in the contemporary European order, and in the Decision on the OSCE Verification Mission of Kosovo of 25 October 1998 it was explicitly noted that the mission to Kosovo was 'devoted to the respect of the sovereignty and territorial integrity of all states in the region' (OSCE, 1998). This principle, however, may subvert the OSCE's claim to impartiality when dealing with conflicts stemming from demands for self-determination. The OSCE upholds the sanctity of recognized territorial boundaries in the Balkans in a bid to prevent the Kosovo crisis from spreading into Macedonia with the potential consequential involvement of Albania, Bulgaria, Greece and Turkey. However, in the eyes of the ethnic Albanian community in Kosovo such a stance appears to endorse the Serbian '… state's firm commitment … to defend Kosovo as a vital state and national interest of Serbia and Yugoslavia' (Gorica Gajevic of the Socialist Party, quoted in the *Daily Telegraph*, 5 February 1998). Thus supporting the principle of territorial integrity may have repercussions for the OSCE's much-vaunted inclusive dialogue as there is little motivation for community representatives, grassroots groups and non-governmental organizations, for example, to enter into a process with an organization that will not countenance the prospect of self-determination for their indigenous constituencies. If their territorial political status is not on the agenda, they have little incentive to engage in the diplomatic process.

The intra-institutional development of the OSCE is irrelevant unless it directly addresses the structural deficiencies of the organization. Internal constraints such as the consensus decision-making process and the lack of an independent enforcement capability clearly limit the OSCE. Moves towards a more flexible decision-making procedure should be consolidated while, in terms of operationalism, it may be useful to abandon thoughts of the OSCE as a provider of security in situations of ongoing conflict. Preventive diplomacy and post-conflict peace-building may be more appropriate. The perceived national interests of the member states constitute a powerful constraint upon OSCE empowerment. The problem of enforcement is related to the status of the OSCE directives which are political rather than legal commitments. The consequences are that in contrast to the violation of 'legally grounded decisions [which] usually give rise to a direct sanction of some sort, infringements of OSCE principles, by contrast, allow a fairly limited response (criticism, exhortation and, in the singular case of Yugoslavia, a suspension of participation)' (Croft et al., 1999, p. 134). The neorealist analysis of the limits of cooperation would appear to be applicable to the functioning of the OSCE in key aspects of conflict management. Relative rather than absolute gains would seem to hold sway when a member state, particularly a great power, perceives its interests as being threatened by a possible OSCE intervention. In addition, the OSCE's commitment to the inviolability of borders precludes meaningful diplomatic dialogue with substate actors seeking self-determination.

## The 'outreach' of international organizations

The capacity of international organizations to stabilize their regional or the global security environment is a critical test of their utility. Here we examine the 'outreach' of two organizations, the EU and NATO. The inclusive nature of the OSCE has meant that our analysis to date has, in effect, been of a corollary activity and need not be repeated.

### The EU
The impact of the EU upon the European regional security system can be seen in two ways: firstly with regard to the impact of CFSP, and secondly in terms of the 'pull' the EU exerts on potential members.

The record of the CFSP has, as we saw in Chapter 4, been modest. In 1995 Santer saw a number of problems: 'the lack of political will, the absence of a common definition of our essential joint interests, the difficulty of activating the unanimous decision-making system, the crippling budgetary procedures, the ambiguity of the roles of the Presidency and the Commission, the European Union's lack of a legal identity and the problem of its external representation have made it very slow to become fully established' (Santer, 1995, p. 7). The problem of realizing a 'European interest' among member states is at the core of CFSP constraints. Members have to conclude that the benefits from common policies outweigh the costs to autonomous action. The EU has adopted 'common positions' and made numerous 'joint declarations'. It has also taken 'joint actions' and been involved in a range of activities from supervising elections in South Africa to the administration of Mostar. At the same time, however, national preferences have been exhibited with unilateral actions. France, for example, unilaterally intervened in Rwanda in June 1994 and, despite condemnation by the majority of EU members, continued nuclear testing in the same year (Gordon, 1997, p. 88). The Greek 1994–95 'economic embargo' of the former Yugoslav republic of Macedonia, Britain's isolated support for US air strikes on Iraq in September 1996, and France and Germany's unwillingness to agree an April 1997 EU resolution critical of China's human rights record (lest it imperil their economic contracts with Beijing) were all further examples of cases in which certain EU states had distinct perceived national interests and pursued national foreign and security policies to protect those interests (ibid.).

The Yugoslav tragedy overtook the formation of CFSP but left significant lessons for the EU's involvement in crisis management. The EU intervened in the former Yugoslavia due to a sense of responsibility, the emergent CFSP, the proximity and interests of Greece and Italy, and concern for the impact of nationalism (Gow, 1999, pp. 24–5). The view that this was a European problem to be solved by Europeans clearly cemented the then European Community's (EC) commitment to Yugoslavia. The EC failed, however, to provide a political solution, proved incapable of finding effective responses to the violence on the ground and looked to the United Nations to supplant the intervention. The Community 'was ill suited for dealing with aggressive nationalism and the use of force within internal boundaries' (Crnobrnja, 1994, p. 204). The EC offers of mediation and diplomatic initiatives failed to be credible solutions to the protagonists who saw separatism and/or the use of force as more tenable means to realize their aims. The EC began by seeking to uphold the unity of Yugoslavia and its democratic transition. The demise of Titoism and Communism, however, had unleashed nationalist forces within the constituent republics which led to demands for independence. Slovenia and Croatia headed the queue for secession, declaring independence on 25 June 1991. Serbia resisted the disintegration of the Federal Republic both politically and with force. The EC sought a peaceful resolution within a federal Yugoslavia but when hostilities commenced between Slovenia and the Yugoslav National Army (JNA) it offered its good offices to broker the Brioni Agreement. The agreement led to a disengagement of forces monitored by the EC but also to an implicit recognition of Slovenia, as independence was not to be implemented for three months. The political precedent of secession was set but, unlike Slovenia, both Croatia and Bosnia had significant Serbian minorities which looked to secure their own autonomy and Serbian protection. As violence mounted in Croatia with the bombardment of Vukovar and Dubrovnik the EC launched the Hague Conference chaired by Lord Carrington. The conference sought to negotiate ceasefires and a political solution on the basis of a new 'looser' federal relationship between the republics. The decision to formally recognize the independence of Slovenia and Croatia taken by the EC in December 1991, following German threats of a unilateral recognition, effectively ended the conference. The principal sanction of the EC, the 'most powerful political weapon the conference had – granting or withholding recognition – was lost' (Crnobrnja, 1994, p. 199). The pattern was soon repeated with Bosnian independence and descent into civil war. The parallel failure to act against Serbia in 1991 encouraged both Milosevic to continue aggression and Tudjman to practice ethnic cleansing in Croatia and the Croatian parts of Bosnia (Sharp, 1997, p. 106). Criticism of the EC role has focused on the lack of consistency and a bureaucratic approach (Carr and Ifantis, 1996, pp. 90–1). The policy of recognition should never have been an end in itself but accompanied by adequate preparation of the indigenous communities for participation in the future state. It could be the case that violence and ethnic cleansing in Croatia and Bosnia would have followed whatever the role of external agencies but a more vigorous and preventive EC strategy may have made a critical difference to the pattern of events.

In contrast to the tribulations of CFSP the prospect of EU membership has had a significant effect upon the wider Europe. In the immediate post-Cold War era the European Community could be seen at the centre of a series of 'concentric economic circles' (Laursen, 1994,

p. 225). The immediate relationship, the first outer ring, was composed of the European Economic Area, an agreement reached in 1992 between the EC and the European Free Trade Association (EFTA) countries. The second circle consisted of states linked to the EC by Association Agreements. Association Agreements can be divided into the Mediterranean group including Turkey, Cyprus and Malta and the Central and East European countries. Beyond that lay a further circle consisting of linkages by Trade and Cooperation Agreements. Countries in this relationship included Russia and other former Communist states. In June 1992 the Commission proposed Partnership and Cooperation Agreements with the members of the Commonwealth of Independent States (CIS) and Georgia. The new agreements were to include political dialogue in addition to economic cooperation. The outer circle essentially anchored the EC's relations with the former Soviet Union while association was seen as a means to assist would-be members to accession.

Applications to join the EC/EU have included: Turkey in 1987; Austria in 1989; Cyprus and Malta in 1990; Sweden in 1991; Finland, Switzerland and Norway in 1992; Hungary and Poland in 1994; Romania, Slovakia, Latvia, Estonia, Bulgaria and Lithuania in 1995; and the Czech Republic and Slovenia in 1996. The response of the EU has for some of the applicants been slow, frustrating and arduous. The EU has sought to protect its interests, policy and law. The attitude of existing member states toward particular applicants, for example Greece to Turkey, has also been important in determining progress. The formal position is that the Council of Ministers can reject an application or request an opinion from the Commission. Commission opinions can be positive, negative or conditional. Positive opinions can lead, subject to Council unanimity, to negotiations on the terms of accession. The treaty of accession finally has to be ratified in the European Parliament, member state Parliaments and the applicant's Parliament. Conditional opinions involve a Commission annual review on progress toward acceptability for accession (see Croft et al., 1999, pp. 60–1). The pattern of application and accession has therefore been variable ranging from the 1995 enlargement involving Austria, Finland and Sweden, to the Turkish rejection in 1997 and the conditionality for the Central and East European Countries (CEECs).

The relationship of the CEECs to the EU has been particularly important to the development of the new European order. The association agreements, known as 'Europe Agreements', were to create 'a special type of relationship reflecting geographical proximity, shared values and increased interdependence' (Commission, 1992, quoted in Gower, 1999, p. 5). The agreements were conditional upon continued progress toward democratization and rewarded the CEECs with favoured access to the EC market. The agreements did not, however, allow unimpeded exports of 'sensitive' goods from the East such as textiles, excluded agriculture and did not guarantee membership.

The Copenhagen European Council in 1993 did offer associated countries in Central and Eastern Europe the prospect of EU membership once key criteria had been met. The Copenhagen criteria were both political and economic. Candidates had to show stability of institutions guaranteeing democracy, the rule of law, human rights and respect for, and protection of, minorities. Candidates had to demonstrate the existence of a functioning market economy, as well as the capacity to cope with competitive pressure and market forces within the Union. Finally membership was seen to presuppose an ability to take on the obligations of political, economic and monetary union. The Copenhagen Council also saw the capacity of the Union to absorb more members as an important factor in the enlargement debate.

The EU's pre-accession strategy for the CEECs consisted of the European Agreements, the PHARE programme of aid and the establishment of 'structured dialogue'. Structured dialogue was to be multilateral and cover all three EU pillars (it was later to be replaced by the European Conference). The meetings were organized on the basis of consultation 'maintaining boundaries while simultaneously offering closer cooperation' (Lippert and Becker, 1998, p. 343).

In 1997 the European Commission published its Opinions on the membership applications from the ten CEECs and published a major report, Agenda 2000, on enlargement, reform of the Common Agricultural Policy, Structural and Cohesion Funds and Union finance. The Commission's assessment was based upon the Copenhagen criteria and found that none of the CEECs fully met the terms but 'Hungary, Poland, Estonia, the Czech Republic and Slovenia could be in a position to satisfy all the conditions for membership in the medium term if they maintain and strongly sustain their efforts of preparation' (Agenda 2000). Slovakia failed the political criteria and Bulgaria, Latvia, Lithuania and Romania were seen to be some way from the economic thresholds. The Luxembourg European Council in 1997 announced an accession process for all ten CEECs plus Cyprus while negotiations with Hungary, Poland, Estonia, the Czech Republic, Slovenia and Cyprus on conditions for entry were to commence in 1998. The Helsinki European Council in 1999 approved negotiations with the five 'second wave' CEECs and Malta to commence in February 2000. The final stages of accession consist of individual Accession Partnerships targeting priorities and inviting annual Commission review on progress. The process involves a close and detailed 'screening' of the *acquis* chapters, pursuit of commonality and then negotiation on securing compatibility between national and European legislation.

The growing relationship between the EU and the wider Europe has become a complex and important element in the stabilization of the European security environment. The EU has specifically linked liberal norms about politics and the economy to association and membership. Political conditionality has been central to the European Agreements and the Copenhagen criteria. The EU has favoured a positive approach to conditionality, tending to reward aspirants that conform to expectations rather than taking sanctions against miscreant states (Smith, 1998, p. 265). Positive conditionality has not, however, always been applied consistently. Decision-making under CFSP can be cumbersome and negative approaches can challenge the commercial interests of key members (ibid., pp. 268–9). Enlargement brings another challenge to the EU, the problem of sustaining governance among a far larger union. The prospect of ten or more new members poses real dilemmas for decision-making and calls for a scale of institutional reform yet to be realized. In short, widening the Union may threaten its deepening agenda and value. At the same time limiting membership threatens new lines of division in Europe. While a variable scale of membership obligation and participation may be the logical outcome it has not been seen to date as an official solution. For some the 'jury is still out' with regard to the EU's ability to manage governance and its boundaries in post-Cold War Europe (Friis and Murphy, 1999, p. 227). Despite the challenges to the EU's external role we need to place the processes of association and enlargement alongside CFSP in our evaluation. The significance of economic and political factors in the new security environment underlines the centrality of the EU to a stable European system and mitigates current weaknesses in the process of CFSP.

## NATO

A key feature of NATO's post-Cold War strategy was to develop a new dialogue with its former adversaries to the East. In December 1991 NATO launched its North Atlantic Cooperation Council (NACC) which included all NATO members, former Warsaw Pact members, the Baltic states and, following the collapse of the Soviet Union, the member states of the CIS. The NACC was organized by an annual work plan which focused on cooperation in areas such as defence conversion, democratic concepts of civil–military relations and command structures. The NACC held one regular meeting per year plus others as required. In 1993 the Work Plan included nuclear disarmament, crisis management and peacekeeping. An Ad Hoc Group on Cooperation in Peacekeeping was created to develop common understandings on conceptual and practical approaches. The NACC further fostered regular political consultation between NACC Partners and the North Atlantic Council and the NATO political committee. The process of consultation and cooperation was extended to military matters, scientific and environmental issues, economic issues and civil emergency planning. While NACC institutionalized relations between NATO and the wider Europe it was not seen to meet the security needs of the CEECs. From 1991 leaders of the Visegrad group had made clear their intention to seek integration with the West and its institutions. The abortive Soviet coup of August 1991 underpinned Polish, Hungarian and Czech perceptions of insecurity, and conflict in the Balkans confirmed their desire to join NATO. The NATO response was cautious, not least because of the need to consider wider security interests vis-à-vis Moscow. The West saw NATO enlargement as potentially destabilizing to the Soviet then Russian reform leadership of Gorbachev and Yeltsin respectively. The last thing NATO wished was to cement an alliance of anti-Western forces in Russian politics which would prompt a return to 'hardline' policies.

The NATO response to the dual need of reassuring the Visegrad countries while not alienating Moscow was the launch of the Partnership for Peace (PfP) in 1994. PfP was established within the framework of the NACC whose members together with those of the CSCE were invited to participate. The objectives of PfP included facilitation of transparency in national defence planning and budgetary processes, ensuring democratic control of defence forces, the maintenance of capabilities to contribute to UN or CSCE operations, the development of cooperative military relations with NATO, and the development of forces that could operate with those of NATO (NATO, *Handbook*, 1995a, p. 52). Membership of PfP requires acceptance of a Framework Document and the development of an Individual Partnership Programme to be agreed between the Partner and NATO. The Framework Document commits signatories to democratic principles, the Universal Declaration of Human Rights, the Charter of the UN, the Helsinki Final Act, the resolution of disputes by peaceful means, territorial integrity and respect for existing borders. The Individual Programme details the level of participation in cooperation activities for the Partner and the steps by which the political goals of the Partnership will be realized. This detailed, almost contractual procedure bound Partner states to NATO and set clear expectations about behaviour. Partners were further invited to send permanent liaison officers to NATO headquarters and the partnership Coordination Cell at SHAPE. The Deputy Secretary-General of NATO was given the task of chairing the PfP Political-Military Steering Committee which could meet in a multilateral or NATO-plus-one-partner formats.

The PfP deepened institutional links with the CEECs but did not extend the full security guarantee of the North Atlantic Treaty. NATO did agree to 'consult with any active participant in the Partnership if that partner perceives a direct threat to its territorial integrity, political independence, or security' (North Atlantic Council, 1994). This was quite different from the Treaty commitments under Article 5 for collective defence. Partners were promised, however, that 'active participation in the Partnership for Peace will play an important role in the evolutionary process of the expansion of NATO' (North Atlantic Council, 1994). While this statement reassured East European leaderships it did little to sustain Russian cooperation. The Visegrad partners signed the Framework Document in February 1994 followed by the Baltic states, Romania, Bulgaria and Albania. Moscow's response was to propose that NATO should be subordinate to the CSCE and the NACC transformed into an independent body.

> Our partnership can contribute to transforming the NACC into an independent body which would be closely linked to the CSCE and which would promote military–political cooperation in the Euro-Atlantic area. Generally speaking, the CSCE should aim at coordinating the activities of NATO, the European Union, the Council of Europe, the WEU and the CIS in the sphere of enhancing stability and security, promoting peacekeeping and protecting human and national minority rights.
>
> (Kozyrev, 1994, p. 4)

Russia also demanded that its special status as a great power be taken into account in any agreement with NATO. When the Alliance used force in Bosnia without consulting Moscow the Russians cancelled their intended visit to sign the PfP in April 1994. Although Russia finally signed the Framework Document in June 1994 a NATO communiqué on enlargement led to the cancellation of agreement on the Individual Partnership Programme. President Yeltsin warned of a 'Cold Peace' in Europe and declared Moscow's opposition to NATO enlargement (Yeltsin, *The Times*, 5 December 1994). President Clinton had moved the agenda forward, however, with clear indications that NATO enlargement was no longer in question; the matter was instead when and how (see Borawski, 1995, pp. 240–1).

Washington had clearly downgraded its 'Russia First' emphasis, taking a 'pragmatic partnership' line and placing Moscow on a more even footing with other American security interests in Europe. This new policy stance reflected changes in American domestic politics and Congressional pressure. Enlargement was made part of the Republican Party 'contract with America' as a key means of renewal of the Alliance (Sloan, 1995). The costs of NATO had to be justified by the Clinton administration to a Congress looking for more equitable burden sharing in the post-Cold War era while, at the same time, the implications of intervention in Bosnia threatened to further undermine the domestic consensus. With 20 million American voters of Eastern European descent NATO enlargement could be seen as a positive electoral asset as well as a means to sustain Congressional support for European policy. The Clinton administration presented enlargement as stabilizing Central Europe, strengthening democracy in the new member states and deterring war (Talbott, 1997). Madeleine Albright warned that a 'decision not to enlarge ... would constitute a declaration that NATO will neither address the challenges nor accept the geography of a new Europe' (Albright, 1997, p. 22).

In September 1995 NATO published its Study on Enlargement. The Study declared that there 'is no fixed or rigid list of criteria for inviting new members to join the Alliance' (NATO, 1995b, p. 23). New members were expected to make certain commitments though, including: conformity to the basic principles of the Washington Treaty, democracy, individual liberty and the rule of law; acceptance of NATO as a community of like-minded nations joined together for collective defence and the preservation of peace and security; and the principles objectives and undertakings of the Partnership for Peace Framework Document (ibid., p. 23). New members would also have to prepare themselves for membership by demonstrating: a commitment to and respect for OSCE norms and principles; a commitment to promoting stability and well-being by economic liberty, social justice and environmental responsibility; appropriate democratic and civilian control of their defence force (ibid., p. 25). States which had ethnic disputes, territorial disputes or internal jurisdictional disputes were to settle those in accord with OSCE principles (ibid., p. 4). In addition, a set of military expectations to ensure conformity to the Alliance doctrine, practice and operability were defined. Active participation in the PfP was also confirmed as an important element in the preparation of new members but would not of itself guarantee access (ibid., p. 12). The Study on Enlargement made clear that decisions on enlargement would be for NATO to decide on 'a case-by-case basis and some nations may attain membership before others' (ibid., p. 4). The timing of future accessions was envisaged as either sequential or in one or more simultaneous sets. The study made clear that the 'Alliance remains open to further accessions by countries not amongst the earliest to be invited to join' (ibid., p. 27).

The study saw that 'cooperative NATO–Russia relations are in the interest not only of NATO and Russia, but of all other states in the OSCE area' (ibid., p. 9). The Russian Individual Partnership Programme in the PfP had been agreed in May 1995 but the Study on Enlargement saw it as desirable that NATO–Russian relations were taken further to form 'another cornerstone of a new, inclusive and comprehensive security structure in Europe' (ibid., p. 9). A new relationship beyond PfP was envisaged in the form of a political framework 'elaborating basic principles for security cooperation as well as for the development of mutual political consultations' (ibid., p. 9). NATO looked to formalize this development in rough parallel to the Alliance's own enlargement.

In May and July 1997 NATO embarked on a round of agreements designed to further institutionalize its cooperative strategies with the wider Europe. The agreements included the 'Founding Act on Mutual Relations' with Russia on 27 May, the launch of the Euro-Atlantic Partnership Council on 30 May and the invitation to the Czech Republic, Hungary and Poland to join NATO on 8 July.

The Founding Act committed NATO and Russia to a number of principles, including:

- development, on the basis of transparency, of a strong, stable, enduring and equal partnership and of cooperation to strengthen security and stability in the Euro-Atlantic area;
- acknowledgement of the vital role that democracy, political pluralism, the rule of law, and respect for human rights and civil liberties and the development of free market economies play in the development of common prosperity and comprehensive security;
- refraining from the threat or use of force against each other as well as against any other state, its sovereignty, territorial integrity or

political independence in any manner inconsistent with the United Nations Charter and with the Declaration of Principles Guiding Relations Between Participating States contained in the Helsinki Final Act;

• mutual transparency in creating and implementing defence policy and military doctrines (Founding Act, 1997, p. 8).

The mechanism to carry out the aims of the Founding Act and to develop common approaches to European Security is the Permanent Joint Council. The central objective of the Permanent Joint Council is to build increasing levels of trust, unity of purpose and habits of consultation and cooperation between NATO and Russia, in order to enhance each other's security and that of all nations in the Euro-Atlantic area...' (ibid., p. 8). The Council is to provide 'a mechanism for consultations, coordination and, to the maximum extent possible, where appropriate, for joint decisions and joint action with respect to security issues of common concern' (ibid., p. 8). Consultation is not, however, to extend to internal matters nor provide a veto over the actions of either partner. The Permanent Joint Council can meet at different levels from head of state to ambassador and in ordinary or extraordinary session. Under the auspices of the Permanent Joint Council military representatives and chiefs of staff meet on a regular basis.

The areas for consultation and cooperation outlined in the Founding Act include: conflict prevention, preventive diplomacy, crisis management and conflict resolution; joint operations, including peacekeeping operations under the auspices of the UN or OSCE; arms control; nuclear safety issues; non-proliferation measures, increasing transparency and mutual confidence regarding conventional forces; joint initiatives and exercises in civil emergency preparedness; and combating terrorism and drug trafficking (see Founding Act, 1997, Section III).

The Euro-Atlantic Partnership Council (EAPC) replaced the NACC to provide an 'overarching framework for consultations among its members on a broad range of political and security related issues, as part of a process that will develop through practice' (Basic Document of the Euro-Atlantic Partnership Council, 1997). The stress was upon 'inclusive organization' and 'self-differentiation', inclusive in that opportunities for cooperation are open to all Allies and Partners equally. The Partners would then decide for themselves the level and areas of cooperation with NATO. The meetings of the EAPC reflect this philosophy being in a full plenary or limited format with NATO meeting an ad hoc group or even an individual state. The EAPC also meets at different levels from ambassador to head of state. Its brief is broad ranging from crisis management to arms control. Consultations have focused on themes including Bosnia, Kosovo, regional security and proliferation matters.

The EAPC was part of a broader NATO strategy of enhancing the PfP. The objectives of PfP enhancement were to strengthen its political consultation element, develop a more operational role and provide for greater participation of partners in decision-making and planning (NATO, *Handbook*, 1998, p. 94). EAPC was one means to enhance political consultation, another was to identify the opportunities for partners to 'associate themselves with the PfP decision-making process, both in the Political-Military Steering Committee on Partnership for Peace and in other relevant bodies' (ibid., p. 94). A new emphasis upon operational aspects of PfP was also launched including an expanded scope for NATO/PfP exercises to address the full range of the Alliance's new missions including Peace Support Operations. PfP Staff Elements (PSEs) have been established at different NATO headquarters and the Alliance has sought to provide possibilities for partner participation in a range of planning modalities including CJTFs.

At NATO's Washington Summit in 1999 measures were taken to make the Partnership more operational and to enhance Partner involvement in appropriate decision-making. The summit announced a Political-Military Framework (PMF) for NATO-led PfP operations which was to enhance Partner roles in political guidance, planning and command arrangements. The PMF is to stand alongside and support CJTF. The summit endorsed an adapted Planning and Review (PARP) which was to enhance the interoperability of Partner forces for PfP activities. A new Operational Capabilities Concept (OCC) was further to be developed within PfP to improve the ability of NATO and Partner forces to operate together in Alliance-led PfP operations. Finally the North Atlantic Council endorsed an outline programme enhancing PfP training and education including a Consortium of Defence Academies and Security Studies Institutes.

At the July 1997 NATO Madrid Summit invitations to commence accession talks were issued to the Czech Republic, Hungary and Poland. The formal accession of the three new members took place on 12 March 1999. The Madrid Summit reaffirmed that NATO remained open to new members and that 'no European democratic country whose admission would fulfil the objectives of the Treaty will be excluded from consideration' (Madrid Declaration on Euro-Atlantic Security and Cooperation, 1997, p. 1). The North Atlantic Council invited aspiring members to participate in EAPC and engage in intensified dialogues covering the range of issues associated with membership. At the Washington Summit in 1999 NATO announced the enlargement process would be reviewed in 2002 and launched a new Membership Action Plan (MAP). The MAP requires aspirant countries to submit an Annual National Programme on preparations for possible membership covering political, economic, defence, security and legal issues. NATO monitors progress, provides political and technical advice and expects full participation in the PfP. Planning targets are set by NATO for each aspirant and the procedures can be seen to draw partners closer to the Alliance. Nine states were participating in the MAP in 2000: Albania, Bulgaria, Estonia, Latvia, Lithuania, Romania, Slovakia, Slovenia and the former Yugoslav Republic of Macedonia.

NATO has also sought to develop cooperative relationships with the Ukraine and the Mediterranean. In 1997 NATO and the Ukraine signed a 'Charter for a Distinctive Partnership' which has led to a number of joint endeavours. In 1994 NATO launched its southern outreach strategy with six Mediterranean countries: Egypt, Israel, Jordan, Mauritania, Morocco and Tunisia. In February 2000 Algeria became a participant. The Dialogue is bilateral but allows for multilateral meetings on a case-by-case basis (NATO, *Handbook*, 1998, p. 105). Its work is organized through an annual work plan and parallels the EU Mediterranean partnership.

The effectiveness of NATO's strategy of institutionalizing cooperative relations is yet to be determined. In a manner similar to the EU, NATO's 'outreach' to the wider Europe has become intertwined with its membership policy. Many of the CEECs have adopted NATO's norms and institutional frameworks in anticipation of membership. Alliance strategies of inclusion have therefore been successful in extending the Western security zone eastward. The institutionalization of this process has been intense and underlines the significance of formalized cooperation to security management. At the same time the Alliance faces the problem of exclusion of states not in the first round or even the possible second round of NATO enlargement and, above all, Russia. In Russia opposition to NATO enlargement united opinion across the political spectrum (see Carr and Flenley, 1999). The Russian leadership perceived NATO's actions as exploiting Moscow's weakness. Russia could do little to prevent NATO enlargement but object and look to the Founding Act to mitigate the worst challenges to Moscow's interests. NATO's commitments not to place nuclear weapons nor station substantial combat forces on the territory of its new members could be seen as the value of the Founding Act. Its limits were exposed in 1999 over NATO action in the Kosovo crisis. The launch of Operation Allied Force, the NATO air bombardment, led to Russian withdrawal from the Permanent Joint Council (PJC). The Russian contribution to KFOR, the NATO-led force under UN auspices dispatched to Kosovo to secure peace, and Moscow's record in SFOR in Bosnia can be seen as positive rejoinders to the negative consequences of the PJC decision. Nevertheless from a Russian perspective the lessons of the Kosovo action are clear. The PJC was not the centre of strategic decision-making, it did not afford access for Moscow's interests and it had failed to institutionalize Russian and NATO security interests (see Croft et al., 2000). The challenge for NATO is to restore Russian interest in the PJC, not just in the resumption of meetings (restarted in May 2000) but in the general value of partnership. NATO may not have enjoyed Moscow's support over Kosovo but needs it in other spheres, particularly arms control.

## Arms control

Throughout the Cold War, the United States and the Soviet Union made notable efforts to manage their nuclear competition and restrict the flow of nuclear weaponry and technology. The threat of a nuclear war, arising either accidentally or through rash design, was deemed a common interest and led to the evolution of a regime architecture of regulation and control. The doctrine of mutual nuclear deterrence characterized the superpower relationship and the arms control process was essential to its maintenance. Throughout the period of Cold War confrontation, then, 'crisis stability' prevailed. Arms control and cooperation facilitated communication, reassurance and a sense of common interest between the superpowers. A series of agreements between the protagonists allowed them to build on this area of mutual interest. In 1972, the Anti-Ballistic Missile (ABM) Treaty placed strict limits on their respective missile defences in an effort to prevent the deployment of missile systems which would raise fears of a enhanced 'first-strike' capacity which would have a destabilizing impact upon the bilateral nuclear relationship. Also in 1972, the Strategic Arms Limitation Talks (SALT I) recognized the strategic nuclear parity of the superpowers and attempted to regulate both the development and deployment of nuclear weaponry. In 1979, SALT II was signed by the Soviet Union and the United States although its ratification by the latter was delayed due to the onset of the Second Cold War following the Soviet invasion of Afghanistan. The appointment of Mikhail Gorbachev as General Secretary of the Communist Party of the Soviet Union in 1985 eventually occasioned 'an extraordinary change in atmosphere' in the superpower relationship and led to an astonishingly radical raft of unilateral initiatives and bilateral agreements with the United States on arms control (Jacobsen, 1990, p. 115). Gorbachev's 'new thinking' on security affairs led to a reconceptualization of Soviet security which, in turn, affected the strategic thinking of other core states within the international system. Recognizing explicitly that neither a nuclear war nor the nuclear arms race was winnable, Gorbachev stressed that 'common' rather than 'national' security had precedence within an increasingly interdependent world. In terms of weaponry, it was now argued that a 'sufficiency' of armaments was appropriate in an age when the notion of absolute security was rendered obsolete. Initially suspicious that such thinking was merely a ploy to lull the West into a false sense of security, the leaders of the core states ultimately conceded that Gorbachev was a man with whom they could do business. In 1987, the Intermediate-Range Nuclear Forces (INF) Treaty was signed, banning all American and Soviet ground-launched ballistic and Cruise missiles with ranges between 500 and 5,500 kilometres. In 1991, both superpowers signed the Strategic Arms Reduction Treaty (START) I. At the time of writing this is being implemented. It will reduce the amount of American and Russian deployed strategic nuclear warheads to around 8,000 each. In 1993, START II was signed which will further reduce their respective totals by more than 50 per cent. In March 1997, at the Helsinki Summit, Clinton and Yeltsin agreed to begin talks on START III which, if attained, would reduce still further their respective arsenals. Both powers have also halted nuclear testing and no longer daily target their warheads against one another. Currently then

> ... the nuclear arsenals of the United States and Russia are shrinking significantly, with physical dismantlement of warheads proceeding at the pace of 1,500 to 2,000 per year on each side.
>
> (Committee on International Security and Arms Control, 1997, p. 16)

While Russia–American cooperation on nuclear arms control has improved in the wake of the Cold War, there still remain issues of concern. In particular, the proliferation of nuclear weaponry and technology is viewed as undesirable.

Throughout the Cold War, it was believed that membership of the 'nuclear club' should not be extended as orthodox opinion held that nuclear proliferation would inevitably undermine the prevailing balance of power and increase the chances of a systemic nuclear war. The need to prevent horizontal nuclear proliferation led to the foundation stone of the regulatory architecture – the non-proliferation regime whose 'normative backbone' is the Non-Proliferation Treaty of 1968. There are various supporting elements to this regime, notably the NSG (Nuclear Suppliers Group, also known as the 'London Club'), the Australia Group, the Treaty of Tlatelolco (1967), the Treaty of Rarotonga (1985), the Treaty of Pelindaba (1997) and the International Atomic Energy Agency (IAEA). The London Club and the Australia Group provide rules covering the trade between states in nuclear material and know-how. The treaties have established nuclear weapons-free zones in Latin America and the Caribbean, the South Pacific and South Africa respectively. The IAEA assists member states of the regime to implement verification procedures. In addition, the Missile Technology Control Regime (MTCR) established in 1987 contributes to the overarching non-proliferation regime through its remit covering the exchange of missiles, either in whole or part, and missile technology. Following the collapse of the bipolar order, there has been a heightened fear of the spread of nuclear arms and technology. In the present international system, there has occurred a redrawing of the politico-military map which has had a notable effect on regional insecurity dilemmas. Changes in patron–client relationships have left some states with a reawakened sense of insecurity. The ongoing nuclear competition between Pakistan and India is representative of this fact. Pakistan now receives less support from the United States while the collapse of the Soviet Union robbed India of its sponsor in the regional power contest. Pakistan fears Indian expansion while India deems itself susceptible to threats from Pakistan and China. As well as regional security competitions, a threat to international stability is seen to emanate from 'rogue' states such as North Korea and Iraq. The finding following the Gulf War that Iraq had an established programme of nuclear development, and its prior use of chemical and biological warfare, exposed the weakness of the non-proliferation regime as Iraq is a signatory of the Non-Proliferation Treaty. The creation of new states following the disintegration of the Soviet Union also led to fears that nuclear weapons and technology and conventional armaments would spread to other countries. In terms of the former category of arms, in the Lisbon Protocol of 1992, Ukraine, Kazakhstan and Belarus agreed to adhere to START I as non-nuclear states and to send back all the nuclear weapons on their respective territories to Russia. Through the Cooperative Threat Reduction or 'Nunn-Lugar' programme, the US provides assistance to Russia, Belarus, Georgia, Kazakhstan, Moldova, Turkmenistan, Ukraine and Uzbekistan to reduce the possibility of the theft of weapons of mass destruction and to make safe the transportation of both missiles and nuclear material back to Russia and to provide for its safe storage upon return. Other measures have been taken to prevent proliferation after the Cold War. The Wassenaar Agreement on Export Controls for Conventional Arms and Dual-Use Goods and Technology is now in force with Russia as a member. However, it has proved difficult at times to attain a consensus between the 28 member states on the appropriate balance to be struck between their respective security and economic interests. The rise of the economic dimension of security has had a pervasive effect on the proliferation issue. Following the Cold War, the expectation of a 'peace dividend' by populaces in the West and the East has led to a reduction of arms purchases by most of the governments concerned. This has resulted in governments and arms manufacturers looking to new markets to sustain domestic arms industries. One feared player on the arms market is non-state groupings as witnessed by the Chechen purchasing of arms from Russian producers (White et al., 1997, p. 116–18) and the use of material from Cold War arsenals in the Balkan wars of the early 1990s. The rise of intra-state conflict has led to an array of potential buyers for a market in search of new customers, as Kaldor (1999, p. 96) notes:

> The new wars could be viewed as a form of military waste-disposal – a way of using up unwanted surplus arms generated by the Cold War, the biggest military build-up in history.

Thus the ending of the Cold War has brought forth a new threat environment wherein the simplicity of a clear, unitary foe is replaced with an array of potential new dangers. In response efforts at regulation and control continue to be made, notably the indefinite extension of the Non-Proliferation Treaty in 1995. Nevertheless, the limits of the non-proliferation regime have been exposed, as noted, especially by the discovery of the Iraqi nuclear programmes following the Gulf War. The various export control arrangements do not cover all states who supply weaponry and even those who are signatories may not offer full and frank disclosure of their sales and purchases. The UN Register of

Conventional Weapons was opened after the Gulf War for all states who wished to participate. Less than 100 states thus far have made information available on their arms activities. In addition, the OSCE plays an important role in the arena of arms control and disarmament both as the repository of arms control agreements and as a proactive player in the field. In the Helsinki Document of 1992, the Forum for Security Cooperation was established with a remit of negotiations and consultations on military security and stability. The mandate of the Forum was extended throughout the early 1990s, notably through the 1994 Budapest Document and the Lisbon Document in 1996, leading to an enhanced role for the OSCE in arms control, transparency in the transfer of weaponry and knowledge, monitoring the exchange of military information and the collection of information from member states on their defence policies and plans. The OSCE acts as a monitor and holder of the Conventional Forces in Europe (CFE) Treaty. This re-adapted treaty establishes limits on conventional forces within post-Cold War Europe and through its Joint Consultative Group the OSCE deals with issues of compliance, interpretation and review and addresses any disputes pertaining to the implementation of the Treaty. The member states are permitted to establish their own limits on the understanding that they adopt a 'restrained approach' and make progress towards the general aim of 'achieving a significant lowering in the total amount of TLE [treaty-limited equipment] in Europe'. One of the central concerns affecting the implementation of this treaty is the Russian stance that they cannot effect compliance until the situation in Chechnya is resolved. Consequently, President Clinton stated that US Senate ratification of the treaty will be dependent upon Russia compliance. The OSCE is involved too in the Open Skies Treaty which establishes a regime of observation flights over the member states' respective territories. Although the Open Skies Treaty is not yet in force due to the ongoing ratification process within individual member states, the OSCE through its Open Skies Consultative Commission (OSCC) facilitates the discussion of any issues about compliance with the Treaty. The OSCE is a significant force within the Confidence and Security Building Measures regime. This work involves action at both the inter-state level and the substate level. In the former, member states are obliged to be open and transparent in their military profiles. It should be noted, however, that compliance is voluntary and not all states make a marked contribution to enhanced communication and a reduction of mistrust. Notably, the Russians violated their commitment to the Code of Conduct on Politico-Military Aspects of Security (1994) in their behaviour over Chechnya. Thus the OSCE description of the Code of Conduct as 'a landmark in the evolution of the OSCE's cooperative concept of security' (OSCE Handbook Online) may be somewhat over-optimistic. Also at the inter-state level the OSCE provides for the implementation and verification of CSBMs within Bosnia and Hercegovina and of a subregional arms control agreement between Bosnia, Hercegovina and the FRY in the area. At the intra-state level, the OSCE is involved in the establishment and execution of CSBMs in post-conflict situations. Within Kosovo, as a part of the UN Interim Administration Mission in Kosovo (UNMIK) it works with the Council of Europe and the UNHCR to facilitate the reconstruction of civil society and the establishment of a pluralistic political community. One of the most central CSBM tasks is the decommissioning of the Kosovo Liberation Army (KLA). While steady progress has been made on this front, there are still incidents of sporadic conflicts between the Albanian and Serb communities within Kosovo. The decommissioning process is clearly hampered, as in all post-ethnic conflict situations, by the inability to distinguish transgressors and to verify disarmament. On the first point, as many of the combatants in the actual conflict were un-uniformed, and may have belonged to irregular and paramilitary forces, the official disarming of the KLA may well not have led to the complete disarmament of all those who wish to participate in terrorist activities. On the second point, poor information and a lack of transparency concerning the amount and location of arms held by former fighters means that much of the material may not be handed in or verified as out of action. This latter issue, the difficulty of verifying compliance with decommissioning procedures, may dog the peace process, as witnessed in the case of Northern Ireland where suspicion remains that the IRA have not decommissioned their entire arsenal and both loyalist and republican paramilitary groupings have clearly got access to weaponry. The various arms control regimes and arrangements, whether at the global, regional or substate level, are as successful as their membership make them. The observance and implementation of the rules and norms are dependent upon the voluntary compliance and good faith of the governments and groupings concerned. No system will provide optimal inter-state security if some of the participants lack the political will to honour their obligations as the Committee on International Security and Arms Control acknowledges (1997, p. 9):

Even the most effective verification system that can be envisioned would not produce complete confidence that a small number of nuclear weapons too had not been hidden or fabricated in secret.

The practice of governments to consider the economic benefits to be gained from the arms trade highlights a possible constraint on the observance of treaty commitments. The ongoing Sino-American dispute over China's sale of missiles to Pakistan attests to differential readings of treaty stipulations. The Americans claim that the trade has violated the MTCR but the Chinese claim that it has not. There are current challenges, therefore, to the non-proliferation regime. Even within the improved US–Russia relationship there are still difficulties. The US commitment to the Strategic Defense Initiative (SDI) has led the Russians to express their concern that the suggested deployment would adversely tilt the nuclear balance in favour of the US and violate the ABM Treaty of 1972. The Russians have formally noted that such an event would constitute grounds for their withdrawal from START I.

Despite ongoing arms reductions and monitoring through both uni-lateral initiatives and bilateral or multilateral arrangements, the US and Russia remain committed to the doctrine of mutual deterrence, as evinced by the US Nuclear Posture Review of 1994 and Russia's new National Security Concept of 1997. Each side still holds a nuclear arsenal which could inflict apocalyptic damage on the other and any third parties. A significant proportion of the existing arsenals is not covered by START and each side holds a 'weapons of last resort' doctrine towards their nuclear forces. This stance permits the first use of nuclear arms if a non-nuclear threat is deemed sufficiently grave. The entire arms control process is a fragile one built as it is on the need for inter-state trust and continued communication, and while the former superpowers have a more constructive relationship now there are still residual mindsets which view one another as potential enemies and which may affect the prospects of greater success in arms control:

> On both sides, the continuing competitive and even confrontational assumptions underlying some official discussions of the US–Russian nuclear relationship, when coupled with the postures of the forces and the potential for destabilizing deployments of ballistic missile defences, pose the risk that the arms control fabric woven during the Cold War and immediately thereafter could in fact unravel.
>
> (Committee on International Security and Arms Control, 1997,
> p. 18)

Given this diagnosis, it is clear that the various arrangements and regimes governing the development, exchange and deployment of arms requires commitment and good faith on the part of their respective memberships. Although there are limitations to this architecture of regulation, it remains the most influential method of ensuring a safer international system. Although member states may differ in their interpretation of the rules and their observance of the norms set, the presence of the regime can and does modify state behaviour, as Muller (1995, p. 383) notes:

> Regimes exert pressure on governments, even on those with reservations about the regime. Not only are regimes powerful behaviour-guides because it is so costly to construct alternatives: the sheer existence of a regime puts an 'extra burden of proof on regime opponents.'

## Conclusion

The post-Cold War European security space is highly institutionalized. International institutions have embraced the new order and sought to develop appropriate strategies to meet the new security environment. For the OSCE the end of the Cold War meant the organization could realize its pan-European rationale. For NATO and the EU the end of the East–West divide predicated new policies toward the wider Europe and questions about their existing rationales. Both the EU and NATO have subsequently undergone a process of rapid institutional adaptation. The changing nature of the security environment has also been conducive to institutional relevance. Military factors have been joined, if not eclipsed, by political and economic issues as priorities for European states. The roles of international institutions in setting norms, regulating behaviour, establishing procedures and facilitating order can therefore be seen as integral to stability in contemporary understandings of security. Institutions can furthermore provide transparency and verification for states in pursuit of agreements to enhance their mutual security. As we have seen, arms control remains a critical instrument for stabilizing the international order and its institutionalization is seen as an essential corollary to its credibility.

The impact of international institutions upon states has, as we have seen, been the subject of substantive debate. The pattern in the new Europe is variable and affected by institution, issue and state. Institutions differ in their political gravity. The leverage they exert is dependent upon the resources they hold and the need or wants of states. International socialization requires a structural asymmetry between the socialization agency and the actor to be socialized. The agency acts as gatekeeper for resources in the social environment which the actor needs or desires to have. In order to get access to these resources, the actor adopts the constitutive beliefs and practices institutionalized in the social environment and taught by the socialization agency.

(Schimmelfennig, 2000, p. 117)

The resources held by the EU and NATO clearly exceed these of the OSCE or Council of Europe. The latter institutions can bestow legitimacy while the former can, in addition, provide more tangible security benefits. Both the EU and NATO have set expectations and left the wider Europe to conform, to socialize themselves, in order to secure rewards. Conforming to international norms can, though, be critically affected by the issue agenda and domestic politics. In the case of Greece and Turkey fundamental divisions have undermined the role of institutions in conflict resolution and left conflict management as the best prospect. In cases where domestic politics is so divided, or where liberal political culture is weak, or where state actors owe their authority to authoritarian or ethno-nationalist orientations, adopting Western norms would undermine the position of political elites (ibid., p. 135). The rule of institutions in these cases is consequently limited and actor compliance will be more likely to reflect deterrence and coercion strategies.

Institutions have to be judged therefore in terms of their relationship with members and non-members, and compliant and 'rogue states'. The politics of inclusion and exclusion have become major issues for the EU and NATO affecting their capacity to exert influence. Drawing boundaries has become critical for both institutions (see Smith, 1996) and blurred boundaries have clear attractions. The EU has enjoyed greater success in sustaining a variable geometry of relationships than NATO where membership alone offers unambiguous security for many states. Nonetheless NATO and the EU have exerted considerable influence in the new Europe. The new democracies of Central and Eastern Europe looked to the West and a 'return to Europe'. This 'strong asymmetrical interdependence' made the CEE states highly susceptible to 'political conditionality', to the granting of material assistance and international legitimacy in return for norm-conforming domestic and international conduct' (Schimmelfennig, 2000, p. 124). For non-compliant states the challenge for institutions is to mobilize resources to prevent or contain conflict. Here the variables of decision-making, resources and political will become discernible features of institutional competence. The ability of institutions to act promptly, to deter and to deploy resources affects the capacity of such organizations to influence non-compliant states or 'rogue states'. International security institutions have been usefully described as 'imperfect unions' (Haftendorn, Keohane and Wallender, 1999, p. 325), since they don't always secure compliance or their own institutional form can hinder cooperation. The political dynamics of institutions may also not lend themselves to crisis management. The limitations of CFSP decision-making can be contrasted with the detail of the Stability Pact for South Eastern Europe in 1999 in which the EU linked its economic resources to the role of other institutions and countries. Institutions may therefore have roles for which they are particularly appropriate. The institutional division of labour following the Dayton settlement for Bosnia-Hercegovina can be seen as illustrative of differential institutional security competences (see Wijk, 1997). Conflict in the Balkans has, though, posed new and fundamental challenges for international institutions. The actors involved in the crises have been substate forces as well as state actors. Intra-state conflict has joined state conflict to produce a complex amalgam. It is to this pattern of conflict and institutional response that we now turn.

# 6
# Managing Intra-State Conflict: the Case of the Former Yugoslavia

## Slovenian and Croatian independence: the EC intervention

The pattern of secession and separatism in the former Yugoslavia set a stern test for Europe's security architecture. In late 1991 the EC-sponsored peace conference was faltering with Slovenia securing independence, Bosnia-Hercegovina seeking recognition and Croatia descending into civil war. Croatia had declared its independence from Yugoslavia on 25 June 1991 and sustained its bid for secession despite the military intervention of the JNA. The divide between EC member states on the question of accepting the fragmentation of Yugoslavia or seeking to maintain its unity clearly impaired the initial international intervention. The division prevented a concerted strategy and revealed a lack of preparation despite open prediction of Yugoslavia's difficulties. The EC and CSCE sought a peaceful settlement and defensive use of force alone while nationalists on the ground, willing to use force, had been in the ascendant for over a year (Woodward, 1995, p. 165). Nor did the EC or CSCE have the capability to intervene physically which left their mediators with little credibility in deterring the conflict. The object of the international intervention became focused on the short term.

> The goal was to stop the fighting, not to establish criteria for judging the right to self-determination among Yugoslav nations and citizens, to reverse the process of a state's disintegration, or to lay the basis for a genuine political negotiation of the conflicts – including borders, if the state did break up.
>
> (Ibid., p. 165).

The Brioni Agreement was a specific measure and not part of a general settlement strategy. It was a means to end the violence between the JNA and Slovenia. Its success masked the end of the Federal Republic, the end of the Slovene–Croat alliance and a basic Slovenian–Serbian understanding with regard to Slovenian secession. The JNA was humiliated in its short war with Slovenia and behind the scenes President Milošević of Serbia and President Kučan of Slovenia determined its withdrawal. The 'diplomatic triumph belonged to Milošević and Kučan, who had, between them agreed Slovenia's departure from the federation at a series of meetings that began, arguably, in Belgrade on 24 January, and ended with the 18 July Presidency session (Silber and Little, 1995, p. 183). Serbian motivation can be understood by an appreciation of the resurgence of Serbian nationalism in the mid-1980s. Milošević had gained power within the Serbian League of Communists on a nationalist programme launched on the question of Kosovo which was soon to embrace the idea of a Greater Serbia. If the international community accepted Slovene independence and 'actually rejected the principle of inviolable external borders and Yugoslavia's territorial integrity, it would provide the excuse, perhaps even the justification, for redrawing internal borders to be more in line with Serb settlements' (Woodward, 1995, p. 26). At the same time the demise of federal authority accelerated the transformation of the JNA into a Serbian-led force.

In Croatia these political trends came together with grave consequences. The 'long-term propaganda campaign emanating from Belgrade since 1988, in particular, was instrumental in intensifying the drift toward armed confrontation by setting the emotional stage early and sharpening the ordinary Serb's mistrust of other ethnic groups in what was a period of change and uncertainty' (Cigar, 1993, p. 306). As the Croatian Democratic Union (HDZ) prepared for independence after the spring 1990 multi-party elections so did the hardline pro-Milošević factions of Croatia's Serbian community.

In the spring of 1991 rebel Serb leaders in Knin, the centre of Krajina, declared independence. As President Tudjman had looked to the international community to protect Croatia's transition to independence he did not launch an offensive or prepare a substantive national defence force. This proved unacceptable to militant Croat paramilitary forces who engaged the Serbs and proved ineffective as a means to prevent the loss of territory. Serbian militias, supported by the JNA, secured by September 1991 between a quarter and a third of Croatian territory. The country was rent by violence with refugees fleeing ethnically mixed areas and the Serbian sieges of Vukovar and Dubrovnik setting precedents for later confrontations in Bosnia.

As the war in Croatia intensified Austria, Canada, Hungary and the Yugoslav Federal President requested the UN Security Council's involvement. The Security Council approved Resolution 713 on 25 September 1991 which called for a complete arms embargo on Yugoslavia and an immediate end to hostilities. The Secretary-General was invited to begin consultations with the Yugoslav government and on 8 October Cyrus Vance was appointed as his personal representative. The United Nations had now joined the EC in seeking to address the conflict. Vance secured a ceasefire in November 1991 which paved the way for the deployment of a classic UN peacekeeping 'interposition' force in March 1992. The settlement was to place UN forces along the ceasefire lines effectively denying Zagreb control of Serbian-held territory. With Croatian independence imminent Milošević had evidently concluded that the UN could protect Serbian interests once the JNA had been obliged to withdraw (see Silber and Little, 1995, p. 217). The Krajina Serbs, moreover, could look to a future unity with Serbia, particularly if Serbian interests in Bosnia-Hercegovina were realized. The UN solution to Croatia then did not resolve the issue of borders. The EC duly recognized a state not in control of its territory and with no guarantees for its Serbian minority. The Badinter Commission was yet to certify that Croatia and the other republics seeking recognition conformed to the CSCE principles on human rights and respect for national minorities but German recognition of Zagreb predated it findings.

The Vance mission marked a new stage in the international intervention. The EC was implicitly recognizing that only the UN had the requisite political authority and legitimacy to respond to the crisis. The EC's divisions weakened its peace conference and deprived its chairman, Lord Carrington, of effective sanctions. The possibility of a comprehensive settlement, which Carrington sought, was therefore lost and attention focused on the immediate manifestations of the conflict. This is not surprising given the priority of containing violence and preventing further civilian casualties. However, in responding in this manner:

> The tragedy of the situation was that the Community's approach did not stop the use of force but made, by its stop-and-go attitude, a lasting and balanced solution more distant and difficult to achieve.
>
> (Crnobrnja, 1994, p. 202)

## Bosnia-Hercegovina: independence and the international community

The conflict in Bosnia-Hercegovina provided the greatest test for international institutions intervening in the former Yugoslavia. The conflict exposed the difficulties of sustaining clear principles of security when complex intra-state divisions join with inter-state. Bosnia's three constituent 'nations' – Bosnian Muslims, Bosnian Serbs and Bosnian Croats – generated 'internal' dynamics to the crisis while Serbia and Croatia provided 'external' forces which clearly affected the evolution of the war. In the period preceding Bosnian independence Milošević and Tudjman had looked to Bosnia for territorial enlargement and partition (Silber and Little, 1995, p. 235). Within Bosnia, Serb and Croat nationalists looked to Serbia and Croatia for support and union. The Bosnian Muslims, the largest ethnic group, with 44 per cent of the population, were in turn portrayed by their opponents as seeking to create an Islamic republic, whilst at the same time there were many ordinary citizens who had lived peacefully with other communities for decades. Bosnian security could therefore be summarized as having three elements: the state and its borders; the 'national' groups and their respective societal security; and the security of individuals. The problem for the West was that the road to self-determination had placed these three elements in conflict. As Woodward argues, recognition of Bosnia-Hercegovina needed to be accompanied by 'positive support for the standards on individual human rights, tolerance for ethnic and cultural diversity, and constitutional arrangements to ensure the principle of self determination ...' (Woodward, 1995, p. 192).

The EC did seek Bosnian compliance with the Badinter Commission's requirements for recognition but failed to respond to the Bosnian Serb boycott of the referendum. The Serbian Democratic Party (SDS) had further declared its own parliament, voting to remain in the 'rump' Yugoslavia. The EC did convene the Lisbon Conference in March 1992 and invited all three leading parties, the SDS, Izetbegovic's Party for Democratic Action (SDA) and the Bosnian branch of the HDZ, to participate. The Lisbon Agreement recognized the existing external borders of Bosnia-Hercegovina but divided the republic on ethnic grounds into 'cantons'. Within days Izetbegovic rejected the agreement as it would permanently divide Bosnia which in practice was the intent of the SDS and HDZ.

The Bosnian referendum was held on 29 February to 1 March 1991 resulting in an overwhelming vote for independence which was formally proclaimed by Izetbegovic on 3 March 1992. The political conflict and violence that had preceded the declaration now became open fighting. The violent clashes were between a number of different forces including, Bosnian Serb units of the JNA, local Bosnian Serb, Bosnian Croat and Bosnian Muslim militias, Croat regular forces and the Bosnian army. The Muslims faced superior Serb and Croat forces and lost territory throughout the first half of 1992. In March the Serbian Republic of Bosnia-Hercegovina was declared with its capital in Banja Luka. Radovan Karadzic became its President and Ratko Mladic the Commander of its armed forces. On 4 July, Mate Boban declared the Croatian community of Herceg-Bosnia. The Bosnian Muslims became trapped in a number of enclaves including Sarajevo. Fighting had begun in the city in March and Bosnian Serb forces soon laid siege to the capital. The world's media focused on the bombardment and the plight of thousands of refugees fleeing 'ethnic cleansing'. The practice of driving other ethnic groups out of chosen regions was by no means the exclusive prerogative of Bosnian Serb forces but in the early phases of the war was most commonly associated with them. The Serbs sought to secure a link between Serbia proper and the western part of Bosnia, Bosanska Krajina, where Serbs were a clear majority of the population. As ethnic cleansing, murder and rape were reported pressure for action mounted in Western capitals.

The response of the international community was to adopt sanctions, conduct humanitarian relief operations and sustain a diplomatic pursuit of a political settlement. On 30 May 1992 the UN Security Council imposed mandatory economic sanctions upon the FRY (Serbia and Montenegro). Sanctions were to be the economic complement to negotiations, to induce a positive response from Milošević. The problem was timing: the impact of sanctions would take effect in the medium to long term while Bosnian Serb military gains were a short-term reality. Sanctions also 'signalled' a preference not to make a military response to military gains. The forces dispatched to Bosnia were only to support the humanitarian mission of the United Nations and not to constitute an intervention in the conflict. UNPROFOR's initial mandates in Bosnia were to open Sarajevo airport for humanitarian aid flights and to support the United Nations High Commissioner for Refugees (UNHCR) convoys under classical peacekeeping rules.

On 29 June 1992 Resolution 761 redeployed 6,000 troops from Croatia to Sarajevo. The role of UNPROFOR was enhanced in August 1992 to ensure humanitarian aid reached its targets. Security Council Resolution 770, echoing the key Gulf War resolution, empowered UNPROFOR to use 'all measures necessary' to deliver humanitarian assistance. This UN commitment was denied credibility, however, by the actions of the key players who had threatened more force than they were prepared to use (Economides and Taylor, 1996, p. 72). Rose has argued that the very reason the UN was deployed in the former Yugoslavia was 'because no nation or military alliance was prepared to fight a war to stop aggression in the Balkans or to impose by armed force a just political settlement on the conflict in Bosnia' (Rose, 1998, p. 3). The London Conference of 1992 reaffirmed sanctions and warned of the total isolation of Serbia and Montenegro but did not threaten force. The message to the protagonists that there were clear limits to the international response was becoming clear. This failure of deterrence not only affected action on the ground but at the conference table.

The Geneva Conference, co-chaired by David Owen for the EC and Cyrus Vance for the UN, proposed a new 'power sharing' constitution for Bosnia-Hercegovina. It was rejected by the Bosnian Serbs who would have had to relinquish territorial gains in northern Bosnia. A second plan was produced by Owen and Stoltenberg (who had replaced Vance) in the summer of 1993. This peace plan divided Bosnia into three ethnic units with a weak overall state structure. The Bosnian government rejected the plan as it was seen to reward military gains and, like the Lisbon proposals before, likely to permanently divide the country. On 31 July 1993 Izetbegovic broadcast that Muslims would now have to fight for territory to ensure their survival as a nation (Woodward, 1995, p. 310). In the summer of 1994 a similar fate befell the Contact Group peace plan. The Contact Group included representatives of the USA, the UK, Russia, France and Germany. Its plan allocated to the recently formed Bosnian Federation of Muslims and Croats (2 March 1994) 51 per cent of the 58 per cent territory claimed. The Bosnian Serbs rejected the plan which would have required ceding a third of the land taken in war. In contrast Milošević urged acceptance of the proposals and sought an end to the sanctions regime. In August 1994 Milošević cut political and economic ties with the Bosnian Serbs accepting international observers to monitor his borders from September. The Security Council in turn approved a selective lifting of sanctions but, as evidence of the complexity of the conflict, Bosnian Serb forces continued to launch offensives.

The consistent failure of the international community to secure an agreement amongst the warring parties meant that the purpose of its mission to Bosnia was frequently questioned. The issue was presented at one level as a choice between peacekeeping and peace enforcement, between a humanitarian role and the military imposition of a settle-ment. The humanitarian role was deemed by all to be vital and 'impar-tiality' the key to its success. Enforcement was believed to end impartiality and consequently, it was argued, would threaten the humanitarian mission. In practice a drift to enforcement or aspects of enforcement became part of the intervention with NATO critical to the use of force.

NATO's role commenced with support for UN sanctions. In June 1992 NATO identified Serbia, Montenegro and the JNA as having primary responsibility for the conflict in Bosnia. In July 1992 NATO and the WEU began to police the sanctions regime in the Adriatic. In October 1992 UN Security Council Resolution 781 banned military flights over Bosnian airspace and on 31 March 1993 the Security Council authorized NATO to enforce the ban. A more direct role for NATO forces, close air support, was heralded by the Security Council decision in May 1993 to declare the Muslim enclaves 'safe areas'. Resolution 824 stated that Sarajevo, Tuzla, Zepa, Gorazde, Bihac and Srebrenica and their surrounds should be treated as safe areas, free from armed attacks. The problem was that the safe areas 'were among the most profoundly unsafe places in the world' (Silber and Little, 1995, p. 303). To protect the safe areas, Security Council Resolution 836 (on 4 June 1993) extended the UNPROFOR mandate to use force in self defence or in deterring attacks against the safe areas. The Council also authorized the use of air power to support UNPROFOR.

The Security Council authorization did not radically change the situ-ation on the ground in Bosnia. NATO allies differed in their views of the utility of air strikes. Washington was reported to be in favour of the use of air power while Britain had major reservations. Britain and other European contributors to UNPROFOR feared the use of force would jeopardize the safety of their troops. A key issue was proportionality, the degree of force used in response to the provocation. Rose lists several aspects of proportionality which divide peacekeeping from war fighting – the 'Mogadishu Line'. He cites the 'goals being pursued, the levels of force, the strategic imperatives facing the combatants and the political circumstances existing at the time' (Rose, 1998, p. 241). Rose argues that the UN mission was primarily humanitarian and needed to deliver aid across a territory held predominantly by the Bosnian Serbs, that UN troops were provided by states keen to limit force levels and that air strikes against strategic targets would have taken the use of force to an unacceptable level (ibid., pp. 242–3). The inactivity of the Alliance, however, was questioned as the media depicted the strangulation of Sarajevo. America's Balkan policy was also contrasted to its enforcement action against Iraq. On 2 August the North Atlantic Council announced it was undertaking immediate preparations for the use of air power. On 9 August NATO refined its position and declared air strikes would be limited to the support of humanitarian aid and would require authorization by the United Nations Secretary-General. The decision clearly rejected the option of an air bombardment against the Bosnian Serbs and ensured a politically acceptable approach to the use of force. It did not mean a rapid response to UNPROFOR's needs. In March 1994 French UN forces in Bihac requested air support but were not assisted largely due to the cumbersome procedures for authorization. Procedures for the 'dual key' were streamlined with authority passing to the UN Secretary-General's Special Representative in the theatre, Yasushi Akashi. The system was still not immediate, however, and its political 'brake' was not lost on the Bosnian Serbs. Bosnian Serb offensives against the safe areas were marked by their 'brinkmanship' with NATO. When air power was finally used on 11 April 1994 to protect UN personnel in Gorazde, Karadzic accused the UN of taking sides in the conflict. Andrei Kozyrev, the Russian Foreign Minister, warned that the 'world could be dragged into an extremely dangerous series of exchanges of strikes' (*The Times*, 12 April 1994). President Yeltsin demanded that President Clinton consult Russia before taking action. Yeltsin's domestic opponents accused the President of accepting Western domination and demanded action. The interrelationship of NATO, the UN, UNPROFOR and Russian politics did little to enhance the deterrent effect of air power.

NATO's involvement in the conflict was deepened with the Sarajevo market mortar bomb attack in February 1994. The North Atlantic Council declared an ultimatum that called for the 'withdrawal, or regrouping and placing under UNPROFOR control, within ten days, all heavy weapons ... of the Bosnian Serb forces located in an area within 20 kilometres of the centre of Sarajevo' (North Atlantic Council, 9 February 1994). NATO warned that any heavy weapons remaining within the exclusion zone not under UNPROFOR control would be subject to air strikes. NATO had put its credibility on the line and threatened direct action. The ultimatum was followed by a Russian initiative to deploy peacekeeping forces to secure a Bosnian Serb withdrawal from Sarajevo. As the Bosnian Serb forces withdrew, Moscow announced there was no need for NATO air strikes. NATO took similar decisions to end the siege of Gorazde in April 1994. On 22 April NATO demanded that Bosnian Serb forces withdraw from Gorazde by 24 April and humanitarian relief convoys be allowed to enter the city. Kozyrev signalled Moscow's acceptance of the ultimatum and the offensive ended with NATO's deadline. These actions reflected UN–NATO responses to 'peaks' of the conflict and threats to the safe areas. The threat of air power assumed a deterrent quality by the build-up in each of the crises. It could not prevent, though, the sustained challenge to the safe areas which could move from Gorazde to Srebrenica or Tuzla. The UN mission was not after all fighting a war, and 'defending a safe area was a war-fighting task for the which the UN was neither mandated, equipped nor trained' (Rose, 1998, p. 110).

The UN Secretariat had asked for 34,000 troops to defend the safe areas and received 7,600 (Shawcross, 2000, p. 133). The mission, in short, was impossible. The Bosnian government could, and did, exploit the UN failure to call for NATO air strikes against the Serbs. At the same time it could use the safe areas to preserve its own armed forces as well as to provoke disproportionate Bosnian Serb responses (ibid., p. 133).

The political difficulties of sustaining the international mission to Bosnia-Hercegovina in 1994 worsened despite the successes of Sarajevo and Gorazde. In the United States the House of Representatives demanded that Washington unilaterally end the arms embargo. As the US Senate increased its pressure in June France intimated it would withdraw its troops from Bosnia. The divisions in NATO grew as fighting on the ground intensified in the autumn. Bosnian government forces took Bihac and Serb counter-offensives threatened the enclave and UNPROFOR personnel. Serb aircraft from Krajina attacked Bihac and the UN Security Council approved Resolution 958 which authorized the use of airpower to support UNPROFOR in Croatia. NATO aircraft struck at Udbina air field in Krajina on 21 November. NATO strikes were also launched against a Bosnian Serb surface-to-air missile site in northern Bosnia on 23 November. The Bosnian Serbs responded by taking UNPROFOR personnel hostage and pressed home their assault on Bihac. In the United States the Bihac crisis stimulated further demands for the use of air power and lifting of sanctions – 'lift and strike'. With the prospect of all factions being rearmed both London and Paris made public the possibility of withdrawing troops. At the same time Croatia began to warn that the UN mandate would be terminated on 31 March 1995. As the international community divided and the situation on the ground deteriorated former President Jimmy Carter's mediation spared further embarrassment by securing a four-month ceasefire.

## Operation Deliberate Force

On 30 August 1995 NATO commenced a sustained air bombardment of Bosnian Serb positions supported by the recently deployed UN Rapid Reaction Force on the ground. NATO air strikes were the largest ever in Bosnia amounting to over 3,400 missions and Alliance action included the use of Cruise missiles. On 14 September the Bosnian Serbs accepted UNPROFOR conditions to end the siege of Sarajevo, remove heavy weapons from the capital's exclusion zone and permit humanitarian relief to be flown into the airport. The NATO action was suspended and plans for a peace conference commenced. Richard Holbrooke, the US envoy, negotiated a ceasefire which took effect on 12 October and laid the foundations for the Dayton Peace Accord of 21 November.

The diplomatic breakthrough in the autumn of 1995 followed significant changes in the strategic situation in Bosnia-Hercegovina. The UN/NATO enforcement action was a major departure from peacekeeping. It was visibly 'triggered' by a Bosnian Serb mortar attack on Sarajevo on 28 August but reflected deeper changes in policy. The attack followed a major American diplomatic initiative and was seen by Holbrooke as the 'first direct affront to the United States' (Holbrooke, 1999, p. 93). America's chief envoy saw his country's response as 'the most important test of American leadership since the end of the Cold War ... not only in Bosnia, but in Europe' (ibid., p. 92). The reassertion of American leadership and credibility coincided with the strong conviction that events had 'reached the absolute end of the line ...' (ibid., p. 103). Since the expiry of the Carter ceasefire the plight of the UN mission had worsened. On 22 May Bosnian Serbs seized artillery held by UN troops near Sarajevo. The capital was shelled and the Bosnian Muslims returned fire. The UN demanded a ceasefire and when the Serbs refused NATO aircraft struck at an ammunition depot near Pale. The Bosnian Serb response was to shell the safe areas and after a second NATO strike take 300 UN soldiers hostage. The UN's weakness was dramatically shown.

> It was a crucial moment. Nothing showed the impotence of the United Nations so vividly as the plight of its soldiers chained to potential targets. And nothing showed so graphically the need to reduce the UN's vulnerability by withdrawing its men from outlying areas.
>
> (Shawcross, 2000, p. 137)

Worse was to follow, however, when Srebrenica fell to the Bosnian Serbs. In a terrible war crime there were mass murders of Muslims by the occupying Serbs. The situation was reviewed by the Contact Group and other UN contributors in London on 21 July. The conference focused on protecting the remaining safe areas and in particular Gorazde. A statement issued at the end of the meeting called for a 'substantial and decisive response' to any attack on Gorazde. While critics of the UN, including the Bosnian government, did not see the summit as a turning point it did modify the dual key arrangements to give Akashi's veto to the commander of UNPROFOR. Military commanders now held the power to call air strikes. A second change after the conference was the deployment of a Rapid Reaction Force. The force, initially agreed in early June, was to compromise two 5,000-strong brigades drawn from British, French and Netherlands troops. Each was armed with artillery, anti-tank weapons and helicopters. The role of the brigades was to protect UNPROFOR. As the new troops were deployed UNPROFOR personnel were progressively moved from vulnerable positions. The final elements in the changing equation were on the ground where the Croatian army was launching a successful offensive. In early August Croat forces retook Krajina. Tudjman was encouraged by the United States and with Bosnian Muslim support sustained the offensive into Western Bosnia (Holbrooke, 1999, p. 160).

The role of air power must be placed in the above context. The decision to use force was the result of several factors: the failure of past policy to contain Bosnian Serb advances, the determination of the American executive to assert leadership, and preparation on the ground to protect UNPROFOR. Air power was an important contributor to the diplomatic breakthrough but not its exclusive broker. The loss of territory and the changing balance of forces against the Bosnian Serbs made, for the first time, negotiations attractive to all parties. Holbrooke's skill was to offer something for each faction and draw them to Dayton.

## Dayton and beyond

Presidents Izetbegovic, Tudjman and Milošević formally signed the Peace Agreement on Bosnia-Hercegovina in Paris on 14 December 1995, after its negotiation in Dayton. The Federal Republic of Yugoslavia (FRY) and the Republic of Bosnia-Hercegovina recognized each other as sovereign independent states within their international borders (Croatia declined to recognize the FRY until Eastern Slavonia was reintegrated with Croatia under international supervision). Bosnia-Hercegovina was to be a democratic state consisting of two 'entities': the Federation of Bosnia and Hercegovina (the Croat–Muslim Federation) and the

Republika Srpska. The Federation occupied 51 per cent and the Republika 49 per cent of the state's territory. Annex 4 of the General Framework Agreement outlined the respective responsibilities of the state and entity institutions. The state was to be responsible for foreign policy, foreign trade, customs policy, monetary policy, finances of the institutions and for the international obligations of Bosnia and Hercegovina, immigration, refugee and asylum policy, international and inter-entity criminal law enforcement including relations with Interpol, the establishment and operation of common and international communications facilities, the regulation of inter-entity transportation, and air traffic control (Article III, annex 4 (1)). The entities could undertake any government functions and powers not expressly assigned to the state and had the right 'to establish special parallel relationships with neighbouring states consistent with the sovereignty and territorial integrity of Bosnia and Hercegovina' (ibid., annex 4 (2)).

State institutions included the Presidency, the council of Ministers, the Parliamentary Assembly and the Constitutional Court. Each was constituted to reflect the ethnic mix of Bosnia-Hercegovina. The Presidency has three members: one Bosniac, one Croat and one Serb. Each is directly elected from their respective constituencies and the member with the highest number of votes takes the chair in the first instance. Decisions have to be reached by consensus and a dissenting member can declare a decision to be destructive of a vital interest of their entity. In such a case the issue would be referred to the respective entity assembly or constituent part of the Federation assembly for decision. If a two-thirds majority confirmed the declaration the proposal would not take effect. The Presidency nominates a Chair of the Council of Ministers who takes office upon approval of the House of Representatives. The Chair in turn nominates ministers who are confirmed in the same way. Not more than two-thirds of ministers may be appointed from the Federation. The Parliamentary Assembly consists of the House of Peoples and the House of Representatives. The House of Peoples comprises 15 members, two-thirds from the Federation (five Bosniacs and five Croats) and one-third from the Republika Srpska. The membership is selected from the respective entity assembly or part thereof. The House of Representatives consists of 42 members elected directly from the entities with two-thirds from the Federation and one-third from the Republika Srpska. The Parliamentary Assembly has complex procedures to protect the vital interests of ethnic groups in tandem with those of the Presidency and Council of Ministers. Finally the Constitutional Court has nine members, four from the Federation, two from the Republika Srpska and three selected by the President of the European Court of Human Rights. The Constitutional Court has exclusive jurisdiction over disputes that arise under the constitution including inter-entity conflicts or entity–state conflicts.

By these constitutional means Dayton sought to reassure each ethnic group that its interests would not be threatened, that they 'would not be endangered minorities and could safely shift from fighting to political activity' (Woodward, 1999, p. 92). The 'veto' procedures were integral to the creation of a weak central state authority accompanied by considerable devolution to the entities. The entities were also regulated by Dayton. The Federation follows a similar model of ethnic balance to state institutions ensuring Muslim and Croat representation. The Republika Srpska was equally regulated by the international community to ensure behaviour according to the philosophy of Dayton. The principle of regulation and sustained intervention was enshrined in the Annexes on Civilian Implementation and Military Aspects of the settlement.

The Civilian Implementation Annex 10 established the post of United Nations High Representative to coordinate the actions of international institutions and to assist local actors. The High Representative has extensive powers to oversee the settlement, to ensure compliance with Dayton and to resolve differences. The network of means for international intervention via the Office of the High Representative (OHR) covers both state and entity levels. The Federation Forum and Federation Implementation Council (FIC) have ensured strong international influence over Federation policy. The FIC has also powers to remove from office those who have been deemed to have violated Dayton (see Chandler, 1999, p. 73). The OHR has directly intervened in the Republika Srpska between Bosnian Serb factions, in economic development and with regard to the degree of autonomy the entity has pursued. The High Representative chairs the Joint Civilian Commission in which the military regime for Bosnia-Hercegovina was also represented.

On the basis of UN Security Council Resolution 1031, NATO was given the mandate to implement the military aspects of the Dayton Agreement. NATO led a multinational Implementation Force (IFOR), including Russian troops, to undertake a number of tasks specified in Annex 1A. The key roles were:

- ensuring continued compliance with the ceasefire;
- ensuring the withdrawal of forces from the agreed ceasefire zone of separation to their respective territories;
- ensuring the collection of heavy weapons into cantonment sites;

- creating conditions for the withdrawal of UN forces;
- controlling the airspace over Bosnia-Hercegovina.

IFOR was given unimpeded movement throughout Bosnia-Hercegovina and a one-year mandate. Within four months of deployment the North Atlantic Council concluded that IFOR had been successful in bringing about a more secure environment. Local forces had been separated, the transfer of territory between the entities completed and a new zone of separation was established along the inter-entity boundary line. The cantonment of heavy weapons was also completed albeit by a revised deadline.

After the 1996 state and entity elections IFOR's role was considered complete but the continuing presence of a military force was seen as important to the implementation of the civilian agreement. Under UN Security Council Resolution 1088 of 12 December 1996 a NATO-led Stabilization Force (SFOR) to replace IFOR was authorized. SFOR was about half the size of IFOR with 32,000 troops. Its task has been to maintain a secure environment and provide support to the organizations and agencies working in Bosnia-Hercegovina.

The international community coordinated its efforts to reconstruct Bosnia through a Peace Implementation Conference. The Conference was held in London in December 1995 and attended by over 50 countries and international organizations. The conference established itself as a Peace Implementation Council (PIC) which meets on a six monthly basis and created a Steering Board chaired by the High Representative. The Steering Board meets on a monthly basis, normally as the senior representatives of the foreign ministries of the member states together with the UN and OSCE. The European Commission and World Bank have coordinated meetings of international donors and inform the Steering Board. Successive PIC meetings have provided detailed analyses of compliance with Dayton and progress toward democratization. The PIC has extended the transition period for Bosnia, enhanced the powers of the High Representative and set deadlines for 'action plans'. In 1998 new indefinite mandates were granted by the PIC to the bodies regulating Bosnia and the enhancement of their powers, including the 'High Representative's powers directly to enact policy, the OSCE's power to install multi-ethnic administrations and stipulate the allocation of governing responsibilities, and the extension of NATO's authority to include policing function beyond SFOR's existing mandate' (Chandler, 1999, p. 55). In this manner Dayton has remained a highly regulated peace process or, as Chandler

puts it, 'an experiment in supplanting democratisation through
extremely imposed strategies' (ibid., p. 36).

The Dayton process has been criticized for being over-regulated.
Chandler has questioned the degree of supervision compatible with
democracy:

> The language of multi-ethnicity and power-sharing has been used to
> justify far-reaching international regulation of Bosnian political life
> but it remains to be seen whether this regulation can promote a
> genuine participatory pluralism based on the stable coexistence of
> different political interests.
>
> (Ibid., p. 89)

The scale of international supervision can be seen as ill suited to a
'bottom-up' democratic transition. A 'top-down' direction of the polity
clearly leaves little room for the emergence of new patterns of participation. Chandler suggests that this pattern of international regulation
is linked to the *raison d'être* of institutions: 'Bosnia was not just NATO's
defining post-Cold War success, but also remains a central focus for
cohering the alliance' (ibid., p. 193). At the same time we can see regulation as a response to redress fear and insecurity in Bosnia-
Hercegovina. The intervention can be seen as needing time to oversee
the divisions generated by a bloody civil war. In this approach outside
help is seen as essential, 'just as individuals suffering severe trauma are
not expected to heal themselves, neither can war-torn and collapsed
states recuperate without careful nurturing over many years' (Sharp,
1997, p. 113). In this vein of thinking the IFOR and SFOR published
exit dates were premature and unlikely to instil confidence. 'Far from
building confidence, this schedule discouraged reconciliation and
simply encouraged former enemies to prepare for the next battle'
(ibid., p. 114). The consequence was the need for international regulation to offset the continuation of war by other means. Far from the
regulation process being seen as exhaustive critics have pointed to its
weaknesses. The scale of the international commitment to law enforcement has been highlighted. Local police forces were left with the
primary responsibility for public order and the small International
Police Task Force entered Bosnia unarmed and ill equipped. Significant
public disorder was not addressed when Serb suburbs of Sarajevo were
transferred to Federation control in February 1996. 'Armed groups of
Serb agitators torched buildings in full view of UN police monitors and
heavily armed – but completely passive – IFOR personnel' (ibid.,

p. 119). Similar arguments have pointed to the failure of the international community to pursue indicted war criminals. The PIC has reaffirmed its support for the International Criminal Tribunal for the Former Yugoslavia (ICTY) (see, for example, PIC London Conference, 1996, p. 4) but its member states have been reluctant to commit forces to detain individuals. Karadzic, for example, was forced to stand down as President of Republika Srpska in 1996 but not arrested. The presence of such political figures in the political systems of Bosnia makes reconciliation and integration between ethnic groups unlikely at best and impossible at worst. Dayton is also committed to an arms control regime but Washington has adopted a 'train and equip' programme for the Federation. The impact of this policy has 'reinforced the perceptions of vulnerability among Bosnian Serbs, encouraged them to cheat on arms control agreements and to maintain a military presence at weak points of their internal frontier, making it more rather than less like an international border, and strengthened their view that protection lay in political and military relations with neighbouring Serbia' (Woodward, 1999, p. 103). In the context of partisan local policing, political insecurity and the politics of partition the difficulties confronting the return of refugees is hardly surprising. During the war approximately 1 million people were displaced in Bosnia-Hercegovina and some 1.2 million outside the country. In 1996 400,000 persons returned, mainly to the Federation, but as the OHR noted in 1998 the 'time of easy returns, ie: voluntary returns to areas controlled by the returnees' ethnic group, is now over' (OHR, 1998, p. 2). Few people have returned to areas in which they would be an ethnic minority. The key reason is political: 'a proper political environment and security are critical pre-conditions' (ibid.).

It has been argued that underpinning the above problems is the Dayton Agreement itself. 'Even if most of the leaders who had no intention of cooperating and still wanted to defect from Bosnia or from Dayton were removed from the scene, the agreement encouraged mobilization along national lines and defensive perceptions and behaviour' (Woodward, 1999, p. 97). The basis of Dayton was to divide Bosnia-Hercegovina on ethnic lines and make ethnicity the basis of political participation. Although this strategy secured agreement among local actors and could be seen to reassure, 'the accords thus appeared to legalise the ongoing partition of the country rather than to soften social and political lines of division' (Woodward, 1999, p. 105). The danger is a perpetuation of ethnic division rather than the creation of meaningful multi-ethnic administration. 'While the ethnicisation of politics has been welcomed, and multi-ethnic administrations formed at all levels the politicisation of ethnicity, the success of political parties which appeal to one ethnic group, has been roundly condemned as a central barrier to the democratisation and the Dayton process' (Chandler, 1999, p. 111).

The record of post-conflict peace-building in Bosnia-Hercegovina demonstrates the challenges for the international institutions and the very real problem of defining an appropriate exit strategy. Dayton has led to a complex process which has yet to realize a stable peace for Bosnia. Its impact upon the broader question of separatism in the FRY is now considered with regard to Kosovo.

## Kosovo

### A brief history of the present conflict

The coming of war to Kosovo in 1996 was not an unanticipated event as Judah notes, 'it has been evident for many years that Kosovo was a catastrophe waiting to happen' (Judah, 1999, p. 5). This troubled province has long been the scene of competition for the right to rule. Over the centuries, struggles have occurred between Serbs and Ottoman Turks, Serbs and Albanians, Serbs and Austro-Hungarians, and the forces of Nazi Germany all seeking to control this 'wretched piece of land' (ibid.). Throughout this turbulent history, as with all disputed territories, claims and counter-claims of rightful ownership have emanated from both sides of the inter-communal divide. The Serbian and Albanian communities have each attempted to trace their ancestral heritage through the mists of time in order to prove the veracity of their respective titles. Serbian claims that their majoritarian presence in Kosovo was a historical reality until the last couple of hundred years are refuted by Albanian assertions that their ancestry in the shape of the Illyrians and Dardanians of the sixth and seventh centuries predates any Slavic presence. In this view, therefore, Kosovo is thoroughly Albanian (see Judah, 2000, pp. 1–33 on this contested history). The Serbs emphasize their dominance in the province during the Middle Ages and point to the many Serbian Orthodox churches and monasteries therein as irrefutable evidence that Kosovo is the cradle of the Serbian nation. In addition, in Serbian folklore the province of Kosovo is regarded as indisputably Serbian and sacred due to the Battle of Kosovo on 28 June 1389. There, according to legend, on the Field of the Blackbirds, Kosovo Polje, the Serbian Prince Lazar chose to die with honour rather than to bear the yoke of the Ottoman Sultan Murat. The inability to verify such myths does not in any way injure their significance to those who hold them dear. Nor does it adversely affect the ability of such myths to fuel nationalism; as Schopflin astutely observes, '… it is the content of the myth that is important not its accuracy as a historical account' (Schöpflin, 1997, p. 20).

It was the ability of Slobodan Milošević to harness Serbian nationalism in the pursuit of his own political goals that led to the most recent bloody contest in this disputed province. Kosovo was never accorded republican status within the Yugoslav Federation. Like Vojvodina to the north, Kosovo was an autonomous province within the republic of Serbia. In the Federation, there was a distinction drawn between those who constituted a 'nation' and those deemed to be a 'nationality'. The former, such as the Macedonians, Montenegrins, Croats, Slovenes and the Serbs were entitled to republican status while the latter, the Kosovo Albanians and the Vojvodina Hungarians respectively, were not accorded republics as each had an existent home state elsewhere. The crucial point about such legal labels is that the theoretical right of secession was held by republics only. Thus any irredentist movements by nationalities were constitutionally illegal (Judah, 2000, p. 37). Following the Second World War, this provincial autonomy for Kosovo had little practical significance as the administrative, political and managerial domains within the province were dominated by the Serbian population therein despite the fact that they were an ethnic minority group. The Federal authorities believed that the state could not depend upon the loyalty of the majority ethnic Albanian community at this time. Indeed, in the immediate aftermath of the War, martial law held for some time, and throughout the 1950s the authorities faced challenges from those campaigning either for greater autonomy within the Federation, for unification with Albania or for statehood for Kosovo. The authorities suppressed such opposition via arrests and imprisonment but, by 1968, a new round of protests proved more difficult to counter. The opposition came from university students whose twin demands were for Kosovo to attain republican status and for an Albanian-language university to be established within Kosovo. The federal government refused the first demand on the traditional legal grounds that the Albanians in Kosovo did not constitute a nation; however, they did accede to the second request and the University of Pristina was duly opened in 1970. Under the federal Constitution of 1974, the legal status of Kosovo was upgraded in that it and Vojvodina were given representation in the Yugoslav Presidency

and, via their representation in the Serbian assembly, could affect legislation within the Serbian Republic. Serbian delegates, however, were
not afforded mutual representation within the autonomous provincial
assemblies and this perceived inequity led to a belief on the part of
some Serbs that Tito's policy of decentralization was aimed at keeping
Yugoslavia strong by keeping Serbia weak (Thomas, 1999, p. 34). From
the late 1960s onwards a process of Albanization occurred within
Kosovo. Increasingly the organs of the province became dominated by
ethnic Albanian communists (Judah, 2000, p. 37). Inter-communal
tensions within Kosovo remained very polarized. At the close of the
1970s, the Serbian minority population accounted for approximately
10 per cent of the total population of Kosovo in contrast to an ethnic
Albanian community of 81.6 per cent. The explanation for this situation lay in a combination of Serbian migration from the province,
generally to Serbia proper, and a very high birth-rate within the ethnic
Albanian community (Thomas, 1999, p. 30). The deterioration of
bicommunal relations was marked by Serbian accounts of ethnic discrimination prompting their departure from Kosovo and such accounts
were to lead to a heightened sense of persecution among Kosovo Serbs
throughout the 1980s and, as we shall see, they came to play a central
role in the mobilization of Serbian nationalism. In dealing with these
claims of migration due to the push factor of discrimination, it should
be noted that there were other factors which may well have influenced
migration levels from Kosovo. One should acknowledge, in particular,
the relative economic deprivation of Kosovo within the Yugoslav federation. Judah notes that the 1979 average income within Kosovo was
$795, in sharp contrast to a national average of $2,365, and Thomas
points out that a decade later Kosovo had an unemployment rate of
54 per cent, nearly triple the national figure (Judah, 2000, p. 46;
Thomas, 1999, p. 29).

### Kosovo after Tito

The death of Tito in May 1980 meant the removal of 'the final arbiter
and the real law of the land' within Yugoslavia (Judah, 1999, p. 8). In
his wake, indigenous politicians throughout the Federal Republic
began to test the structures and tenets of Titoism without Tito. In
Kosovo, protestors took to the streets. Ethnic Albanians staged nationalist demonstrations in the spring of 1981, with the students of the
University of Pristina leading the calls for republican status for the
province. Soon these students were joined by high school students and

industrial workers. The response of the authorities was, once again, to 'manage' the situation via mass indiscriminate arrests and long prison sentences. In addition, protestors were expelled from their places of education or employment. Throughout the 1980s, however, the call for greater autonomy for Kosovo continued and was accompanied by political developments within the ethnic Albanian community. In 1982, the Popular Movement for Kosovo (LDK) was established as a focus for the campaign for republican status for the province. As Judah notes, this campaign should not be viewed as an inter-ethnic campaign between Serbs and Albanians within Kosovo but as an intra-ethnic competition within the Albanian community: 'It is vitally important, however, that, at this critical juncture, and indeed until 1989, it was not Serbs who were in charge in Kosovo. It was Albanians' (Judah, 2000, p. 41).

The response of Serbs in Kosovo was to feel a heightened sense of insecurity within the province. From the early 1980s, they sought to bring their perceived plight to the attention of the government in Belgrade. The campaign for the address and redress of their situation did not go unheeded but attracted support from politicians, intellectuals and the Orthodox Church (see Judah, 2000, p. 48; Thomas, 1999, pp. 38–42; Malcolm, 1998, pp. 339–40). In 1982, Orthodox priests within Kosovo produced a petition asking 'for the protection of the spiritual and biological essence of the Serbian people in Kosovo' which they alleged was being systematically undermined by ethnic Albanians. In 1985, a petition was presented demanding protection for the Kosovo Serbs and implicitly suggesting that those Albanians who had migrated to Kosovo from Albania since 1941 should be repatriated. Another petition was circulated in 1986 by Serbian intellectuals asking that Belgrade take 'decisive measures' to combat 'Albanian aggression' in the province. The most noted expression of solidarity with the Kosovo Serbs came from SANU, the Serbian Academy of Arts and Sciences. Although a secret document, extracts from it were printed in the press in September 1986. This 'Memorandum' was a highly emotive piece of prose protesting at what it described as the 'physical, political, juridical and cultural genocide' of Serbs in Kosovo and demanding that the Belgrade authorities take action to facilitate the return of those Serbs who had been forced out of their homeland. The fundamental premise of the 'Memorandum' was that the constitutional arrangements of Yugoslavia led to pervasive discrimination against the Serbian nation. It accused Serbian politicians of 'inveterate opportunism' in putting self-interest before the well-being of the

Serbian nation. Ominously, the authors warned that if the exiled Serbs felt unable to return to Kosovo, that is if a more benign environment were not created for them, 'then this part of the Republic of Serbia and Yugoslavia will become a European issue, with the gravest possible unforeseeable consequences' (Judah, 2000, p. 50). Thus had the issue of the Serbs in Kosovo entered the national political arena.

In response to such petitions, as well as demonstrations in Belgrade by the Kosovo Serbs themselves, the then Serbian President Ivan Stambolic sent his protégé, Slobodan Milošević, then Chairman of the Serbian Communist Party, on a fact-finding mission to Kosovo. Thomas notes that Milošević 'was to be the critical actor in achieving the fusion between 'opinion' and 'power' (Thomas, 1999, p. 42). This visit, on 24 April 1987, afforded Milošević the opportunity to begin his conversion from communist to nationalist. Witnessing scuffles between the local police and the Kosovo Serbs, he announced that 'No one should dare beat you' and, casting himself as the defender of Kosovo, he proclaimed that:

> Yugoslavia does not exist without Kosovo!
> Yugoslavia would disintegrate without Kosovo!
> Yugoslavia and Serbia are not going to give up Kosovo.
>
> (Judah, 2000, p. 52)

As Freedman notes, however, in fact it was the dissent within Kosovo which led to the disintegration of Yugoslavia, as it 'provided Slobodan Milošević with his opportunity for a power play, in the process losing whatever hope there was for holding the federation together' (Freedman, 2000, p. 345). It should be noted too that Milošević displayed what was to become an enduring character trait even at this stage – his ability to gauge his audience's needs and perform accordingly. Despite professing his solidarity with the Kosovo Serbs, two months later, in June 1987, addressing a meeting of Yugoslav secret police, he described the 'Memorandum' as 'nothing else but the darkest nationalism' (Judah, 2000, p. 50).

### Playing the Kosovo card

Milošević lost little time in exploiting the issue of the Serbs in Kosovo to his own political advantage. In September 1987, at the Eighth Session of the Central Committee of the League of Communists in Serbia, he ousted Pavlovic to become chief of the Belgrade Communist Party. With his star on the rise, he moved in December 1987 against his former mentor Stambolic and became President of Serbia. Using the issue of the Kosovo Serbs, he organized a series of mass demonstrations, known as 'Truth Rallies', throughout the summer of 1988 to the spring of 1989 wherein the central theme of a Greater Serbia predominated. Milošević also moved to consolidate his political base elsewhere. In early October the respective governments of Vojvodina and Montenegro resigned en masse allowing Milošević to organize their replacement with more 'friendly' forces. The myth of Kosovo now was fully utilized by Milošević in building and maintaining his personal political position. At a mass rally in November 1988, he declared that:

> Every nation has a love which eternally warms its heart. For Serbia it is Kosovo. That is why Kosovo will remain in Serbia.
> 
> (Judah, 2000, p. 55; Malcolm, 1999, p. 343)

Demonstrating such a commitment to Kosovo, Milošević now attempted to change the constitutional status of Kosovo to bring it entirely under Serbian control via the elimination of its residual autonomy. Belgrade's efforts to revoke the 1974 Constitution led to protests by the ethnic Albanians within Kosovo. In February 1998, the miners of Trepca refused to surface from their mines and went on hunger-strike. Soon the protests spread throughout the province. Milošević and his security forces proved stronger than such opposition and on 23 March 1989, in accordance with the legal requirements, the Kosovo assembly endorsed the proposed constitutional changes and, less than a week later, the Serbian parliament ratified the new constitutional arrangements. The autonomy of Kosovo was now eradicated.

Now firmly in control, Milošević enacted a series of measures designed to 'rectify' the situation in Kosovo. A raft of discriminatory legislation was ushered in removing various rights from the ethnic Albanian community. In an effort to prevent further Serbian migration from the province, Albanians could no longer buy houses or land from Serbs. In March 1990, the 'Programme for the Realization of Peace and Prosperity in the Socialist Autonomous Province of Kosovo' was introduced. Its aims were to encourage Albanians to leave and Serbs to stay or return. Two months later, the 'Law on the Activities of Organs on the Republic in Exceptional Circumstances' or 'temporary measures' was passed. This law facilitated the dismissal of thousands of ethnic Albanians from state employment, the closure of the main Albanian newspaper and the closure of the Kosovo Academy of Arts and Sciences. The Serbian curriculum was to be taught in schools although the financing of Albanian schools was stopped and, eventually, Albanian teachers and their students were prevented from entering schools altogether.

### Passive resistance: Rugova and the LDK

In this climate of repression, the Albanian delegates of the Kosovo assembly made their move. As the provincial assembly had been reduced to a mere rubber-stamping organ, the remaining Albanian members resigned from it. Two months later, outside a locked parliament building, they reconvened to declare that Kosovo was now a republic – 'an equal and independent entity within the framework of the Yugoslav Federation'. Their audacity in perpetrating 'this illegal act' was greeted by the immediate dissolution of the Kosovo assembly by the Serbian parliament. Undeterred the Albanian delegates met secretly in September 1990 and voted for a Constitution of the Republic of Kosovo and followed this move, a year later, by voting for a Resolution on the Independence and Sovereignty of Kosovo. In the ensuing referendum, boycotted unsurprisingly by the Serbs in Kosovo, 99.87 per cent of the vote favoured independence. Subsequently, in October 1991, the parliament of Kosovo declared Kosovo to be a republic and, by May 1992, in secretly conducted elections, the LDK polled 76.4 per cent of the vote and Ibrahim Rugova was duly elected President of the new Republic of Kosovo.

Throughout these proceedings, the Serbian authorities took the line of least resistance in that they did not interfere in the various polls. In June 1982, however, the Serbian police moved to prevent the convening of the new Kosovo 'parliament'. The general attitude of non-interference by the Serbian authorities is explicable when one considers the strategy employed by Rugova and the LDK. Lacking the resources and the political will to engage in a violent confrontation with the Serbian forces, the Albanians pursued a policy of passive resistance. Also, Milošević was faced with more pressing challenges elsewhere. By 1991, the FRY was no more and war was on the horizon. Belgrade had more urgent business to attend to and, as Judah observes, 'may have calculated, rightly, that if the pacifist "President" were removed from office, radicals preaching violence would fill the leadership vacuum' (Judah, 1999, p. 11). Rugova thus maintained his position at home and maintained contact with his government in exile led by Bujar Bukoshi. The policy of pacifism extended to Rugova and Bukoshi denying requests from Croatian President Tudjman and Bosnian President Izetbegovic for the Kosovo Albanians to open a third front against Serbia during the Balkans wars (ibid., p. 12). Aware of their precarious situation and their lack of resources to defeat the Serbian forces, the Kosovo Albanian leadership pursued a triad strategy: 'to prevent violent revolt; to "internationalize" the problem ... and to deny systematically the legitimacy of Serbian rule ...' (Malcolm, 1999, p. 348). Pursuant to this latter aim, a shadow state was established, notably in the fields of education and health. Using monies levied from ethnic Albanians working or running businesses abroad, the LDK funded, somewhat haphazardly, a parallel education system and parallel health provision. Using the pre-1990 curriculum, classes for students from primary to tertiary levels were taught by teachers in private homes. Mother Teresa clinics provided a basic level of health care though not all Albanians rejected state provision, especially for more serious medical matters. Approximately half of the medical personnel in the state facilities were ethnic Albanians as their presence was essential to the running of the state health service. Rugova's attempt to place the issue of Kosovo on the international political agenda involved his meeting many foreign leaders but rendered little substantive benefit. The international community refused to consider that Kosovo had a rightful claim to secession. In 1991, Kosovo, like the republics of Yugoslavia, requested diplomatic recognition from the EC. The request was rejected as it was held that the secession of Kosovo would violate the UN Charter. The republics, conversely, could be recognized because the Yugoslav Federation was deemed to have dissolved and so, in effect, they had nothing to secede from (Caplan, 1998, pp. 747–8). Despite this denial of recognition, the Rugova government believed that eventually the international community would recognize an independent Kosovo. After all, they reasoned, initially the US and the EU had refused to recognize any of the former Yugoslav republics as sovereign states. When, in 1992, recognition was given, a lesson was learned by the Kosovo Albanians: it meant that, from then on, Kosovars never believed that Kosovo did not have the right to independence because of its provincial status (Judah, 2000, p. 76). This belief that eventual international recognition would come was shored up by President Bush's 'Christmas warning' to the Serbs in 1992, when a cable was sent reminding Serbia that '... in the event of conflict in Kosovo caused by Serbian action, the United States will be prepared to employ military force against Serbians in Kosovo and Serbia proper' (ibid., pp. 73–4).

Preventing violent conflict proved fairly successful for the Rugova government initially as the KLA remained a marginalized grouping.

Formed in 1991, its early activities in 1996 had little impact. Popular support was for Rugova and his policy of patience and also the KLA was overwhelmingly outgunned by the Yugoslav forces. Indeed, up until 1997, Rugova argued that the KLA was a fiction – 'a provocation whose origins can be found in Serbian extremist circles' (Thomas, 1999, p. 400). The fortunes of both the LDK and the KLA were set to change. The turning point came in the form of the Dayton Agreement in 1995.

## Kosovo post-Dayton

As noted, from the inception of the international community's efforts to resolve the Balkan wars, Kosovo was deemed to merit no more than a return to autonomy within Serbia. At the London Conference on the Former Yugoslavia in August 1992, Carrington invited Rugova to attend 'if you are planning to be in London at the time'. He was offered meetings with both Carrington and Cyrus Vance but was not offered access to the conference itself (Carrington, cited in Weller, 1999, p. 18). Despite such treatment, the Kosovo Albanian leadership still held out hopes of inclusion within the settlement and a change of attitude on the part of the international community. Such hopes were to be dashed. Kosovo simply was not on the agenda at Dayton. Caplan (1998, p. 750) notes two reasons for its omission: 'First, it was felt that there was simply too much to negotiate already; ... second, no one wanted to alienate Milošević, the 'peacemaker'. Milošević led the joint FRY/Republika Srpska negotiating team and oversaw an agreement which created a Bosnian state comprising two territorial elements, namely the Republika Srpska and the Muslim-Croat Federation, with the latter granted full control over Sarajevo. In effect, Milošević had distanced himself from the Pale Serbs. His treatment of these Serbs had culminated in his imposing economic sanctions on the Republika Srpska and allowing international monitors to witness their efficacy. His pressuring of the Bosnian Serbs to accept the Dayton Agreement won him plaudits from the international community and charges of treason from some at home. The motivation behind Milošević's abandonment of the Bosnian Serbs may have been largely a matter of economics. International sanctions had been imposed on Serbia in May 1992 and had been progressively strengthened throughout 1993, to the extent that by the end of that year, ' ... Serbia had achieved the dubious distinction of exceeding the inflation rate of Weimar Germany in the early 1920s and unemployment had more than doubled' (Thomas, 1999, pp. 164–5). The international community was keen now to cast Milošević as a man of peace with whom they could do business. The Serbs in Kosovo were less than reassured. Their sense of insecurity was heightened as they witnessed Bosnian Serbs leaving Bosnia and recalled the exodus of the Krajina Serbs. They worried that Milošević's commitment to their cause would prove similarly flexible. For the Kosovo Albanians, Dayton was a wake-up call:

> Suddenly Kosovo Albanians realized that passive resistance had failed as a strategy. They were not to be rewarded – in fact, they felt themselves penalized for eschewing violence.
>
> (Judah, 1999, p. 12)

Richard Holbrooke remains defiant that the exclusion of Kosovo from the Dayton process did not adversely affect developments later in the province:

> Kosovo would have happened anyway, and it is the part of the mythology that Dayton was responsible and I don't believe it. What really drove this thing was Rugova's failure to produce results and the Serb crackdown.
>
> (Cited in Judah, 2000, p. 124)

This is a harsh judgement indeed upon Rugova as it is clear that the failure of Dayton to address the Kosovo question radicalized Albanian nationalist sentiment. Caplan speculates that a possible further reason that Kosovo was not considered at Dayton was that 'in the absence of war in Kosovo it was thought that there was no urgent need to deal with the question' (Caplan, 1998, p. 751). This point is appreciated by Freedman too: 'a conflict boiling over into violence can capture international attention; one merely simmering can be put off for another day' (Freedman, 2000, p. 346). If this was so, then the situation was to be rectified. Rugova's policy of persistent patience now lay in tatters. The international community had ignored Kosovo, still maintaining that it should receive only 'special status' within Yugoslavia given its majority ethnic Albanian population. Such 'status' was in accordance with Helsinki norms of human rights observation and the creation of a pluralistic political culture and civil society. It was viewed as completely inadequate by the Kosovo Albanians who saw no end to their repression while other ethnic majority populations within the FRY had won statehood or, like the Republika Srpska in Bosnia, had attained a high degree of autonomy through the use of arms. Consequently,

'Kosovo's Albanians increasingly lost faith in the patient ways of their leadership and gravitated towards arms struggle' (Caplan, 1998, p. 752). Moreover, the KLA was soon in a position to wage such a struggle. In the spring of 1997, the Albanian state imploded following the collapse of financial pyramid schemes. The Albanian army similarly collapsed leading to the theft of much military material left unguarded in arsenals throughout the country. Using monies gathered from the Albanian diaspora, the KLA bought such weaponry and began a more substantive campaign of armed resistance against the Yugoslav forces within Kosovo. In turn, Milošević launched a repressive counter-insurgency strategy in the spring of 1998.

## Milošević returns to the Kosovo issue

Milošević was faced with other difficulties too. Despite the suspension of sanctions against Yugoslavia as part of the Dayton Agreement, Serbia still was experiencing economic hardship. Excluded from the International Monetary Fund, and with industrial unrest besetting the country throughout the spring of 1996, Milošević attempted to reassert his authority within Serbia. In November 1996, local election results confirmed that Milošević's Socialists were losing support to a coalition of opposition political parties. Milošević refused to recognize the results which led to mass daily protests on the streets of Belgrade (see Thomas, 1999, pp. 285–318 for coverage of this 'Happening of the Citizens'). The international community, principally the OSCE and the Council of Europe, beseeched their 'man of peace' to recognize the democratically expressed will of the people and endorse the electoral results. Milošević remained intransigent and held out until the end of February 1997 when he finally acquiesced in the face of continuing widespread popular unrest and protest. Despite such domestic difficulties, Milošević was immeasurably helped by the other political parties as they could not manage their internal divisions to present a consistent and coherent opposition to his rule. In addition, the leading opposition figures were as committed as Milošević to the maintenance of Serbian control of Kosovo. It was to the issue of Kosovo that Milošević now turned to restore his credibility and political fortunes:

> He calculated that, as on previous occasions in his career, the rhetoric and symbolism of nationalism could be used to rally popular support behind him.
>
> (Thomas, 1999, p. 405)

Any fear that the international community would look dimly upon still greater repression of the Kosovo Albanians arguably was lessened when the US envoy to the Balkans, Robert Gelbard, told a press conference on 23 February 1998 that the KLA was nothing more than a terrorist group. However unintentionally, this disclosure was regarded 'as being a "green light" for a security crackdown in Kosovo' (Thomas, 1999, p. 406).

### The international community and the Kosovo crisis

The international community reacted promptly to the latest Serbian campaign in Kosovo but it remained hamstrung to a certain extent by its persistent view that Kosovo was and should remain a part of Serbia:

> ... We have made it very clear to Milošević and the Kosovars that we do not support independence for Kosovo – that we want Serbia out of Kosovo, not Kosovo out of Serbia.
>
> (Madeleine Albright, cited in Weller, 1999b, p. 278)

This commitment to the principle of territorial integrity was backed by a fear that the granting of independence to Kosovo would lead to challenges from ethnic majority populations elsewhere within the international order. In addition, it was feared that the instability within the Balkans would spread, especially with the pressure of huge refugee flows into neighbouring countries, particularly Albania and Macedonia. There were fears that this relatively contained conflict would 'spill over' and possibly drag in Albania, Bulgaria and, most pointedly, the two NATO allies Greece and Turkey. However, as the Serb campaign continued with no diminution of its ferocity, it became increasingly difficult to maintain that Serbia had jurisdiction over a population whose rights it systematically and most brutally violated. As time passed the case for respecting such state sovereignty was weakening while the view that there existed 'a moral duty' to intervene grew steadily stronger.

Throughout the summer of 1998, the UN Security Council and the Contact Group repeatedly urged Milošević to heed the demands of the international community. He was to withdraw Serbian Special Forces from Kosovo, to facilitate the return of displaced peoples and to enter into meaningful political talks with the ethnic Albanian leadership. Failure to comply with these demands would result in the use of military force against Serbia. At the end of September, the United States announced that it was reviewing the military means at its disposal for dealing with the Serbs, including the use of Cruise missiles (*Daily Telegraph*, 1 October 1998). In October, via UNSCR 1199, the United Nations announced that the situation in Kosovo represented a threat to international peace and security and demanded that the Serbs and Kosovo Albanians should start immediate talks. Also, in October, NATO issued an activation order– ActOrd– for air strikes if Milošević did not comply with the demands made upon him. By now 200,000 Kosovo Albanians had been displaced from their homes and many were living in mountain camps in appalling conditions. The approach of winter threatened an even greater humanitarian crisis. The international community, notably the Western powers, were increasingly coming to accept that Serbian sovereignty could and should be abrogated due to the state's persecution of its nominal citizens. Forcible humanitarian action thus was a legitimate response to this situation: 'the humanitarian situation constitutes a reason that can justify an exception to a rule, however strong and firm it might be' (Jacques Chirac, cited in the *International Herald Tribune*, 7 October 1998). Some states, however, were less convinced of the legality of such a position. China and Russia, in particular, were relatively more supportive of Serbian claims that as an independent state it had the right to tackle 'terrorism' how it saw fit within the boundaries of its own sovereign territory. The Russians insisted that any military action against Serbia would require another UN Security Council Resolution for authorization and made it clear that they would use their veto to ensure that such a resolution would never pass:

> The Russian government finds it necessary to emphasize that the use of force against a sovereign state without an appropriate sanction from the Security Council would be a gross violation of the UN Charter and would torpedo the system of international relations.
> (Russian government statement aired on ITAR-TASS and cited in the
> *Daily Telegraph*, 5 October 1998)

Nevertheless, despite such public rhetoric in support of their Orthodox kin, privately Russian politicians were saying something much different. Judah cites Holbrooke recounting the words of the Russian Foreign Minister Igor Ivanov telling a collection of others involved in the diplomatic efforts at resolution that: 'If you take it to the UN, we'll veto it. If you don't we'll just denounce you'. As Judah concludes, 'the Russians had, in effect, told NATO that it would do nothing if it were to bomb' (Judah, 2000, p. 183). The Russian position is explicable when one considers the leverage that was used against them. The US was quick to point out that the substantial financial assistance given to Russia should not be treated as an independent variable in any calculations about whom it should support in this matter. In addition, 'the Russian establishment had never forgiven Milošević for his support of the coup plotters who sided against Boris Yeltsin ... in 1991' (Judah, 2000, p. 272).

The Serb response to the demands of the international community was to engage in brinkmanship, moving heavy artillery from time to time while maintaining that the doctrine of state sovereignty should be respected. Throughout the crisis the Contact Group, originally established to coordinate policy on Bosnia, remained involved in diplomatic efforts at resolution. The involvement of the Contact Group proved useful as it afforded a role to Russia which had better relations with Serbia than many of the Western powers. In October 1998, Milošević made an agreement with the American envoy, Richard Holbrooke, wherein he agreed to respect the demands of the international community on condition that NATO cancel its order of authorization for air strikes. Presumably recognizing Milošević's usual way of doing business, NATO merely suspended the order for the time being. As part of the deal, Milošević accepted the presence of the KVM (Kosovo Verification Mission) of the OSCE within Kosovo. Initially there were hopes that the Holbrooke deal would hold; as an unnamed American diplomat noted:

> We're getting very positive signs. There is increasing evidence that 40,000 Serbian police have pulled out. More of the military is returning to base. But we're concerned about increasing signs of the KLA.
> (*Daily Telegraph*, 28 October 1998)

The diplomat was right to be concerned. As and when the Serbian forces pulled out, the KLA moved in to take possession of the territory. Ultimately, the Holbrooke deal did not hold. The Serbs refused to respect it and continued their campaign of repression against the KLA and the general population of Kosovo Albanians. The discovery in January 1999 at Racak of a mass grave of Kosovo Albanian civilians was testimony to the continuation of the Serbian 'counter-insurgency' strategy. The fact that such an atrocity was carried out while the KVM was within the province undermined the efficacy of the OSCE. Moreover, when the head of the KVM, William Walker, accused the

Serbs of 'a crime against humanity' in Racak he was promptly declared *persona non grata* by the Serb government which insisted that the KLA had faked the Racak incident. The KVM reflected poorly on the ability of the OSCE to play a proactive conflict-prevention role in a theatre of ongoing conflict. Although it managed to attain some ceasefires between the warring parties these inevitably proved to be less than complete and of very short duration. During the deployment of the KVM, which incidentally never reached the initial figures, killings and abductions on both sides were commonplace, and seemed to prove the sound judgement of John Sandrock, the head of the OSCE advance party, when he stated that 'we are unarmed and can operate only in a benign environment. We will not penetrate an area where there is hostile action' (*Daily Telegraph*, 19 October 1998). It was clear that the remit of the KVM could not possibly be executed in such a hostile situation. The deployment of the KVM, however, did serve a purpose as 'the fact that the KVM was tried, and failed, was an important step in building consensus for the eventual use of force' (Judah, 2000, p. 188).

Given the apparent failure of the diplomatic process to resolve the Kosovo crisis, steps were being taken to facilitate the use of force against Serbia. US Secretary of State Albright commented, 'one of the keys of good diplomacy is knowing when diplomacy has reached its limits and we are rapidly reaching that point in Kosovo' (*Daily Telegraph*, 9 October 1998). It appeared by now that the Milošević government no longer cared about its portrayal in the West. The head of the International Criminal Tribunal for the former Yugoslavia, Judge Louise Arbour, was refused entry to Serbia and Western television screens continued to be dominated by scenes of human loss and misery. Faced with the defiance of the Serbs, the suffering of the Kosovo Albanians and growing public outrage at the lack of action, it was becoming increasingly apparent to the international community that 'something' had to be done.

Thus using the prospect of an even greater humanitarian catastrophe, in late January 1999 the North Atlantic Council informed Milošević that either he complied fully with the Holbrooke agreement or Serbia would be subject to air strikes (Weller, 1999b, p. 416). The Kosovo Albanians were informed that they too were to heed the international community's calls for meaningful dialogue between the two parties or else NATO would 'take all appropriate measures' to address such a failure. Thus the North Atlantic Council's statement of 30 January 1999 was clear: the Serbs and the Kosovo Albanians were instructed to present themselves at Rambouillet, outside of Paris, so that a diplomatic settlement of their conflict could be made:

The crisis in Kosovo remains a threat to peace and security in the region. NATO's strategy is to halt the violence and support the completion of negotiations on an interim political settlement, thus averting a humanitarian catastrophe. Steps to this end must include acceptance by both parties of the summons to begin negotiations at Rambouillet by 6th February 1999 and the completion of the negotiations on an interim political settlement within the specified timeframe ...

(Cited in Weller, 1999a, pp. 222–223)

## The Rambouillet Conference

In the face of such threats, both the Serbs and the Kosovo Albanians agreed to participate at the Rambouillet Conference. The ethnic Albanians were not immune to threats issued towards them either, namely that the KLA would be regarded by the international community as a terrorist outfit and all efforts would be made to stifle their profitable drugs trade. Given the amount of coercion used to get both sides to the negotiating table, and most importantly, the fact that neither side had tired of their war, the prospects for a successful and durable agreement at Rambouillet were slight indeed. Judah cites the astute observation of a British Foreign Office member concerning the contrast between Dayton and Rambouillet:

> In Bosnia everyone was ready – they were all exhausted. And, don't forget that three peace plans had already failed before we got to Dayton. The problem here is that we are trying to get them to agree to a deal before the war has really started. What we are concerned on is a deal. It ought to satisfy both sides if they are rational about it ... but both sides have not yet fought each other to a standstill ...'

(Judah, 2000, p. 198)

In effect, then, there was no 'hurting stalemate' to urge the protagonists to make a peace. The Rambouillet Conference did not make the most auspicious beginning due to the absence of the Albanian delegation. Some of the KLA contingent within the Albanian negotiating team were still in the field and, moreover, they lacked passports. The announcement by the Serb delegates that they intended to arrest such 'criminals' if and when they arrived did little to create a mutually reassuring diplomatic environment. In the event, carrying French-issued visas, the Albanian delegation was eventually brought to Rambouillet. Still the climate was one of a tragi-farce: having declared that they would not talk to the Albanian delegates due to the inclusion of the KLA in its ranks, the Serbs now demanded that they would only enter into talks on a face-to-face basis. Within the Albanian ranks, there were tensions between its different factions. It included LDK and government-in-exile members, and representatives from the KLA among others, and, as previously, noted there were serious intra-Albanian differences of opinion concerning the way ahead. The negotiating teams were presented with two documents at Rambouillet. The first was a set of 'non-negotiable principles' and 'basic elements' which they had to accept. The material was based on the commitment to the territorial integrity of Yugoslavia, the need for the protection and promotion of human rights within Kosovo and the position that any emergent agreement from the conference would be an interim one for three years. The second paper was the Interim Agreement for Peace and Self-Government in Kosovo and it was concerned with the need for a permanent ceasefire and the political structures for a post-conflict Kosovo (see Weller, 1999a, for details on such contents). Attempts to reach a settlement failed, despite the extension of the conference, because of two central issues. Firstly, the Kosovo Albanian delegation would not sign up to an interim agreement which did not contain a mechanism for the review of the whole procedure at the end of the set three-year period. Effectively, if the implementation of the agreement did not also make provision for a referendum at the end of the set period, then there was no hope of satisfying the expressed popular will for self-determination. The Serbs refused to accept Annex B which provided for the deployment of a NATO force on the grounds that they opposed the presence of foreign troops on Serbian sovereign territory. Despite the Contact Group granting a time-extension to the conference, it thus proved impossible to reach a deal. However, the Albanian Kosovo delegation noted that they would indeed sign the deal, with the inclusion of an independence referendum at the end of the three-year period, following time to consult their constituents at home. Their letter to the conference hosts made their position clear:

> This declaration is given with full consensus. The delegation of Kosova with consensus understands that it will sign the agreement in two weeks after consultations with the people of Kosova, political and military institutions.
>
> (Judah, 2000, p. 218)

In light of this development and in an effort to encourage Serbia to adopt a more constructive approach to the proposed settlement, a round of follow-up talks was organized in Paris from 15 March. On the opening day of the talks, the Kosovo Albanians declared their willingness to sign the agreement. However, they were prevailed upon to delay their signing as the diplomats sought to give more time and space to the Serbian delegation in a bid to obtain their endorsement of the agreement (Weller, 1999a, p. 234). Far from signing the agreement, the Serbian delegation attempted to supplant it with an entirely revised document, as one of the international diplomats present explains:

> ... it presented on the first day its own version of the Agreement. The fact that the first change proposed in that version was to strike the word 'peace' from the title did not augur well for the acceptance of the Rambouillet accord.
>
> (Weller, 1999a, p. 234)

After three days, the Kosovo Albanian delegation signed the agreement but the Serbian negotiating team refused to do so. The scene was set for a resort to military force to prove that the diplomatic objectives of the international community would not be denied as the statement of the Chairmen of the Rambouillet/Paris process counselled:

> We solemnly warn the authorities in Belgrade against any military offensive on the ground and any impediment to the freedom of movement and of action of the KVM, which would contravene their commitments. Such violations would have the gravest consequences.
>
> (Cited in Weller, 1999a, p. 236)

## The bombing of Serbia

Prior to the onset of military measures against Serbia, a final attempt at diplomacy was made. On 22 March Holbrooke and the other diplomats visited Milošević in Belgrade to urge him to accept the Rambouillet Agreement. They received a less than favourable welcome when, according to Holbrooke, Milošević informed him somewhat fatalistically:

> No more engagement, no more negotiations, I understand that, you will bomb us. You are a great and powerful country, there is nothing we can do about it.
>
> (Holbrooke, *Newsnight*, 20 August 1999)

Two days earlier the KVM left Kosovo for Macedonia aware that their mission was completely untenable by now. On 24 March NATO began its campaign against Yugoslavia because 'all efforts to achieve a negotiated, political settlement to the Kosovo crisis having failed, no alternative is open but to take military action' (Solana, quoted in the *Daily Telegraph*, 23 March 1999).

Stating its *casus belli* as a wish to avert a humanitarian catastrophe, NATO reactivated the pending ACTORD and initiated its aerial bombardment of Serbia. Deterrence strategies clearly had failed. Now a coercive strategy would be deployed to force Milošević to comply with the oft-stated demands of the international community. Given the way in which the issue of Kosovo had been exploited by Milošević in his political career, its centrality in Serbian mythology and Serbians' self-perception of themselves as stalwart rebels against any foreign yoke, it was perhaps unsurprising that Milošević opted for war:

> NATO political leaders seem to have blinded themselves to how the Serbs would react to the threat and the actuality of a bombing campaign. The Serbs have always been proud of their ability to fight in defence of their interests and their capacity to absorb punishment.
>
> (MccGwire, 2000, p. 19)

While the humanitarian impulse may have afforded NATO the legal grounds for intervention, there were other factors which came into play. In terms of its credibility and institutional relevance, NATO could not afford to ignore the crisis in Kosovo. Judah notes that NATO leaders were aware of the credibility issue, citing a report circulated at the annual Anglo-German Konigswinter Conference which explicitly noted that: 'NATO's credibility will be destroyed if it dithers indefinitely and fails to deliver on its threats' (Judah, 2000, p. 235). There were other factors too which influenced NATO's decision to use force. NATO had not emerged from the Bosnian debacle with any great credit. In particular its refusal to supply supporting troops to assist UN troops in their protection of the supposedly 'safe' areas of Srebrenica had led to an institutional 'sense of revulsion and guilt' (MccGwire, 2000, p. 13). Although ultimately NATO 'had managed to contain the Bosnian conflict and bring it to some sort of conclusion [this was] only after being witness to terrible suffering – and Dayton hardly constituted a "lasting settlement"' (Freedman, 2000, p. 345). Moreover, NATO arguably was anxious to ground its new strategic concept, unveiled at its 50th birthday party in April. NATO now was able to act without specific authorization from the UN. Its aerial campaign against Serbia was legitimate, therefore, in its own eyes at least, as it was covered by the spirit of UNSCR 1160 and UNSCR 1199 if not the actual letter of a new targeted resolution (MccGwire, 2000, p. 9).

The onset of Operation Allied Force had the effect of boosting support within Serbia for Milošević. A 'blitz spirit' descended upon Belgrade as the people rallied to publicly demonstrate their defiance of Serbia's latest potential 'overlords'. While Milošević undertook measures to suppress internal dissent from the media, the intelligentsia or any other quarters, there were mass rallies to demonstrate public support, though it is arguable that these were demonstrative of defiance of NATO rather than displays of endorsement for Milošević's regime. If the Alliance had hoped that its action would create an anti-Milošević movement and lead to his downfall, they were unfamiliar with the lessons of history:

> Indeed, a recurring historical lesson is that attempts to force an adversary's hand by targeting its populace's will to resist may backfire. Coercion often stiffens an adversary's determination, as the leadership and the country as a whole unite against the coercer.
> (Byman and Waxman, 2000, p. 20)

While Milošević may have suppressed dissent at home, in most of the domestic constituencies of NATO member states the CNN effect was increasingly influential. The televisual scenes of hundreds of thousands of Kosovo Albanian refugees fleeing into Albania and Macedonia and the piteous plight of those displaced to the mountains of Kosovo led to increased public support for the perceived morality of NATO's action. In general Western populaces had already concluded that the Serbs were the villains of the piece given the earlier coverage of the Balkan Wars: 'this was not wholly unfair given the history of Yugoslavia's dissolution and their superior military strength as the bullies and instigators of the practices of "ethnic cleansing"' (Freedman, 2000, p. 344).

Some commentators attributed blame to NATO for the increased flow of refugees: as Jamie Shea acknowledges, 'we were faced by accusations of turning a disaster into a catastrophe' (Judah, 2000, p. 253), but others have found that it was evidence of Serb pre-planning in the event of air strikes. Throughout the months of diplomacy leading to the use of force, Belgrade had increased its military forces in the region and had adopted a policy of forcibly reducing the Albanian Kosovan population to a level that would assure the manageability of the unruly province (Freedman, 2000, p. 352). The Potkova 'horseshoe plan' is cited as irrefutable proof that the Serbs were ready to increase their efforts at reducing the indigenous Albanian community in Kosovo. While this renewed campaign to expel them was more savage following the onset of NATO's airstrikes, the culpability for the refugees' situation lies with Belgrade: 'the evidence then is reasonably conclusive. It is not the case that NATO airstrikes prompted the campaign against the Kosovan Albanians' (ibid., p. 352). The level of public support among the populaces of the West meant that when NATO made 'mistakes' such as the bombing of refugee convoys, a television station in Serbia and the Chinese Embassy in Belgrade, these generally were treated as genuine errors rather than as evidence of NATO personnel acting deliberately. The fog of war, it seemed, was sufficient explanation for most television audiences and newspaper readers: 'if anything the Western public got more bored with the war, as it acquired a routine quality, than indignant. When bombs went astray they saw it as evidence of ineptitude but not malevolence' (ibid., p. 356).

The aerial campaign against Serbia lasted for 78 days during which over 30,000 missions were flown and a total of 25,000 bombs, both 'smart' and ordinary campaign, were dropped. When considering why Milošević opted for war, it is speculated that he, like the leaders of the West, believed that the campaign would be short, a matter of days rather than weeks or months. Possibly basing his calculations on the precedent of Desert Fox against Iraq in December 1998, Milošević thought that he could endure such a short offensive and accrue benefits in its wake (Judah, 2000, pp. 228–9). Possibly too he believed that the 'body-bags' effect would limit the Alliance, particularly the US, in its conduct of the war. In a sense, this may have been the case as far as a ground war was concerned but given the high aerial tactics of NATO, the prospect of Alliance personnel casualties receded as the campaign progressed. Milošević's gamble for war may also have been influenced by his faith in his Russian ally and in potential internal dissension within NATO. As noted previously, Russia's support for Serbia was hardly resolute given its wish for financial assistance from the West, and the prospect of NATO paralysed by internal division did not materialize. Greece appeared to assume a more pro-Serbian stance than its NATO colleagues if one takes the popular demonstrations against NATO as conclusive evidence of the government's position but, in fact, the Greek administration 'made the crude calculation that it feared the Turks more than it liked the Serbs' (ibid., 2000, p. 254). Indeed, like the Russians, the Greeks adopted a public/private dichotomy in their attitude towards the Serbs, a fact appreciated by an unnamed NATO source:

The Greeks were wonderful. We understood their situation. Their leaders made fiery speeches in Greece which we didn't mind and in exchange they never broke the consensus. They worked very hard with their bilateral contacts with the Serbs and with Milošević but in the end, they realised there was no alternative strategy.

(Ibid.)

Milošević's hopes for NATO division were not to be realized: cohesion increased as the campaign intensified and 'the NATO campaign did not so much sputter and die as take on an added intensity of its own' (Freedman, 2000, p. 356). That is not to say that there were not debates within the organization. One of the most central of these concerned the most appropriate military strategy for the situation. While some were committed to air strikes, others favoured the committal of ground troops. In retrospect, some commentators have claimed that the surrender of Milošević proves that air power coercive strategies are the way ahead for dealing with recalcitrant leaders who ignore the international community. However, as Byman and Waxman note, it is more accurate to see Milošević's capitulation as a consequence of several factors:

... the bombing of strategic targets inside Serbia, the threat of a ground invasion, and the failure of Serb counter-coercive strategies against NATO countries (particularly Belgrade's inability to gain Moscow's support) contributed greatly to the success of coercion.

(Byman and Waxman, 2000, p. 17)

Thus the threat of a ground offensive was sufficient, in tandem with other factors, to force Milošević to concede defeat. Despite some misgivings, especially in the initial stages of the campaign, this was a credible threat. NATO already had troops stationed in Macedonia as an 'extraction force' for the earlier KVM and throughout the air strikes these were reinforced. Although US President Clinton had said at the start of NATO action, 'I do not intend to put our troops in Kosovo to fight a war', the British Prime Minister Tony Blair was a public advocate of a ground invasion and as the campaign progressed President Clinton made it clear that 'all options are on the table'. Indeed, 'Milošević came to terms on the day that President Bill Clinton planned to discuss ground options with his US generals' (Byman and Waxman, 2000, p. 26). Despite the conjuncture of several factors influencing Milošević's decision, however, there remains a tendency to believe in the infallibility of air strikes as a conflict-resolution strategy, especially as high-level flights protect the pilots concerned. Cohen wryly explains the comfort of such a view: 'Air power is an unusually seductive form of military strength, in part because, like modern courtship, it appears to offer gratification without commitment' (Cohen, 1994, p. 109).

On 9 June, Milošević accepted a peace deal brokered by the Russian envoy Viktor Chernomyrdin, a former Russian premier, and President Martti Ahtisaari of Finland. NATO air strikes were suspended on 10 June, the same day as UNSCR 1244 was passed authorizing NATO troops to enter Kosovo while guaranteeing the sovereignty of Yugoslavia. An interesting postscript to the conclusion of the military campaign was the departure of 200 Russian troops from SFOR in Bosnia to 'secure' the Slatina airport in Kosovo. Judah notes the claim that this action was taken to facilitate a Russian presence in the north of Kosovo which would allow Milošević to retain that area if Kosovo were to be partitioned in the future. Whether or not this is the case, it was hardly an auspicious sign when 'within days, the Russian troops at the airport had to ask the British for bread' (Judah, 2000, p. 285).

Milošević attempted to 'spin' the story of surrender in his tele-visual address:

> Our nation is a hero. That may be the shortest conclusion about this war ... Earlier this year there were numerous rallies throughout our country. One slogan could have been heard there: we won't give up Kosovo. We haven't given up Kosovo ...
>
> (Quoted in Judah, 2000, p. 285)

Despite de jure Yugoslav sovereignty over Kosovo, there is little doubt that de facto sovereignty rests with those international institutions now administering the province.

### The Institutional Governance of Kosovo

The temporary governance of Kosovo is under the central authority of the UN via UNMIK (UN Interim Administration Mission in Kosovo. Its mandate is UNSCR 1244 from June 1999 which orders the withdrawal of Yugoslav forces from Kosovo, the return of displaced persons, the demilitarization of the KLA and the creation of a multi-ethnic province with 'substantial autonomy and self-governance'. UNMIK is assisted by an international military presence, KFOR, made up of NATO and non-NATO countries including Russia. The OSCE is present to assist in the creation of democratic governmental structures and civil society.

One of the first priorities for UNMIK was to facilitate the return of refugees. In the first year of its operation, 1,300,000 displaced persons have returned to the province (Robertson, 2000). While the return of Kosovo Albanians has been welcomed, new refugees have been created as the Serbian migration has increased substantially. The responsibility for the safety of those who remain is assumed by KFOR which currently allocates over half of its manpower to ensuring that ethnic minorities, primarily though not exclusively Serbs, are defended from attack by ethnic Albanians. KFOR was responsible too for the demilitarization of the KLA. It confiscated and destroyed any illegally held weaponry found either through the discovery of arms dumps or through the searching of individuals. By December 1999, 10,000 weapons had been decommissioned but there remained fears that former KLA members had retained some of their arms. The transfer of KLA personnel and armaments over the common border with Macedonia demonstrated that such fears had proved well-founded. The KLA has been stood down with some of its membership joining the KPC (Kosovo Protection Corps), 'a civilian organisation designed to assist the people of Kosovo in the event of man-made or natural disasters'. There have been charges, however, that KPC members are responsible for attacks on indigenous Serbs and other ethnic minorities. One area, in particular, remains a place of high inter-ethnic tension. The city of Mitrovica has become an enclave of Kosovo Serbs and is a regular scene of inter-communal protest and violence, and UNMIK have appointed a regional administrator there to try to build up inter-communal confidence. As the incidents of ethnic violence are still continuing, it would seem that the task is far from complete. Jean-Marie Guehenno, the Under-Secretary for Peace-Keeping Operations, has noted that Kosovan Serbs 'suffer disproportionately from major crimes and ethnically-motivated acts of intimidation' (*Daily Telegraph*, 22 June 2001). In areas of ongoing ethnic conflict, UNIP (UN International Police) has been deployed. While the OSCE and the UNHCR (July 1999) have lamented the creation of 'mono-ethnic enclaves', it would appear that NATO views such a development as a legitimate method of conflict management. On a NAC fact-finding mission to Kosovo in July 2000, Roberston put forward an arguably strange strategy for the protection of an inclusive multi-ethnic society:

> Don't underestimate our determination. We are going to protect a multi-ethnic society here and we'll do it if necessary by making sure that the individual groups are protected in their homes and communities. If it involves building walls around them, giving them the protection they need, then we'll do it.
>
> (Robertson, 2000)

Although the level of criminal activity within Kosovo has fallen, it remains of great concern to the international bodies. Trafficking in drugs, weaponry and women are the central problems. UNMIK has attributed the inability to tackle such crime forcefully to the shortage of police and judges within Kosovo. To this end, efforts have been made to create a multi-ethnic police force and judiciary. The OSCE established a police school in September 1999 and has striven to deliver an ethnically representative police force. To date, over 1,000 officers have graduated and while some members of minority communities have joined, ethnic Albanians constitute its majority. UNMIK has appointed over 100 new judges and prosecutors for the municipal courts. Again, most of the judiciary has an ethnic Albanian background as Serbs have been reluctant to participate.

In order to restore autonomy to Kosovo, measures are currently under way to establish a provincial assembly. Robertson (2000) has noted, however, that local leaders from all communities must demonstrate 'their commitment to the goal of a fair and multi-ethnic Kosovo'. Municipal elections were held on 28 October 2000. The OSCE played the lead role in UNMIK's Civil and Voter Registration process. Despite declaring its first phase to be a success, it was boycotted by Serbs in the province. Other institutional apparatus, such as the JIAS (Joint Interim Administrative Structures), which were designed to foster bi-communal governance, were similarly boycotted by their Serb members at times. Through such testing times, the international institutions concerned remained committed to the creation of a multi-ethnic polity within Kosovo. The ousting of Milošević from power and the assumption of office by the Kostunica administration improved the prospects for the realization of this end goal. The present Serbian government has publicly declared its support for a multi-ethnic, self-governing province and has urged Kosovar Serbs to participate in the province-wide elections of mid-November 2001. In addition, Kosovar Serbs, supported by the Belgrade administration, are represented on the Joint Working Group on the Legal Framework for Provisional Self-Government.

It is clear that the problems in Kosovo are far from resolved, however, with sporadic inter-ethnic violence continuing. It is obvious that the international institutions present are there for the foreseeable future. There have been appeals to the international community to provide further support and funding for the reconstruction project:

> It is in the international community's interest to provide the necessary resources, both personnel and funds to overcome the existing

shortfalls. Governments, including NATO governments, must do more in this respect.

(Robertson, 2000)

The road to building a multi-ethnic, self-governing Kosovo will be difficult. There are elements within the Albanian community who have not surrendered their aspirations for self-determination. Thus far, the international community has emphasized to the Albanians that the state boundaries within the region are not subject to change. Significantly, in April 2001, the head of UNMIK, Hans Haekkerup, stressed that there would not be a referendum to decide the status of Kosovo within the foreseeable future. He noted that UNSCR 1244 makes no mention of a referendum and that while the Rambouillet Agreement refers to the will of the people within the province, it does not detail how this is to be expressed. He concluded that:

> The issue of final status has to be negotiated by the future leaders of Kosovo with the international community.
>
> (*Daily Telegraph*, 19 April 2001)

This commitment to the territorial integrity of the states within the region has been strengthened by the spillover of ethnic tension into neighbouring Macedonia in 2001. Macedonia had managed to avoid violent internal dissension during the collapse of the former Yugoslavia. During the war in Kosovo, however, the indigenous Albanian community within the republic was radicalized in their attitudes towards the state. The ethnic Albanian community within Macedonia constitutes a significant minority at almost one-third of the population. The exodus of Kosovar Albanians into Macedonia increased this community both in terms of numbers and its desire for a new set of arrangements within the state. The transfer of KLA troops and armaments over the common border led to overt political violence in a number of cities. Such developments exacerbated already existing inter-ethnic tensions within Macedonia. In 1998, a US State Department Report had explicitly noted the prevailing situation:

> Ethnic tensions and prejudices are present in society. The Government is committed to a policy of peaceful integration of all ethnic groups in society but faces political resistance and the persistence of popular

prejudices. Parts of the political opposition object to even modest steps to meet the needs of ethnic minorities.

(US State Department, 1998)

Ethnic Albanians suffered discrimination in terms of welfare and educa-tion provision, land sales and employment within the public services, notably the police and security forces. As the international community managed to reduce levels of political violence within Kosovo, it appeared as if the conflict was being reborn within Macedonia. During the war in Kosovo, the Macedonian government had permitted NATO troops to be stationed on its territory but, notwithstanding such actions, there was consistent anti-Western feeling among sections of both political and popular opinion. There were fears that the Western powers would coerce the administration into a settlement with the ethnic Albanians. The emergence of the NLA (National Liberation Army) and the state's attempt to deal with this challenge to its authority solely by military means alarmed the West. The Macedonian Army was holding off the Nationalist Liberation Army in general but, especially in north-western Kosovo, the ethnic Macedonian community was suffering the effects of ongoing clashes between the two sides. Returning to the notion of a moment of 'ripeness' as a prerequisite for successful mediation, this intra-state conflict arguably had not reached this stage. Instead, the international community was insistent that there should be no evolution into a full-scale civil war within the republic. Preventive intervention was required to stop the igniting of inter-communal war engulfing the region once again. Essentially, the standpoint of the international community was that the government in Macedonia had to implement the constitutional safeguards for minority ethnic communities in general and, specifically, had to augment the rights of the indigenous Albanians. Initially, the Macedonian government did not respond positively to such insistences. Both the Interior and the Defence Ministers, Vlado Buckovski and Ljube Boskovski, stated that the NLA had to retreat from its positions as an unconditional precursor to negotiations on political matters (*The Guardian*, 26 July 2001). As NATO Secretary-General Robertson and EU foreign policy leader Solana engaged in a round of shuttle diplomacy in the region, there were large anti-Western demonstrations, including the storming of the Macedonian parliament on 25 July 2001. Populist percep-tions, fuelled by local media and political hardliners, believed that the government would be forced to 'sell out' the Macedonian people in the face of international pressure. This radicalization of Macedonian senti-ment directly affected the work of the international institutions within

Kosovo as the Macedonian government closed its border with the province, cutting off supply lines for troops and other personnel. The fear of the indigenous Macedonian people and their government was that the nationalist calls for more rights for the ethnic Albanians inevitably would lead to the break-up of their state. Danilo Gligorovski, a member of parliament from the main governing party, the VMRO, expressed such fears:

> I have no problem giving Albanians any number of rights. What I am against, however, is the never-ending story until a Greater Albania comes.
>
> (*Daily Telegraph*, 30 August 2001)

Despite such misgivings within the elite and masses, the Macedonian government did succumb to Western pressure, not least to its economic leverage. They agreed to restart the political process and to implement a ceasefire with the NLA. The issue of the decommissioning of the NLA arsenal became a sticking point, much as in the case of IRA arms within Northern Ireland. The NLA initially refused to surrender arms before the implementation of Albanian minority rights and an amnesty against prosecution for its soldiers. In the Ohrid Agreement, the Macedonian government agreed to expand the official usage of the Albanian language, agreed a minimum of minority votes for passing legislation in the parliament, and accepted the principle of increased Albanian representation within the police force. In return the NLA agreed to decommission and give their weapons to NATO troops in Operation Essential Harvest. This operation would be British-led and constitute a force of about 3,500. The agreement was rejected by a breakaway faction of the NLA, the ALA (Albanian National Army), who remained committed to continuing a war against the Macedonian state. Macedonia and the NLA now had their version of the Real IRA. In the light of this circumstance and the grudging accommodation of the central domestic actors, there was a notable lack of faith in the prospects for a successful operation. An anonymous Western official opined:

> This is going to be one of the hardest ever NATO missions and already, even at this planning stage, it's got 'disaster' written all over it.
>
> (*Daily Telegraph*, 11 August 2001)

Operation Essential Harvest was planned to last for only 30 days and to be withdrawn immediately if it came under fire. Given the need to institute and embed confidence-building measures to accomplish the mission, such a short stay seemed hopelessly inadequate. Inevitably parallels were drawn with the decommissioning of the KLA in Kosovo. In that case, the surrender of arms was clearly minimalist, given that much of it showed up in Macedonia, and two years on, KFOR had still not managed to close down cross-border transfers and could not guarantee security for the minority Serb and Roma communities. The planned short stay of the NATO troops in Macedonia did not accord either with the hopes of the NLA. Commander Matoshi stated its expectations clearly:

> We expect NATO to come for more than 30 days. In return for handing over arms, NATO will protect us from the Macedonian police.
> (*Daily Telegraph*, 18 August 2001)

Despite the ceasefire-in-place within Macedonia, there continued to be truce violations which demonstrated at least a partial lack of faith in the hopes for a peaceful resolution of the conflict. In order to keep the Macedonian authorities on side, and in keeping with the West's often-stated commitment to territorial integrity of the states within the region, NATO quickly reaffirmed the nature of the mission:

> It is not a peacekeeping mission. It is not an intervention force. It will not separate fighting parties. NATO will not do anything which could lead to partition.
> (Danish Major-General Gunnar Lange, commander of the disarma-ment forces, cited in the *Observer*, 19 August 2001)

The NLA honoured their commitment to surrender their weapons. NATO stated that it expected to receive 3,300 weapons in total; however, hardline Macedonian politicians insisted that this was a ridiculous underestimation of the NLA arsenal. They argued that 85,000 arms was more reasonable. This disparity in estimates was seized upon by the local media to demonstrate that NATO was biased in favour of the NLA and stoked popular perceptions that, far from removing weapons from the NLA, it was illicitly arming it:

> We've seen what they've done in Kosovo and Bosnia. They helped the Albanians and Bosnian Muslims and banished the Serbs. They're playing the same game here.
> (Macedonian civilian, quoted in the *Daily Telegraph*, 28 August 2001)

At the time of writing, NATO troops remain in Macedonia, in excess of the 30-day deadline. There are claims that they will remain until the end of 2001 at least. Sporadic inter-communal violence continues in north-western Macedonia, though at a lesser level than previously, leading to a growing consensus that a follow-on operation will be needed to keep the uneasy peace. The Macedonian parliament has agreed to seriously debate the granting of further rights for ethnic Albanians but there remains an implementation gap between what is said and what is practised. There is no general acceptance that the ethnic Albanian community should be accorded nationality status and so the Albanian Liberation Army continues to appeal to more radical espousers of a Greater Albania and may well appeal to moderates if the implementation gap is not overcome.

## Conclusion

'No one starts a war – or rather, no one in his senses ought to do so – without first being clear in his mind what he intends to achieve by that war and how he intends to conduct it' (Clausewitz, 1976, p. 579). This advice should be heeded by international institutions commencing upon interventions. The lesson of the interventions in the former Yugoslavia is the need for a strategy combining political objectives with agreed means and an exit pathway. While this may be true of all interventions it is arguable that the constraints of intra-state conflict make a clear political strategy an even greater imperative. The decentralized nature of authority in intra-state conflicts leaves international institutions with difficulties regarding accountability and responsibility. As the state itself can be a source of insecurity it may be of limited value as a partner to institutions. 'If the state cannot protect the interests of all ethnic groups, then each group will seek to control the state, decreasing the security of other groups and decreasing the ability of the state to provide security for any group' (Saideman, 1996, p. 23). Missions can then drift as the intervening forces become the authority to regulate the behaviour of factions within the state. Under Dayton it has been argued that the 'extension of the international institutional mechanisms of regulation during the process of democratisation, to transition to democracy and self rule, has meant that the Bosnian state bodies have had little influence over either policy development or its implementation' (Chandler, 1999, p. 64). This bodes ill for an early international departure from Bosnia. The problem for institutions is to determine the pace at which autonomy can be granted to Bosnia and the implementation of an exit strategy. The issue, whatever one's view of the international presence in Bosnia, is the timescale of the commitment. Kosovo, like Bosnia, also holds the potential for a long-term involvement of the international community and a difficult exit point.

The problem of finding an appropriate strategy for an intervention in the former Republic of Yugoslavia was caused by both the complexities of the local situation and differences of opinion among the key international players. In Bosnia and Kosovo interventions were affected by divergences over both objectives and means. The question of recognition divided the European Community's objectives toward the former Yugoslavia but, once settled, led to acute problems over policy. The question ceased to be whether self-determination should guide the policy of the international community but where would it end? Would it be for constituent republics or groups within such republics including the Kosovans? The principle in itself did not answer the question and local actors sought to implement an agenda that was not mutually acceptable. Divergences over the means of response to local conflict soon developed with respect to sanctions, air power and the humanitarian mission. Divergences facilitated brinkmanship and undermined the credibility of institutions. Indeed the credibility of NATO became an issue for the Alliance which complicated the intervention and relations with the UN in coordinating the mission. The presence of Russia, Greece and Turkey brought wider security agendas into the equation which further complicated the role of institutions. The mission to the former Yugoslavia became the 'art of the possible' rather than the desirable. Relationships had to be found with the erstwhile 'enemy' Milošević while the media called for action and deterrent threats failed. The 'possible' became a series of strategies responding to the local crises. Proactive or preventive strategies were not realized in preparation for Croatian or Bosnian independence. An important exception was the UN deployment of a preventive peacekeeping force in Macedonia (UNPREDEP) in 1993. The force, composed firstly of Canadians then Scandinavians and US troops, exhibited a foresight absent from the other interventions in the former Yugoslavia. As we have seen, however, subsequent events in Macedonia demonstrated that the spillover of ethnic tension may not be an immediate process. Foresight needs to look to the longer term if prevention is to prove successful. This critique is not to denigrate the efforts of those involved in UNPROFOR and the pursuit of a viable peace; it is rather to point to the challenges for institutions to become real security providers in the new Europe.

# 7
# Conclusion

The nature of international order has profoundly changed since the Cold War. The Cold War was structured by superpower confrontation which dominated firstly European and then secondly global politics. The Soviet system of formal and informal empires was joined by the American strategy of containment which together demarcated respective spheres of influence. The system was mutually reinforcing in ideological, economic and strategic terms. The arms race and balance of nuclear forces sealed the confrontation and its immobilism. Détente institutionalized superpower conflict to secure stability but did not undermine the pillars of the Cold War order. In this structure of international order international institutions were, in the main, incapable of enhancing international security. The 'overlay' of superpower conflict reached out from the central balance of power to affect local and regional balances. The prospect of United Nations intervention was therefore diminished by superpower interest and potential veto. The world body was effectively paralysed except in a minority of cases where both Moscow and Washington saw the services of a UN operation as beneficial. A similar fate befell the CSCE which could not bridge the European divide and fulfil its Helsinki agenda. Institutions within the respective superpower 'blocs' were the focus of greater interest as they directly contributed to the superpower order. NATO and the EC, for example, had a demonstrable relevance within the Cold War system. Realism and neorealism were the prevalent analyses through which international order and institutions were judged. The intensification of economic agendas in the international system of the 1970s did reorientate attention to the management of interdependence, institutions and regimes but superpower confrontation remained an underlying theme of international order. It was only with the collapse of the Cold War system that international institutions could begin to fulfil their promise.

The United Nations, once freed from Cold War constraints, embarked on a scale of activity hitherto unseen. The CSCE could also begin to realize its pan-European role. NATO and the EC also began a process of rapid institutional change to sustain relevance in markedly different international conditions. The retreat of Moscow's influence in Europe left some institutions such as the Warsaw Treaty Organization without purpose and enhanced the relevance of others. The transition in America's global role and the growing regionalization of Washington's security interests has also affected the role of institutions. Organizations such as NATO and the EU have become more directly important for the structure of the international system rather than means to demarcate superpower spheres of interest. Institutions still face constraints and the United States clearly remains the 'core power' within NATO. While Cold War immobilism has ceased to inhibit global and regional organizations, political will is still a critical factor in determining action. The United Nations post-Cold War role has been constrained by funding and the international intervention in the former Yugoslavia was constrained by choice of means and intra-organizational difficulties. Member states or organizations may also face domestic constraints which can affect their policy position. It would also be an error to perceive of a world completely free from spheres of interest and open to institutional regulation. Moscow has sought to define the former Soviet Union as its sphere of influence. Intervention in the 'Near Abroad' has been stridently declared as Moscow's prerogative. The capacity of the OSCE to moderate Russian behaviour in the former Soviet Union has consequently been limited and a NATO intervention is unthinkable. NATO enlargement has re-inforced this 'dividing line' leaving areas such as the Baltic states in a highly sensitive position between their Western aspirations and Russia's desire to sustain its interests. Yugoslavia, largely due to Tito's policies, was a halfway house between East and West and therefore more open to the international community's actions.

Institutions have become more relevant to states as the nature of security has changed after the Cold War. The transition from threats to risks and the growing importance of political, societal and economic elements in security and stability have made the functions of institutions integral to order. Institutions can contribute to the regulation and management of economic transactions, set norms, rules and expectations for political behaviour and codify compliance. The importance of membership of institutions, such as NATO and the EU, to the states of Eastern and Central Europe is clear. The new security environment both permits and encourages the growth of institutions and their functions. In this new context absolute gains are seen as positive and the old agenda of security, dominated by the arms race and deterrence, which made relative gains a premium, has been eclipsed. Institutional development, adaptation and growth has dominated the post-Cold War era in Europe. The commitment given to institutional building by states is testimony to their importance. The EU integration agenda has been reinvigorated with respect to both 'deepening' and 'broadening' the institution. EU integration has not been a linear progression but new layers of commitment have been realized including the transition from CFSP to CEPSD. NATO has embraced a fundamental revision of its strategic rationale and opened its doors to new members. Both institutions have embraced an 'outreach' programme to the wider Europe including the Mediterranean region.

The institutional provision of security has therefore become a critical component of the contemporary European order. In the security community of Western Europe institutions have become the means by which member states resolve conflicts and deal with distributional issues. In this world institutions have increased in importance since the Cold War. Core powers remain important to institutions – Germany, France and Britain to the EU and the USA to NATO – and this is an important reflection of how such states see their interests being served. But placing those interests in an institutional context affects how those interests are both articulated and realized. The prism of institutional processes can affect the most powerful, leading to commitments such as those within the Dayton Agreement.

The European security architecture has limitations, however, not just in terms of its geographical competence, but with respect to the 'hold' institutions can exert over their members and other actors. The capacity of institutions to regulate the behaviour of their members varies according to perceptions of need, vulnerability to sanctions and the degree to which institutional norms are embedded in the state. In the case of Greece and Turkey institutions may have only moderated at best policies of conflict which have transcended the Cold War era. NATO's relationship with Russia has been vulnerable to the impact of domestic politics and policy differences in the wider Europe. NATO's action over Kosovo circumscribed the institutionalization of the Founding Act despite common interests in arms control and European stability. Where institutions have little leverage to exert over states their capacity to influence is limited. The OSCE can cajole, publicize and report but generally lacks the institutional means to deter or coerce. The socialization of the wider Europe has been variable and we found those institutions with resources to offer, NATO and the EU, to be the most effective. Institutions have also had to target new actors in contemporary Europe. The major contemporary challenge for international institutions is intra-state conflict and the actors are factions or groups. Although not unique to the post-Cold War era intra-state conflict has become the predominant issue in the development of European security. Institutions formed to address the security of states are now having to adapt to the politics of conflict below as well as between states. The new challenge often presented in terms of ethnic politics has affected strategies of peacekeeping, enforcement and peace-building.

Inter-state 'heroic warfare' has been supplanted by 'post-heroic warfare' among non-state actors (Luttwak, 1995, p. 109). Often intra-state conflict arises as a consequence of weak or failing states wherein the leaking of state authority and erosion of state capacity leads to the emergence of a security dilemma in which ethnicity plays a central role. International institutions now face the challenge of an international order in which sovereignty itself is in a process of transition. Such institutions have had to adapt their apparatus and revise their remits to respond to trans-sovereign issues:

> The end of communism has opened the door to the spread of weapons of mass destruction and lifted the lid on ethnic and religious conflicts. The growing openness that we so cherish also benefits a host of equal opportunity destroyers – terrorists, international criminals, drug traffickers, and those who do environmental damage that cross national borders. None of these problems has any particular respect for the borders of the nation ... Because the Cold War is over, some of these challenges are underestimated.
>
> (Clinton, 1996)

Tackling such challenges has called into question the concept of national sovereignty and the principle of non-interference in the domestic affairs of the state. During the Cold War, the international order rested upon the inviolability of state sovereignty. Traditional peacekeeping or 'first-generation' peacekeeping was premised upon the willingness of the disputing parties to accept intervention. In general an invitation to intervene was mandatory, a ceasefire should be in place and the UN troops would enter as a lightly armed force to act as a buffer between the protagonists. In this way, they created a space in which the two sides could channel their political will to reach a settlement. In the present international environment, no such clarity of mandate exists. Intervention now generally occurs in a situation of ongoing conflict, there may well be no party authorized to offer an invitation, and usually there will be a notable lack of political will to resolve the dispute via diplomacy. Thus 'second generation' peacekeeping and peace-building is a fundamentally different task. In intra-state conflicts the mandate is often not to keep the peace but to make it, not to maintain a ceasefire but to enforce one, and not to assist indigenous groups to find a settlement but to impose one. Most pointedly, the mandate is often open-ended. Once a settlement is imposed, an environment must be created in which it will become self-sustaining.

International institutions have taken on the mantle of establishing democratic political systems and creating inclusive civil societies. These are complex and long-term tasks as both the structural and perceptual dimensions of a protracted social conflict must be addressed by the intervenors and new forms of thinking and behaviour be fostered:

> ... intervention can provide the capability to monitor and enforce new institutional arrangements during a transitional period until locals' expectations converge on the new pattern and vested interests in the new status quo emerge.
>
> (Synder and Jervis, 1999, p. 27)

Given the subjectivity of 'democratization', there appears to be no specific point at which one can say that a society is fully on the road to democracy and that local parties can be entrusted with their own affairs. Equally significant, there may well be a lag between establishing 'new institutional arrangements' and the requisite altered thinking and behaviour of the indigenous people. The holding of free and fair elections may well result in the return of unreconstructed individuals who have used stereotypical perceptions of 'otherness' to fuel their political campaigns. The security dilemma between contending groups thus may still prevail despite the new institutional structures. In tackling the perceptual aspects of conflict, the challenge for security providers is extremely difficult. One primary task is the disarming of the contending groups but there are problems inherent to the decommissioning process as we have seen in Northern Ireland, Kosovo and Macedonia. Armed parties may resist the surrender of their arms until their security fears are assuaged. Alternatively, as in Macedonia, there may be dis-agreements between the parties over the estimates of weapons held and the logistics of their surrender. Such stances then may be inter-preted as a lack of sincerity of some or all of the parties in terms of their commitment to the politics of peace.

To meet these challenges and fully address the security dilemma, intervenors need to demonstrate their credibility and their commit-ment to making peace work. There has to be a recognition that the making of a democracy is a time-expansive endeavour:

> Outsiders, therefore, should refrain from pushing for a 'quick and easy' democratization process and understand that they cannot simultaneously end a civil war and set up a fully liberal democracy without some sort of transition in between.
>
> (Walter, 1999, p. 59)

This clearly has implications for the execution of peace-building. Instead of concern over 'mission creep', the initial mandates should explicitly recognize the long-term nature of the commitment and insti-tutions should be prepared to resource the intervention fully. The constituent parties of the institutions involved need to be ready to pay for the tasks, both in terms of finance and personnel, if the 'capability-expectations' gap is to be breached:

> … there must be a convergence between the *expectations* placed on … [them] … , the *resources* allocated by member states to fulfil these expectations, and the *political will* of member states to follow through on … initiatives.
>
> (Tafe, 2000, p. 249).

The resolution of intra-state conflicts thus is a demanding business and, as we have seen, generates tension within alliances and organiza-tions. Arguably, it is not made any easier by the confusion surrounding the notion of state sovereignty and the potentially competing recipi-ents for security. The present international order has witnessed a diminution of state sovereignty in some cases but the primary unit of order remains the state and, consequently, policy-makers still operate in a geopolitical statist mindset. Thus we see the containment of conflict as a rationale for intervention in some places and a refusal to intervene in others, notably Russia's 'Near Abroad'. This selectivity demonstrates the continuing tension between the interests of states and human rights:

We are clearly witnessing what is probably an irresistible shift in public attitudes towards the belief that the defence of the oppressed in the name of morality should probably prevail over frontiers and legal documents. We must now ponder this in a manner that is at once prudent and bold. In a prudent manner, because the principles of sovereignty cannot be radically challenged without international chaos quickly ensuing.

> (Pérez de Cuéllar, cited in Thomas and Reader, 1998, p. 124)

It is arguable that efforts to provide security for states, groups and individuals are inherently futile as often, especially in intra-state conflict, the demands of such potential recipients are incompatible. Thus there are calls for an 'end to business as usual' by international institutions and 'a profound reorientation' in their thinking on intervention:

> First, the notion of humanitarian intervention as a quick fix, military or otherwise, needs to be abandoned. Second, a much more society-oriented perspective on conflict situations is required. Statist perspectives, forever percolating within the orbit of sovereignty, national interest and international security, cannot address society's security problems ... New forms of public action and synergies are required, both local and transnational, between public and private social development efforts.
>
> (Pieterse, 1998, pp. 259–60)

Until, however, someone can articulate the explicit nature of such actions and synergies, and policy-makers authorize their implementation, it will be a case of more of the same. Moves to establish the new International Criminal Court to further promote human rights by strengthening the international community's ability to prosecute war criminals suggest that state interests still dominate the international agenda. In particular, the reluctance of the United States to lend its support to the project, fearing that its peacekeepers may be subject to controversial prosecutions, demonstrates that the post-Cold War international order is not as fundamentally different from its predecessor as was initially thought. Primacy of security remains with states on the whole despite the rhetoric of power to the people.

Several themes emerge from the above analysis. Firstly, institutional theory must encompass the challenge of intra-state as well as inter-state conflict. The neorealist and neoliberal debate on institutional relevance needs to be revised to address contemporary conflict patterns.

As the nature of the security environment has changed state conflicts have afforded institutions a new relevance but simultaneously substate conflict has revealed new limitations. Secondly, strategies of conflict management and resolution developed for inter-state conflicts have had a difficult translation to intra-state crises. The instruments of state power – sanctions, deterrence and force – have proven unwieldy in their application to the new conflict paradigm. Thirdly, when institutions resort to enforcement there are questions concerning the point at which the organization becomes a participant in the ongoing conflict. The line is affected by both context and actor perception. This clearly affects the composition and mandate of the mission. Fourthly, 'new wars' are media wars in that they are conveyed instantaneously to global audiences thereby prompting demands for action. Fifthly, as institutions have sought to adapt to new roles they still have to discharge older responsibilities. The agendas of inter-state conflict and cooperation remain relevant to the new Europe even if they are not front-page news.

International institutions, therefore, have enjoyed enhanced relevance in the post-Cold War era as security providers but are not free from constraints either internally as organizations or from the new security environment. Their record to date suggests limited success in enhancing the security of individuals or societies. The violation of human rights in the former Yugoslavia drew world attention, but desperately slow progress was made on the ground by the international community's agencies. Humanitarian aid was not accompanied by decisive diplomacy or intervention until the tragedy had truly developed. Societal insecurity is clearly a difficult phenomenon to curtail but the Balkan wars point to a larger failure of strategy for the people of the former Yugoslavia. The conflicts in Croatia, Bosnia, Kosovo and Macedonia, however, have been contained to date which may point to a different conclusion. International institutions can be seen to have served states by limiting the wars to intra-state and not inter-state levels, restricting the costs to the local region and isolating the zone of conflict. In conclusion, the capacity and effectiveness of institutions remains the prerogative of their member states:

> We cannot assume that either barbarism or civility is embedded in human nature. Whether we can learn to cope with the new wars and veer towards a more optimistic future depends ultimately on our own behaviour.
>
> (Kaldor, 1999, p. 152)

# Bibliography

Adomeit, H. (1995) 'Russia as a Great Power in World Affairs: Images and Reality', *International Affairs*, vol. 71, no. 1, pp. 35–68.

Albright, M. (1997) 'Enlarging NATO', *The Economist*, February, pp. 21–3.

Alperovitz, G. (1985) *Atomic Diplomacy* (Harmondsworth: Penguin).

Andersen, S. and Eliassen, K. (eds) (1993) *Making Policy in Europe: The Europefication of National Policy-Making* (London: Sage).

Anderson, J. and Goodman, J. (1993) 'Mars or Minerva? A United Germany in a Post-Cold War Europe', in Keohane, R., Nye, J. and Hoffmann, S. (eds), *After the Cold War: International Institutions and State Strategies in Europe, 1989–1991* (Cambridge, MA: Harvard University Press).

Andò, S. (1993) 'Preparing the Ground for an Alliance Peacekeeping Role', *NATO Review*, vol. 41, no. 2, pp. 4–9.

Aron, R. (1975) *The Imperial Republic: The United States and the World 1945–1973* (London: Weidenfeld & Nicolson).

Aron, R. (1966) *Peace and War* (London: Weidenfeld & Nicolson).

Azar, E. (1990) *The Management of Protracted Social Conflict: Theory and Cases* (Aldershot: Dartmouth).

Azar, E. (1985) 'Protracted International Conflicts: Ten Propositions', *International Interactions*, vol. 2, no. 1, pp. 59–70.

Azar, E. (1983) 'The Theory of Protracted Social Conflict and the Challenge of Transforming Conflict Situations', *Monograph Series on World Affairs*, vol. 20, no. 2, pp. 81–99.

Azar, E. and Burton, J. W. (1986) *International Conflict Resolution: Theory and Practice* (Sussex: Wheatsheaf).

Azar, E. and Moon, C. (1986) 'Managing Protracted Social Conflicts in the Third World: Facilitation and Development Diplomacy', *Millennium*, vol. 15, no. 3, pp. 393–406.

Baehr, P. and Gordenker, L. (1999) *The United Nations at the End of the 1990s* (London: Macmillan).

Bercovitch, J. (ed.) (1996) *Resolving International Conflicts: the Theory and Practice of Mediation* (Boulder, CO: Lynne Rienner).

Bercovitch, J. (1986) 'International Mediation: a Study of the Incidence, Strategies and Conditions of Successful Outcomes', *Cooperation and Conflict*, vol. 21, pp. 155–68.

Bercovitch, J. (1984) *Social Conflicts and Third Parties: Strategies of Conflict Resolution* (Boulder, CO: Lynne Rienner).

Berdal, M. R. (1993) 'Whither UN Peacekeeping?', *Adelphi Paper 281* (London: International Institute for Strategic Studies).

Bernstein, B. and Matusow, A. (eds) (1966), *The Truman Administration: A Documentary History* (New York: Harper Row).

Betts, R. K. (1994) 'The Delusion of Impartial Intervention', *Foreign Affairs*, vol. 73, no. 6, pp. 20–33.

Blair, T. (1999) *NATO, Europe and our future security,* http://www.fco.gov.uk/text-only/news/speechtext.

Blair, T. (1998) *NATO's Role in the Modern World,* http://www.fco.gov.uk/text.

Bloed, A. (2000) 'OSCE Chronicle' *Helsinki Monitor,* vol. 11, no. 2, The Netherlands Helsinki Committee and the International Helsinki Federation for Human Rights: The Hague, pp. 58–62.

Bloomfield, D. (1997) *Peacemaking Strategies in Northern Ireland: Building Complementarity in Conflict Management Theory* (London: Macmillan – now Palgrave).

Borawski, J. (1995) 'Partnership for Peace and Beyond', *International Affairs,* vol. 71, no. 2, pp. 233–46.

Boutros-Ghali, B. (1995) *Supplement to An Agenda for Peace: Position Paper of the Secretary-General on the Occasion of the Fiftieth Anniversary of the United Nations* (New York: United Nations).

Boutros-Ghali, B. (1992) *An Agenda for Peace* (New York: United Nations).

Bowen, W. and Dunn, D. (1996) *American Security Policy in the 1990s* (Aldershot: Dartmouth).

British Strategic Defence Review (1998) *Modern Forces for the Modern World,* http://www.mod.uk/policy/sdr.

Brown, M. (ed.) (1996) *The International Dimensions of Internal Conflict* (Cambridge, MA: MIT Press).

Brown, M., Coté, O., Lynn-Jones, S. and Miller, S. (1998) *Theories of War and Peace* (Cambridge MA: MIT Press).

Bryson, J. M. and Crosby B. C. (1992) *Leadership for the Common Good: Tackling Public Problems in a Shared-Power World* (San Francisco: Jossey-Bass).

Brzezinski, Z. (1967) *The Soviet Bloc: Unity and Conflict* (Cambridge MA: Harvard University Press).

Buergenthal, T. (1990) 'The Copenhagen Meeting: A New Public Order for Europe', *Human Rights Law Journal,* vol. 2, pp. 213–25.

Bull, H. (1979) *The Anarchical Society: A Study of Order in World Politics* (London: Macmillan).

Bulmer, S. and Paterson, W. (1996) 'Germany in the European Union: Gentle Giant or Emergent Leader?', *International Affairs,* vol. 72, no. 1, pp. 9–32.

Burton, J. W. (1990a) *Conflict: Resolution and Prevention* (London: Macmillan).

Burton, J. W. (1990b) *Conflict: Human Needs Theory* (London: Macmillan).

Burton, J. W. (1987) *Resolving Deep-Rooted Conflict: A Handbook* (Lanham, MD: UPA).

Burton, J. W. and Dukes, F. (eds) (1990) *Conflict: Readings in Management and Resolution* (London: Macmillan).

Buszynski, L. (1995) 'Russia and the West: towards Renewed Geopolitical Rivalry?', *Survival,* vol. 37, no. 3, pp. 104–25.

Buzan, B. (2000) 'Change and Insecurity Reconsidered', in Croft, S. and Terriff, T. (eds), *Critical Reflections on Security and Change* (London: Frank Cass).

Buzan, B. (1993) *People, States and Fear: The National Security Problem in International Relations* (Chapel Hill: University of North Carolina Press).

Buzan, B. and Diez, T. (1999) 'The European Union and Turkey', *Survival,* vol. 41, no. 1, pp. 41–57.

Buzan, B., Wæver, O. and Wilde, J. (1998) *Security: A New Framework for Analysis* (London: Lynne Rienner).

Byman, D. L. and Waxman, M. C. (2000) 'Kosovo and the Great Air Power Debate', *International Security*, vol. 24, no. 4, Spring, pp. 5–38.

Caplan, R. (1998), 'International Diplomacy and the Crisis in Kosovo', *International Affairs*, vol. 74, no. 4, October, pp. 745–61.

Carr, E. H. (1981) *The Twenty Years Crisis 1919–1939* (London: Macmillan).

Carr, F. and Flenley, P. (1999) 'NATO and the Russian Federation in the New Europe: the Founding Act on Mutual Relations', *Journal of Communist Studies and Transition Politics*, vol. 15, no. 2, pp. 88–110.

Carr, F. and Ifantis, K. (1996) *NATO in the New European Order* (London: Macmillan, now Palgrave).

Carr, F. and Massey, A. (eds) (1999) *Public Policy in the New Europe* (Chelthenham: Edward Elgar).

Chandler, D. (1999) *Bosnia: Faking Democracy After Dayton* (London: Pluto).

Chryssochoou, D. (1999), 'Eurogovernance: Theories and Approaches to the European Union', in Carr, F. and Massey, A. (eds), *Public Policy in the New Europe* (Cheltenham: Edward Elgar).

Cigar, N. (1993) 'The Serbo-Croatian War, 1991: Political and Military Dimensions', *Journal of Strategic Studies*, vol. 16, no. 3, pp. 297–338.

Claude, I. (1962) *Power and International Relations* (New York: Random House).

Clausewitz, C. (1976) *On War*, eds Howard, M. and Paret, P. (Princeton NJ: Princeton University Press).

Clinton, President W. J. (1996) *Remarks by the President at the United States Coast Guard Academy Commencement* (Washington DC: White House Documents, Office of the Press Secretary, 22 May).

Cohen, E. A. (1994) 'The Mystique of U.S. Air Power', *Foreign Affairs*, vol. 73, no. 1, pp. 109–24.

Cohen, W. (1999) *Annual Report to the President and the Congress*, http://www.dtic.mil/execsec/adr1999/.

Committee on International Security and Arms Control (1997) *The Future of U.S. Nuclear Weapons Policy* (Washington DC: National Academy of Sciences, National Academy Press).

Cook, R. (1999) *Speech by the Foreign Secretary, House of Commons, 1/12/1999*, http://www.fco.gov.uk/news/speechtext.

Coser, L. (1957) 'Social Conflict and the Theory of Social Change', *British Journal of Sociology*, vol. 8, no. 3, pp. 197–207.

Coufoudakis, V. (1996), 'Greek Foreign Policy in the Post-Cold War Era: Issues and Challenges', *Mediterranean Quarterly*, vol. 7, pp. 26–41.

Cragg, A. (1996) 'The Combined Joint Task Force Concept: a Key Component of the Alliance's Adaptation', *NATO Review*, vol. 44, no. 4, pp. 7–10.

Crnobrnja, M. (1994) *The Yugoslav Drama* (London: Tauris).

Crockatt, R. (1996) *The Fifty Years War* (London: Routledge).

Croft, S., Howarth, J., Terriff, T. and Webber, M. (2000) 'NATO's Triple Challenge', *International Affairs*, vol. 76, no. 3, pp. 495–518.

Croft, S., Redmond, J., Wyn-Rees, G. and Webber, M. (1999) *The Enlargement of Europe* (Manchester: Manchester University Press).

CSCE (1990), *The Charter of Paris for a New Europe*. http://www.osce.org/docs/english/1990–1999/summits/paris90e.htm

CSCE Budapest Decisions (1994) *CSCE Budapest Document 1994* (Vienna: CSCE).

Cusimano, M. K. (2000) *Beyond Sovereignty: Issues for a Global Agenda* (New York: St. Martin's Press, now Palgrave).

Cutileiro, J. (1997), 'Address to the WEU Assembly', quoted in Kintis, A. (1998), 'NATO–WEU: An Enduring Relationship', *European Foreign Affairs Review*, vol. 3, pp. 537–62.

Dalby, S. (1997) 'Contesting an Essential Concept: Reading the Dilemmas in Contemporary Security Discourse' in Krause, K. and Williams, M. (1997), *Critical Security Studies: Concepts and Cases* (London: UCL Press).

Dawisha, K. and Parrott, B. (eds) (1997) *Politics, Power and the Struggle for Democracy in South-East Europe* (Cambridge: Cambridge University Press).

Dawisha, K. and Parrott, B. (1994) *Russia and the New States of Eurasia* (Cambridge: Cambridge University Press).

DED (Department of Economic Development) (1999) *Strategy 2010: Report by the Economic Development Strategy Group on Northern Ireland* (Belfast: Department of Economic Development).

Delors, J. (1991) 'European Integration and Security', *Survival*, vol. 33, no. 2, pp. 99–109.

Deutscher, I. (1967) *Stalin* (London: Oxford University Press).

Dobbie, C. (1994) 'A Concept for Post-Cold War Peacekeeping', *Survival*, vol. 36, no. 3, pp. 121–48.

Dulles, J. F. (1954) ' Policy for Security and Peace', *Foreign Affairs*, vol. 32, no. 3, pp. 353–64.

Dumoulin, A. (1995) 'Defence and Disarmament Memorandum 1994/1995', quoted in Kintis, A. (1998), 'NATO–WEU: An Enduring Relationship', *European Foreign Affairs Review*, vol. 3, pp. 537–62.

Economides, S. and Taylor, P. (1996) 'Former Yugoslavia', in Mayall, J. (ed.), *The New Interventionism 1991–1994* (Cambridge: Cambridge University Press).

Eibl-Eibesfeldt, I. and Salter, E. (eds) (1998) *Indoctrinability, Ideology and Warfare: Evolutionary Perspectives* (Oxford: Berghahn).

Etzioni, A. (1995) *The Spirit of Community: Rights, Responsibilities and the Communitarian Agenda* (London: Fontana Press).

Etzold, T. and Gaddis, J. (1978) *Containment: Documents on American Policy and Strategy, 1945–1950* (New York: Columbia University Press).

European Commission (1997) 'Agenda 2000', *Bulletin of the European Union*, Supplements 5–15/97.

European Council (1999a) *Presidency Conclusions Cologne European Council Annexe III*, http://europa.eu.int/council/off/conclu/June 99.

European Council (1999b) *Presidency Conclusions Helsinki European Council*, http://europa.eu.int/comm/external_relations/news/12-99/doc_99_16htm.

Evriviades, M. (1998), 'Turkey's Role in United States Strategy During and After the Cold War', *Mediterranean Quarterly*, vol. 9, pp. 30–51.

Falk, R. A. (1995) *On Humane Governance* (Cambridge: Polity).

Fisher, R. J. and Keashly, L. (1991) 'The Potential Complementarity of Mediation and Consultation within a Contingency Model of Third Party Intervention', *Journal of Peace Research*, vol. 28, no. 1, pp. 29–42.

Foreign and Commonwealth Office (1998) *Joint Declaration on European Defence*, http://www.fco.gov.uk/text.

Forster, A. and Wallace, W. (1997) 'Common Foreign and Security Policy', in Wallace, H. and Wallace, W. (eds), *Policy-Making in the European Union* (Oxford: Oxford University Press).

Founding Act (1997) *On Mutual Relations, Cooperation and Security Between the North Atlantic Treaty Organisation and the Russian Federation* (Brussels: NATO Office of Information and Press).

Freedman, L. (2000) 'Victims and Victors: Reflections on the Kosovo War', *Review of International Studies*, vol. 26, no. 3, pp. 335–58.

Friis, L. and Murphy, A. (1999) 'The European Union and Central and Eastern Europe: Governance and Boundaries', *Journal of Common Market Studies*, vol. 37, no. 2, pp. 211–32.

Gaddis, J. (1998) *We Now Know: Rethinking Cold War History* (Oxford: Oxford University Press).

Gaddis, J. (1982) *Strategies of Containment* (Oxford: Oxford University Press).

Gaddis, J. L. (1987) *The Long Peace* (New York: Oxford University Press).

Galtung, J. (1996) *Peace by Peaceful Means: Peace and Conflict, Development and Civilization* (London: Sage).

Gelb, L. H. (1994) 'Quelling the Teacup Wars', *Foreign Affairs*, vol. 73, no. 6, pp. 2–6.

Gelpi, C. (1999) 'Alliances as Instruments of Intra-Allied Control', in Haftendorn, H., Keohane, R. and Wallender, C., *Imperfect Unions: Security Institutions Over Time and Space* (Oxford: Oxford University Press).

Glaser, C. and Kaufmann, C. (1998) 'What is the Offense–Defense Balance and Can We Measure It?', *International Security*, vol. 22, no. 4, pp. 48–82.

Goldman, M. (1992) *What Went Wrong with Perestroika* (London: Norton).

Gompert, D. and Larrabee, S. (1997) *America and Europe* (Cambridge: Cambridge University Press).

Goodrich, L. (1972) 'The UN Security Council', in Barros, J. (ed.), *The United Nations: Past, Present and Future* (London: Collier-Macmillan).

Gorbachev, M. (1988) *Perestroika* (London: Fontana).

Gordon, P. (1997) 'Europe's Uncommon Foreign Policy', *International Security*, vol. 22, no. 3, pp. 74–100.

Gow, J. (1999) 'Security and Democracy: the European Union and Central and Eastern Europe', in Henderson, K., *Back to Europe: Central and Eastern Europe and the European Union* (London: UCL Press).

Gower, J. (1999) 'European Union Policy to Central and Eastern Europe', in Henderson, K., *Back to Europe: Central and Eastern Europe and the European Union* (London: UCL Press).

Graham, T. W. and Mullins, A. F. (1991) *Arms Control, Military Strategy, and Nuclear Proliferation*, paper presented at the conference on 'Nuclear Deterrence and Global Security in Transition', University of California, Institute on Global Conflict and Cooperation, La Jolla, California, 21–23 February.

Grant, R. (1996) 'France's New Relationship with NATO', *Survival*, vol. 38, no. 1, pp. 58–80.

Grieco, J. (1995) 'Anarchy and the Limits of Cooperation: a Realist Critique of the Newest Liberal Institutionalism', in Kegley, C., *Controversies in International Relations Theory* (New York: St. Martin's Press, now Palgrave).

Grieco, J. (1993) 'The Relative-Gains Problem for International Cooperation', *American Political Science Review*, vol. 87, no. 3, pp. 729–735.

Grieco, J. (1988), 'Anarchy and the Limits of Cooperation: A Realist Critique of the Newest Liberal Institutionalism', *International Organization*, vol. 42, pp. 485–507.

Griffiths, M., Levine, I. and Weller, M. (1995) 'Sovereignty and Suffering', in Harriss, J. (ed.), *The Politics of Humanitarian Intervention* (London: Pinter), pp. 33–90.

Gurr, T. R. (1970) *Why Men Rebel* (Princeton, NJ: Princeton University Press).

Gurr, T. R. and Harff, B. (1994) *Ethnic Conflicts in World Politics* (Boulder, CO: Westview Press).

Guzzini, S. (1998) *Realism in International Relations and International Political Economy* (London: Routledge).

Haftendorn, H., Keohane, R. and Wallender, C. (1999) *Imperfect Unions: Security Institutions Over Time and Space* (Oxford: Oxford University Press).

Hall, J. A. (1996) *International Orders* (Cambridge: Polity Press).

Halliday, F. (1989) *The Making of the Second Cold War* (London: Verso).

Hampson, F. O. (1996) *Nurturing Peace: Why Peace Settlements Succeed or Fail* (Washington, DC: United States Institute of Peace Press).

Harriman, W. and Abel, E. (1976) *Special Envoy to Churchill and Stalin, 1941–1946* (London: Hutchinson).

Hartmann, F. (1967) *The Relations of Nations* (New York: Macmillan).

Helman, G. and Ratner, S. (1992/93) 'Saving Failed States', *Foreign Policy*, vol. 89, pp. 3–30.

Hiro, D. (1992) *Desert Shield to Desert Storm* (Hammersmith: Paladin).

Hix, S. (1999) *The Political System of the European Union* (London: Macmillan, now Palgrave).

Hoffmann, S. (1978) *Primacy or World Order* (New York: McGraw-Hill).

Holbrooke, R. (1999) *To End a War* (New York: Random House).

Holsti, K. (1991) *Peace and War: Armed Conflicts and International Order, 1648–1989* (Cambridge: Cambridge University Press).

Holsti, K. J. (1996) *The State, War, and the State of War* (Cambridge: Cambridge University Press).

House of Commons Foreign Affairs Committee (1992–93) *The Expanding Role of the United Nations and its Implications for United Kingdom Policy* (London: HMSO).

Hunter, R. (1969) *Security in Europe* (London: Elek).

Huntington, S. (1999) 'The Lonely Superpower', *Foreign Affairs*, vol. 78, no. 2, pp. 35–49.

Ifantis, K. (1996) 'Greece and the USA after the Cold War', in Featherstone, K. and Ifantis, K., *Greece in a Changing Europe: Between Europe's Integration and Balkan Disintegration* (Manchester: Manchester University Press).

Ignatieff, M. (1993) *Blood and Belonging: Journeys into the New Nationalisms* (London: Chatto & Windus).

Ikenberry, J. (1998) 'Institutions, Strategic Restraints, and the Persistence of American Postwar Order', *International Security*, vol. 23, no. 3, pp. 43–78.

Jacobsen, C. G. (1990) 'Soviet Strategic Policy Since 1945' in Jacobsen, C. G. (1990), *Strategic Power: USA/USSR* (London: Macmillan), pp. 106–20.

Jervis, R. (1999) 'Realism, Neoliberalism, and Cooperation', *International Security*, vol. 24, no. 1, pp. 42–63.

Jervis, R. (1993) 'Security Regimes', in Krasner, S. (ed.), *International Regimes* (Ithaca, NY: Cornell University Press).

Johnstone, I. (1994) *Aftermath of the Gulf War: An Assessment of UN Action* (London: Lynne Rienner).

Judah, T. (2000) *Kosovo: War and Revenge* (New Haven, CT and London: Yale University Press).

Judah, T. (1999) 'Kosovo's Road to War', *Survival*, vol. 41, no. 2, pp. 5–18.

Kaldor, M. (1999) *New and Old Wars: Organised Violence in a Global Era* (Cambridge: Polity Press).

Kegley, C. W. and Wittkopf, E. R. (1999) *World Politics: Trend and Transformation* (New York: St. Martin's Press, now Palgrave).

Kennedy-Pipe, C. (1998) *Russia and the World 1917–1991* (London: Arnold).

Kennedy-Pipe, C. (1995) *Stalin's Cold War* (Manchester: Manchester University Press).

Keohane, R. (1993b) 'The Demand for International Regimes', in Krasner, S. (ed.), *International Regimes* (Ithaca, NY: Cornell University Press).

Keohane, R. (ed.) (1986) *Neorealism and Its Critics* (New York: Columbia University Press).

Keohane, R. (1984) *After Hegemony: Cooperation and Discord in the World Political Economy* (Princeton NJ: Princeton University Press).

Keohane, R. and Hoffmann, S. (1991) *The New European Community: Decisionmaking and Institutional Change* (Boulder, CO: Westview).

Keohane, R. and Nye, J. (1993) 'Introduction: the End of the Cold War in Europe', in Keohane, R., Nye, J. and Hoffmann, S. (eds), *After the Cold War: International Institutions and State Strategies in Europe, 1989–1991* (Cambridge, MA: Harvard University Press).

Keohane, R. and Nye, J. (1989) *Power and Interdependence* (New York: HarperCollins).

Khalilzad, Z. and Ochmanek, D. (1997) 'Rethinking US Defence Planning', *Survival*, vol. 39, no. 1, pp. 43–64.

Kissinger, H. (1982) *Years of Upheaval* (London: Weidenfeld & Nicolson).

Kissinger, H. (1957) *Nuclear Weapons and Foreign Policy* (New York: Harper & Bros).

Kohler-Koch, B. (1996) 'Catching Up with Change: the Transformation of Governance in the European Union', *Journal of European Public Policy*, vol. 3, no. 3, pp. 359–80.

Kozyrev, A. (1994) 'Russia and NATO: a Partnership for a United and Peaceful Europe', *NATO Review*, vol. 42, no. 4, pp. 3–6.

Krasner, S. (ed.) (1993) *International Regimes* (Ithaca, NY: Cornell University Press).

Krause K. and Williams, M. (1997) *Critical Security Studies: Concepts and Cases* (London: UCL Press).

Kühne, W. (1994) 'Fragmenting States and the Need for Enlarged Peacekeeping', in Taylor, P., Daws, S. and Adamczick-Gerteis (eds), *Documents of Reform of the United Nations*, (Aldershot: Gower).

Lapidus, G. (1998) 'Contested Sovereignty', *International Security*, vol. 23, no. 1, pp. 5–49.

Laursen, F. (1994) 'The European Community in Europe's Future Economic and Political Architecture', in Andersen, S. and Eliassen, K., *Making Policy in Europe: The Europeification of National Policy-Making* (London: Sage).

Lederach, J. (1995) *Preparing for Peace: Conflict Transformation Across Cultures* (New York: Syracuse University Press).

Lepingwell, J. (1994) 'The Russian Military and Security Policy in the Near Abroad', *Survival*, vol. 36, no. 3, pp. 70–92.

Lijphart, A. (1991) 'The Power-Sharing Approach', in Montville J. V. (ed.), *Conflict and Peacemaking in Multiethnic Societies* (New York: Lexington Books), pp. 494–520.

Lippert, B. and Becker, P. (1998) 'Structural Dialogue Revisited: the European Union's Politics of Inclusion and Exclusion', *European Foreign Affairs Review*, vol. 3, pp. 341–365.

Luard, E. (1982) *A History of the United Nations: the Years of Western Domination* (London: Macmillan).

Luttwak, E. N. (1995)'Towards Post-Heroic Warfare', *Foreign Affairs*, vol. 74, no. 3.

McAuley, M. (1992) *Soviet Politics 1917–1991* (Oxford: Oxford University Press).

McCalla, R. (1996) 'NATO's Persistence after the Cold War', *International Organisation*, vol. 50, no. 3, pp. 445–75.

MccGwire, M. (2000) 'Why Did We Bomb Belgrade?', *International Affairs*, vol. 76, no. 1, January, pp. 1–23.

McSweeney, B. (1996) 'Identity and Security: Buzan and the Copenhagen School', *Review of International Studies*, vol. 22, pp. 81–93.

McSweeney, B. (1999) *Security, Identity and Interests* (Cambridge: Cambridge University Press).

Malcolm, N. (1998) *Kosovo: A Short History* (London: Macmillan, now Palgrave).

Mandelbaum, M. (1998) 'Is Major War Obsolete?', *Survival,* vol. 40, no. 4, pp. 20–38.

Mandell, B. S. (1992), 'The Cyprus Conflict: Explaining Resistance to Resolution', in Salem N., (ed.), *Cyprus: a Regional Conflict and Its Resolution* (New York: St. Martin's Press, now Palgrave).

Manning, N. (1989) *The Cauldron of Ethnicity in the Modern World* (Chicago: Chicago University Press).

Mansfield, E. D. and Snyder, J. (1995) 'Democratization and War', *Foreign Affairs*, vol. 57, pp. 79–97.

Mason, D. (1992) *Revolution in East-Central Europe: The Rise and Fall of Communism and the Cold War* (Boulder, CO: Westview Press).

Mastanduno, M. (1997) 'Preserving the Unipolar Movement: Realist Theories and US Grand Strategy after the Cold War', *International Security*, vol. 21, no. 4, pp. 49–88.

Matthews, K. (1993) *The Gulf Conflict and International Relations* (London: Routledge).

Matthews III, J. (1996) 'Current Gains and Future Outcomes', *International Security*, vol. 21, no. 1, pp. 112–46.

Mayall, J. (ed.) (1996) *The New Interventionism 1991–1994* (Cambridge: Cambridge University Press).

Mayall, J. (1992) 'Nationalism and International Security after the Cold War', *Survival*, vol. 34, no. 1, pp. 18–35.

Mearsheimer, J. (1990) 'Back to the Future', *International Security*, vol. 15, no. 1, pp. 5–56.

Miall, H. (1993) *Shaping the New Europe* (London: Pinter).

Miall, H., Ramsbotham, O. and Woodhouse, T. (1999) *Contemporary Conflict Resolution: The Prevention, Management and Transformation of Deadly Conflicts* (Cambridge: Polity Press).

Miller, L. (1994) 'The Clinton Years: Reinventing US foreign policy', *International Affairs*, vol. 70, no. 4, pp. 621–34.

Millon, C. (1996) 'France and the Renewal of the Atlantic Alliance', *NATO Review*, vol. 44, no. 3, pp. 13–16.

Monar, J. (1997) 'The European Union's Foreign Affairs System after the Treaty of Amsterdam: A Strengthened Capacity for External Action?', *European Foreign Affairs Review*, vol. 2, pp. 413–36.

Montville, J. V. (ed.) (1991) *Conflict and Peacemaking in Multiethnic Societies* (New York: Lexington Books).

Moravcsik, A. (1999) *The Choice for Europe* (London: UCL Press).

Moravcsik, A. (1991) 'Negotiating the Single European Act: National Interests and Conventional Statecraft in the European Union', *International Organisation*, vol. 45, no. 1, pp. 19–56.

Morgan, R. (1974) *The Unsettled Peace* (London: BBC Publications)

Morgenthau, H. (1971), 'The Four Great Intellectual Errors of American Postwar Policy', in Sanders, B. and Durbin, A. (eds), *Contemporary International Politics: Introductory Readings* (New York: John Wiley).

Morgenthau, H. (1967) *Politics among Nations* (New York: Alfred Knopf).

Muller, H. (1995) 'The Internalization of Principles, Norms, and Rules by Governments: The Case of Security Regimes', in Rittberger, V. (1995), *Regime Theory and International Relations* (Oxford: Clarendon Press).

NATO (1998) *Handbook* (Brussels: NATO Office of Information and Press).

NATO (1997) *Basic Document of the Euro-Atlantic Partnership Council* (Brussels: NATO Office of Information and Press).

NATO (1995a) *Handbook* (Brussels: NATO Office of Information and Press).

NATO (1995b) *Study on NATO Enlargement* (Brussels: NATO Office of Information and Press).

Natsios, A. (1995) 'NGOs and the UN in Complex Emergencies: Conflict or Cooperation', *Third World Quarterly*, vol. 16, no. 3, pp. 405–19.

Nicholas, H. (1979) *The United Nations as a Political Institution* (Oxford: Oxford University Press).

Niklasson, T. (1994) 'The Soviet Union and Eastern Europe, 1988–9; Interactions between Domestic Change and Foreign Policy', in Pridham, G. and Vanhanen, T. (eds), *Democratization in Eastern Europe* (London: Routledge).

Nordlinger, E. (1972) *Conflict Regulation in Divided Societies* (Cambridge, MA: Harvard University Center of International Affairs).

North Atlantic Council (1999a) *Washington Summit Communiqué*, http://www.NATO.int/docu/pr/1999/p99-064e.htm.

North Atlantic Council (1999b) *The Alliance's Strategic Concept,* http://www.NATO.INT/docu/pr/1999/p99-065e.htm.

North Atlantic Council (1997a) *Madrid Declaration on Euro-Atlantic Security Cooperation* (Brussels: NATO Office of Information and Press).

North Atlantic Council (1997b) 'Madrid Declaration on Euro-Atlantic Security and Cooperation', *NATO Review*, vol. 45, no. 4 (special insert).

North Atlantic Council (1996) 'Ministerial Meeting of the North Atlantic Council Berlin', *NATO Review*, vol. 44, no. 4, pp. 30–5.

North Atlantic Council (1994) *Declaration of the Heads of State and Government Participating in the Meeting of the North Atlantic Council Held at NATO Headquarters, Brussels, 10–11 January 1994,* Press Communiqué M-1 (94) 3.

North Atlantic Council (1991a) 'Partnership with the Countries of Central and Eastern Europe', *NATO Review*, vol. 39, no. 3, pp. 28–9.

North Atlantic Council (1991b) 'Ministerial Meeting of the North Atlantic Council, Copenhagen', *NATO Review*, vol. 39, no. 3, pp. 30–1.

North Atlantic Council (1991c) *NATO's Core Security Functions in the New Europe* (Brussels: NATO Office of Information and Press).

North Atlantic Council, (1991d) *The Alliance's Strategic Concept* (Brussels: NATO Office of Information and Press).

North Atlantic Council (1990) *London Declaration on a Transformed North Atlantic Alliance* (Brussels: NATO Office of Information and Press).

Nuttall, S. (1992) *European Political Cooperation* (Oxford: Clarendon Press).

OHR (1998) *RRTF: Report March 1998*, http://www.ohr.int/rrf/r9803-01.htm.

Organski, A. F. K. (1968) *World Politics* (New York: Knopf).

OSCE (1999) *Charter for European Security*, http://www.OSCE.org/e/docs/summits/istachart99e.htm.

OSCE (1998) *Ministerial Declaration: Statement on Kosovo*, http://www.osce.org/e/docs/mincon/7oslo98e.htm.

OSCE Ministerial (1998) *Seventh Meeting of the Ministerial Council*, http://www.OSCE.org/e/docs/mincon/7OSLO98e.htm.

OSCE Ministerial Council (1997) *Decisions of the Copenhagen Ministerial Council Meeting*, http://www.OSCE.org/e/docs/mincon/6cope97e.htm.

Parrott, B. (1997) Perspectives on Post Communist Democratisation', in Dawisha, K. and Parrott, B. (eds), *Politics, Power and the Struggle for Democracy in South-East Europe* (Cambridge: Cambridge University Press), pp. 1–39.

Peace Implementation Conference (1996) *Making Peace Work*, Lancaster House, London. http://www.NATO.int/ifor/general/D961205B.HTM

Peterson, J. and Bomberg, E. (1999) *Decision-Making in the European Union* (London: Macmillan, now Palgrave), pp. 4–7.

Peterson, N. (1997) 'Towards a European Security Model for the 21st Century', *NATO Review*, vol. 45, no. 6.

Pieterse, J. N. (ed.) (1998) *World Orders in the Making: Humanitarianism and Beyond* (London: Macmillan, now Palgrave).

Posen, B. (1993) 'The Security Dilemma and Ethnic Conflict', *Survival*, vol. 35, no. 1, pp. 27–47.

Primakov, Y. (1996) *Interview with Izvestiya*, http://search.rferl.org/nca/features/1996/03/F.RU. 96030714280566.html

Prodromov, E. (1998) 'Reintegrating Cyprus: the Need for a New Approach', *Survival*, vol. 40, no. 3, pp. 5–24.

*Report of the Quadrennial Defense Review* (1997) United States Department of Defense, http://www.defenselink.mil/pubs/qdr/.

Reynolds, P. A. (1971) *An Introduction to International Relations* (London: Longman).

Richardson, L. (1960a) *Arms and Insecurity* (Pittsburg, PA: Boxwood Press).

Richardson, L. (1960b) *Statistics of Deadly Quarrels* (Pittsburg, PA: Boxwood Press).

Roberts, A. (1994) 'The Crisis in UN Peacekeeping', *Survival*, vol. 36, no. 3, pp. 93–120.

Roberts, A. and Kingsbury, B. (eds) (1993) *United Nations, Divided World: The UN's roles in International Relations* (Oxford: Clarendon Press).

Robertson, G. (2000) *NAC Factfinding Mission to Kosovo*, www.nato.int, 26 July.

Robertson, G. (1999) *Speech to the RIIA Conference, European Defence: The Way Ahead*, http://www.mod.uk/news/speeches/sofs/99-10-07.htm.

Rose, M. (1998) *Fighting for Peace: Bosnia 1994* (London: Harvill Press).

Rostow, W. W. (1960) *The Stages of Economic Growth* (Cambridge: Cambridge University Press).

Ruggie, J. G. (1996) *Winning the Peace: America and World Order in the New Era* (New York: Columbia University Press).

Saideman, S. (1996) 'The Dual Dynamics of Disintegration: Ethnic Politics and Security Dilemmas in Eastern Europe', *Nationalism and Ethnic Politics*, vol. 2, no. 1, pp. 18–43.

Santer, J. (1995) 'The European Union's Security and Defence Policy', *NATO Review*, vol. 43, no. 6, pp. 3–9.

Schake, K., Bloch-Lainé, A. and Grant, C. (1999) 'Building a European Defence Capability', *Survival*, vol. 41, no.1, pp. 20–40.

Schimmelfennig, F. (2000) 'International Socialization in the New Europe: Rational Action in an Institutional Environment', *European Journal of International Relations*, vol. 6, no. 1, pp. 109–39.

Schmidt, H. (1999) 'The Transatlantic Alliance in the 21st Century', *NATO Review 50th Anniversary Commemorative Edition* (Brussels: NATO office of Information and Press).

Schöpflin, George (1997) 'The Functions of Myth and a Taxonomy of Myths' in G. Schöpflin and G. Hosking (eds) (1997), *Myths and Nationhood* (London: Hurst).

Schwarz, H. (1994) 'Germany's National and European Interests', *Daedalus*, vol. 123, no. 2, pp. 81–105.

Shafir, M. (1987) 'Eastern Europe', in McCauley, M. (ed.), *Khrushchev and Khrushchevism* (London: Macmillan).

Sharp, J. (1997) 'Dayton Report Card', *International Security*, vol. 22, no. 3, pp. 101–137.

Shashenkov, M. (1994) 'Russian Peacekeeping in the Near Abroad', *Survival*, vol. 36, no. 3, pp. 46–69.

Shawcross, W. (2000) *Deliver Us from Evil: Warlords and Peacekeepers in a World of Endless Conflict* (London: Bloomsbury).

Sheehan, M. (1996) *The Balance of Power; History and Theory* (London: Routledge).

Sherman, F. (1987) *Pathway to Peace: The United Nations and the Road to Nowhere* (Pennsylvania State University: Pennsylvania).

Sherwin, M. (1975) *A World Destroyed: the Atomic Bomb and the Grand Alliance* (New York: Random House).

Silber, L. and Little, A. (1995) *The Death of Yugoslavia* (London: Penguin).

Silva, M. (1998) 'Implementing the Combined Joint Task Force Concept' *NATO Review*, vol. 46, no. 4, pp. 16–19.

Simkin, W. E. (1971) *Mediation and the Dynamics of Collective Bargaining* (Bureau of National Affairs: Washington DC).

Singer, D. (1996) 'Armed Conflict in the Former Colonial Regions: from Classification to Explanation', in van de Goor, L., Rupesinghe, K. and Sciarone, P. (eds), *Between Development and Destruction: An Enquiry Into the Causes of Conflict in Post-Colonial States* (New York: St. Martin's Press, now Palgrave).

Singer, D. and Small, M. (1972) *The Wages of War, 1816–1965: A Statistical Handbook* (New York: Wiley).

SIPRI (1997) *SIPRI Yearbook*, (Oxford: Oxford University Press/Stockholm International Peace Research Institute).

Sivard, R. L. (1996) *World Military and Social Expenditures 1996* (Washington DC: World Priorities).

Sloan, S. (1995) 'US Perspectives on NATO's Future', *International Affairs*, vol. 71, no. 2, pp. 217–31.

Smith, K. (1998) 'The Use of Political Conditionality in the European Union's Relationship with Third Countries: How Effective?', *European Foreign Affairs Review*, vol. 3, pp. 253–74.

Smith, M. (1996) 'The European Union and a Changing Europe: Establishing the Boundaries of Order', *Journal of Common Market Studies*, vol. 34, no. 1, pp. 5–28.

Snidal, D. (1991) 'Relative Gains and the Pattern of International Cooperation', *American Political Science Review*, vol. 85, no. 3, pp. 701–26.

Snow, D. (1996) *Uncivil Wars: International Security and the New Internal Conflicts* (Boulder, CO: Lynne Rienner).

Sperling, J. and Kirchner, E. (1998) 'Economic Security and the Problem of Cooperation in Post-Cold War Europe', *Review of International Studies*, vol. 24, no. 2, pp. 221–37.

Spero, J. (1980) *The Politics of International Economic Relations* (London: George, Allen & Unwin).

Stearns, M. (1993) 'The Greek–American–Turkish Triangle: What Shape After the Cold War?', *Mediterranean Quarterly*, vol. 4, pp. 16–29.

Stein, A. (1993) 'Coordination and Collaboration: Regimes in an Anarchic World', in Krasner, S. (ed.), *International Regimes* (Ithaca, NY: Cornell University Press).

Stewart, P. (1999) 'Northern Ireland: Between Peace and War?' *Capital and Class*, no. 69, autumn, pp. vi–xiv.

Stokes, G. (1993) *The Walls Came Tumbling Down* (Oxford: Oxford University Press).

Stokes, G. (1991) *From Stalinism to Pluralism* (Oxford: Oxford University Press).

Synder, J. and Jervis, R. (1999) 'Civil War and the Security Dilemma', in Walter, B.F. and Synder J. (eds), *Civil Wars, Insecurity and Intervention* (New York: Columbia University Press), pp. 15–37.

Tafe, U.C. (2000) 'Intergovernmental Organisations', in Cusimano, M. K., *Beyond Sovereignty: Issues for a Global Agenda* (New York: St. Martin's Press, now Palgrave), pp. 221–52.

Talbott, S. (1997) 'The Case for Expanding NATO', *Time*, vol. 150, no. 2, p. 31.

Tharoor, S. (1995) 'United Nations' Peacekeeping in Europe', *Survival*, vol. 37, no. 2, pp. 121–34.

Thomas, C. and Reader, M. (1998) 'Human Rights and Intervention: a Case for Caution', in Pieterse, J.N. (ed.), *World Orders in the Making: Humanitarian Intervention and Beyond* (London: Macmillan, now Palgrave).

Thomas, R. (1999) *Serbia Under Milosevic: Politics in the 1990s* (London: Hurst).

Treverton, G. (1985) *Making the Alliance Work* (London: Macmillan).

Tuschhoff, C. (1999) 'Alliance Cohesion and Peaceful Change in NATO', in Haftendorn, H., Keohane, R. and Wallender, C. (eds), *Imperfect Unions: Security Institutions over Time and Space* (Oxford: Oxford University Press).

UN (1990) *The Blue Helmets: A Review of United Nations Peace-Keeping* (New York: United Nations Publications).

US State Department Country Report – Macedonia 1998, cited in M. Komac, 'The House on the Historical Fault', *Cambridge Review of International Affairs*, vol. XII, spring/summer 1999, pp. 94–108.

Wæver, O. (1996) 'Europe's Three Empires: a Watsonian Interpretation of Post-Wall European Security', in Fawn, R. and Larkins, J. (eds), *International Society after the Cold War* (London: Macmillan, now Palgrave)

Wallander, C. and Keohane, R. (1999) 'Risk, Threat, and Security Institutions', in Haftendorn, H., Keohane, R. and Wallender, C. (eds), *Imperfect Unions: Security Institutions over Time and Space* (Oxford: Oxford University Press).

Waller, M. (1993) *The End of the Communist Power Monopoly* (Manchester: Manchester University Press).

Walter, B. F. (1999) 'Introduction', in Walter, B. F. and Synder, J. (eds), *Civil Wars, Insecurity, and Intervention* (New York: Columbia University Press), pp. 1–12.

Waltz, K. (2000) 'Structural Realism after the Cold War', *International Security*, vol. 25, no. 1, pp. 5–41.

Waltz, K. (1995) 'Realist Thought and Neorealist Theory', in Kegley, C. (ed.), *Controversies in International Relations Theory* (New York: St. Martin's Press, now Palgrave).

Waltz, K. (1986) 'A Response to My Critics', in Keohane, R. (ed.), *Neorealism and Its Critics* (New York: Columbia University Press).

Waltz, K. (1959) *Man, the State and War* (New York: Columbia University Press).

Watson, A. (1984) *Diplomacy: The Dialogue Between States* (London: Methuen).

Weiss, T. G. (1998) 'Humanitarian Action in War Zones: Recent Experience and Future Research', in J. N. Pieterse (ed.), *World Orders in the Making: Humanitarian Intervention and Beyond* (London: Macmillan, now Palgrave), pp. 24–68.

Weiss, T. and Collins, C. (1996) *Humanitarian Challenges and Intervention: World Politics and the Dilemmas of Help* (Boulder, CO: Westview Press).

Weller, M. (1999) 'The Rambouillet Conference on Kosovo', *International Affairs*, vol. 75, no. 2, April, pp. 211–51.

WEU (1994) *Preliminary Conclusions on the Formulation of a Common European Defence Policy* (WEU: Press and Information Service).

WEU (1992) *Petersberg Declaration* (WEU: Press and Information Service).

White, B., Little, R. and Smith, M. (eds) (1997) *Issues in World Politics* (London: Macmillan, now Palgrave).

Wight, M. (1979) *Power Politics* (Harmondsworth: Penguin).

Wijk, R. (1998) 'Towards a New Political Strategy for NATO', *NATO Review*, vol. 46, no. 2, pp. 14–18.

Wijk, R. (1997) *NATO on the Brink of the New Millennium* (London: Brassey's).

Windsor, P. (1969) *German Reunification* (London: Elek).

Wohlforth, W. (1999) 'The Stability of a Unipolar World', *International Security*, vol. 24, no. 1, pp. 5–41.

Woodward, S. (1999) 'Bosnia and Herzegovina: How Not to End a Civil War', in Walter, B. and Snyder, J. (eds), *Civil Wars, Insecurity, and Intervention* (New York: Columbia University Press).

Woodward, S. (1995) *Balkan Tragedy: Chaos and Disorder after the Cold War* (Washington: Brookings Institution).

Wörner, M. (1991) 'The Atlantic Alliance in the New Era', *NATO Review*, vol. 39, no. 1, pp. 3–10.

Wyllie, J. (1997) *European Security in the New Political Environment* (London: Longman).

Yeltsin, B. (1990) 'Speech to the Russian Federation Congress of People's Deputies, Moscow, May 22, 1990', in Dallin, A. and Lapidus, G. (eds), *The Soviet System from Crisis to Collapse* (Boulder, CO: Westview Press).

Yergin, D. (1980) *Shattered Peace* (Harmondsworth: Pelican).

Young, O. (1993) 'Regime Dynamics: the Rise and Fall of International Regimes', in Krasner, S. (ed.), *International Regimes* (Ithaca, NY: Cornell University Press).

Zartman, W. (1985) *Ripe for Resolution: Conflict and Intervention in Africa* (New York: Oxford University Press).

Zartman, W. and Rasmussen, J. (eds) (1997) *Peacemaking in International Conflict: Methods and Techniques* (Washington, DC: United States Institute of Peace).

Zartman, W. and Touval S. (1985) *International Mediation in Theory and Practice* (Boulder, CO: Westview Press).

# Index

219